Reading and Spelling
Pure & Simple

Reading and Spelling Pure & Simple

Phonics-Based Lessons for Elementary, Teen, and Adult Students

by

Deede Hinckley Cauley

The Real Reading Company

Big Spring, Texas

www.realreading.com

Edited by Cathrynn Novich Brown

Cover design and illustrations by Grayson Cauley

Printed by Action Printing Company, Lubbock, Texas

Printed in USA

ISBN: 978-0-9847666-1-1

15 14 13 12 11 10 9 8 7 6

"Thy word is a lamp unto my feet, and a light unto my path."
Psalms 119:105 KJV

Many people have contributed to the development of
Reading and Spelling Pure & Simple
but the book would not exist without the special contributions of
three faithful, dedicated women:
Janet Wolfe, Reta Faught, and Cathrynn Novich Brown.
You each know the labor of love you have given.

I appreciate my husband Richard's willingness to put up with this time-consuming but fascinating adventure. I value the amazing work, including terrific graphics, which have been contributed by our son, Grayson.

I am indebted to my students for their working through each lesson and pushing me to create the next lessons. Their interest and success drove the curriculum to completion and made the journey amazingly gratifying for me.

Contents

Pre-Unit: Preparing for Lesson 1 with Lessons A Through E

Unit 1: Short-Vowel Words

Unit 2: Long-Vowel Words and |ü|

Unit 3: More Vowel and Consonant Variations

Unit 4: Putting It All Together

Additional Support and Information

Documentation

Why This Book?

It is said that necessity is the mother of invention. In searching for teaching material to use with students who needed to develop basic reading skills, I discovered that most curricula were not particularly effective with my students, and so I started devising my own lessons. Through trial and error and after fifteen years of fine tuning, I was ready to publish *Reading and Spelling Pure & Simple: Phonics-Based Lessons for Elementary, Teen, and Adult Students.* This is the book that you have in front of you.

In my weekly meetings with struggling readers or non-readers, I noticed that most of them tried to read by guessing at words. This was troublesome, because guessing, instead of genuinely reading words on a page, does not constitute real reading. My students inspired me to create a program that would meet their needs and literally take the guesswork out of reading.

This book provides:

- Complete instructions for teaching students of any age how to read and spell.
- Lessons designed for one-on-one instruction that can be applied also with small groups.
- Lessons configured so that students may learn at their own pace.
- The introduction of alphabet letters in a sequence that enables students to read at least seven words by the end of the first lesson.
- An easy-to-teach format designed so that anyone who is literate can give the lessons. (This was important for our remedial reading program since the instructors differed from week to week.)
- An emphasis on comprehension and spelling. Reading and spelling are skills ideally learned at the same time.
- A format that eliminates the option of guessing. Pictures and illustrations are absent from our lessons to keep students from having clues that might facilitate guessing. Students are given no choice but to focus on the letters of the words.
- A system for documenting student achievement, using an at-a-glance format.

Reading and Spelling Pure & Simple develops reading, comprehension, and spelling skills in 90 lessons. The core of the program is a mere 77 pages. That's it! The rest of the book is support material for the tutor or teacher.

The lessons in this book have been used with success with students in public and private schools, home schools, church ministries, and literacy programs. Students learning English as a second language (ESL) have done well with this material, as have persons diagnosed with attention deficit disorders and dyslexia. By Lesson 90, students typically will be reading at an advanced level and will have a sizeable vocabulary.

I wish to emphasize that these lessons are based on many hours of research and observation from my many years of teaching experience. Educators at all levels of instruction and a broad band of professionals reviewed the material and helped hone it.

—Deede Cauley
March 2012

Reading Is All About Patterns

English is a pattern-based language. Words are constructed from letters of the alphabet, with each of the letters representing one or more sound patterns. The behavior of letters and letter combinations is actually quite consistent and reliable, and this means that students who learn the sound and spelling patterns have the tools to read and spell. In all there are 26 alphabet letters, less than 50 sound patterns, and some 250 spelling patterns. The beauty of knowing patterns is that it eliminates the need to memorize words one-by-one and truly makes every word of English accessible.

This reading curriculum methodically teaches the sound and spelling patterns of English. A cardinal rule is that letters, syllables, and words are read (and spelled) from left to right. Reading is meant to be an orderly process, a one-way, left-to-right procession. No other approach is as sure-footed. This rule seems obvious to people who have been taught it, but it's shocking how many of today's students have not been given this most basic of instructions. Again, the unbendable rule that we will teach from Day One is that we always read and spell from left to right!

Instruction begins with short-vowel words because the short-vowel pattern is easy to learn. More than half of the syllables and words in English follow this pattern. All 32 lessons of Unit 1 are devoted to short-vowel words. Unit 2 introduces most of the long-vowel patterns. A few more patterns are introduced in Unit 3, at which point your student will know more than three-quarters of the patterns found in English. Unit 4 covers irregular sounds and spellings, including so-called sight words. Unit 4 also puts all the pieces together and practices all the concepts and patterns. Practice is vital to your student becoming a self-assured reader. If you faithfully follow the instructions, by Lesson 90, your student will be reading and spelling five- and six-syllable words with ease and comprehending their meaning.

Sound and spelling patterns are like building blocks. We will introduce one pattern at a time. Most students will become excited and energized as they apply the patterns and discover that it is not difficult to learn to read and spell.

We have structured this program to develop and improve literacy in persons of any age. **Success is attainable by students who have a willingness to learn, a caring tutor, and a well-designed reading program**. With *Reading and Spelling Pure & Simple* an instructor has all of the tools needed to promote reading and spelling success.

In this book, we refer to the student as "he."
The instructor may use "he" and "she" interchangeably.

General Information About the Program

1. You do not have to prepare lesson plans for any of the lessons in this book. The planning has already been done for you. The teaching protocol, consisting of four steps, is the same for all 90 lessons.

2. Every lesson has a brief set of instructions, never more than one page long. Included are teaching tips, insights about learners, and explanations about our teaching method. Your effectiveness as an instructor will be enhanced by your knowing the reasons we approach the teaching of reading as we do. Rest assured that our method is thoughtfully designed, systematic, sequential, and research-based. We try to explain fundamental reading concepts succinctly, giving you the information you need to help your student be successful. (The aim of the support material is to equip you to be an effective reading instructor, not necessarily to be a scholar.)

3. There are some excellent teaching tips in the Pre-Unit! (You have the option of skipping the Pre-Unit if your student already knows the alphabet letters and their basic sounds.) If you will not be using the Pre-Unit, we encourage you to thumb through this section to capture the instructional nuggets. For example, the overview contains a sample dialog for teaching a letter sound. In Lesson B, we suggest a way you can help a distracted student gain focus. We also explain how to use a No. 2 pencil to control lesson flow and give your student positive, non-verbal feedback. There is also a note about why it is important for you to monitor your student's eye movement.

More teaching tips are interspersed throughout the book. The first 23 lessons are especially so endowed. Take a few minutes to scan these pages before you begin teaching your first lesson. You will gain a sense of how the program flows. Practical and easy-to-implement ideas for the classroom teacher are provided on pages 201-205.

4. Signposts are provided on all of the instruction pages to guide you. You will see headings like these:

NEW CONCEPT	**LEARN**
NEW PATTERN	**PRACTICE**
INTRODUCE	**REVIEW**

Just follow these markers. The lessons are progressive, meaning knowledge of reading and spelling patterns will build. Review exercises are presented frequently to help your student achieve mastery. Feel free to share some of the background information from the instruction pages with your student. Use your judgment in deciding what to mention.

5. This reading program has no speed limits! *Please do not rush through the lessons.* DO STAY on a lesson for as long as it takes for your student to become highly proficient. (You even have the option of doing a "go back" and starting over if you think it wise.) Proceed at a pace that enables your student to excel.

The next several pages provide a bird's-eye view of the curriculum and will help you get ready to teach the lessons.

The 48 Sounds of English

There are 48 sounds of the English language that will be taught in this book, distributed over four units. The sounds and a sample word for each are as follows:

Pre-Unit and Lesson 1

(18 Sounds)

|ă|	apple
|b|	baseball
|f|	fish
|g|	guitar
|h|	hat
|j|	jacket
|l|	light bulb
|m|	money
|n|	nose
|p|	pen
|r|	run
|s|	sun
|t|	tent
|v|	vase
|w|	web
|ks|	box
|y|	yoyo
|z|	zebra

Unit 1

(14 Sounds)

|ĭ|	igloo
|ŏ| (|ô| or |ä|)	on / off
|ŭ| (|ə|)	umbrella
|ĕ|	egg
|d|	dog
|k|	key
|khw|	question mark
|ngk|	ink
|ng|	ring
|sh|	ship
|ch|	chair
|hw|	whistle
|th|	thumb
|th|	this

Unit 2

(7 Sounds)

|ē|	east
|ā|	acorn
|âr|	hair
|ō|	oval
|ī|	ice
|ū|	cube
|ü|	moon

Unit 3

(8 Sounds)

|ů|	foot
|ô|	saw
|ä|	car
|ə|	balloon
|ōē| or |ōĭ|	coin
|ow|	clouds
|ər|	earth
|zh|	garage

Unit 4

(1 Sound)

|gz|	exit

Procedure for Teaching the Lessons

The teaching template is the same for all 90 lessons. More detailed instructions are available at the start of the Pre-Unit and at the start of Unit 1. Here is a brief overview of the four steps for teaching each lesson.

Teaching Template for All 90 Lessons

1. Read.
2. Discuss word meanings.
3. Spell.
4. Mark the chart.

Step 1 **READ.** To begin a lesson, point with a sharpened pencil to the first letter (left side) of the first word in Roman numeral I, so that your student knows where to focus his eyes. Tell him that, in English, we always read in one direction, from left to right. Direct your student to sound out the letters in the word and not skip any letters. Next, in the same manner, point to the left side of the other words in the list and have your student read these words out loud.

Step 2 **DISCUSS WORD MEANINGS.** Discuss the meaning of words as you go through each lesson. This is important! Keep a dictionary handy for reference.

Step 3 **SPELL.** Call out (recite) the words in the lesson and have your student write them on notebook paper. Continue practicing the lesson words until your student writes them accurately and without hesitation.

When you are finished with a lesson, ask your student if he wants to read the entire lesson again or reread one or more of the word lists. *Total mastery of the word patterns is more important than speed!*

Step 4 **MARK THE CHART.** Use one of the completion (progress) charts supplied at the back of this book to keep a record of your student's achievement. Enter a 100 each time he succeeds in accurately reading and spelling a word list.

Advice for Teachers and Tutors: Relax. Smile! Keep It Simple

An instructor does not need to have all the answers or instantly understand every concept in this book. The teacher just needs to be able to read the words in the current lesson and follow simple instructions.

Do check a dictionary if a word's meaning is unknown or difficult to explain.

Do not let the information in this curriculum overwhelm or stress you. Can you read the words in the list? If so, you are qualified to teach the lesson.

Teacher Preparation (Critical Information)

Because all of the lessons in this book will be taught following the same four steps, the preparation for teaching is greatly simplified. You will be asking your student to **read** and **spell** and **know the meaning** of the words in each lesson. To track your student's progress in these skill areas, you will make notations on one of the **completion charts** provided at the back of the book.

Lesson Pages. Each lesson introduces a new pronunciation and spelling pattern or reviews a previously introduced pattern. Since each segment builds to the next, students will receive the most benefit by learning the lessons in order. Each lesson is divided into six or fewer word lists organized by Roman numeral (I, II, III, IV, V, and VI). This arrangement allows flexibility in pacing the lessons. Your student will be expected to read and spell all of the words listed in a lesson before you sign off on that lesson.

Sound Charts. Sound charts are provided at the front of the Pre-Unit and units 1, 2, 3, and 4. The charts are intended as backup and support for the teacher or tutor. We seldom use these charts with students. Allowing students to refer back and forth from a sound chart to the lesson words is usually unnecessary and cumbersome. This "two-stepping" is analogous to an ESL student interpreting a word in his native language, then crossing over into English. Our goal is to have students make an immediate, automatic connection between letter and sound.

Completion Charts. Before you begin the lessons, you will need to select a completion (progress) chart to use with your student. The charts are found starting on page 273. Completion charts are visually rewarding for both student and teacher.

Progress Monitoring Table. If you are using these lessons for Response to Intervention (RTI), you might want to keep records on the Progress Monitoring Table supplied at page 277. It has space for your notes and impressions and comes with a convenient word tabulator (page 281).

Supply List. A supply list is found on page xviii. A glance at this page will remind you of the items you will need for each lesson. One item you surely must have is a good dictionary. Dictionaries that feature pronunciation helps, usage notes, and word illustrations are the most useful. We highly recommend *The American Heritage Dictionary of the English Language*, fourth edition, published by Houghton Mifflin Harcourt.

Instruction Pages. Instructions for each lesson are always located adjacent to the lesson page. A boxed summary is provided. Spelling patterns are indicated with **bold** and sometimes underlined letters; pronunciations and sound patterns are identified inside vertical lines: | |. A comprehensive sound chart for the forty-eight sounds taught in this book is provided on page xiv.

Desk and Chairs. Provide a solid surface, preferably a desk or table, for reading and writing the lessons. If either of these is not available, use a hardback book. Sit side by side so that the lesson page can be seen by the instructor and the student. The instructor needs to be able to comfortably point to the left side of each word while working with the student and must be able to observe the student's spelling of words so that corrections can be made immediately.

Meeting Place.   Determine the best available place to conduct the lessons. Find a location that has good lighting and as few distractions as possible.

Meeting Times.   Daily lessons are always better than weekly. More than once a day is optimal, especially if your student has to overcome bad reading habits, such as the tendency to guess. The transition to left-to-right reading will be easier for your student if his outside reading is limited as much as possible. If working at home or tutoring a student elsewhere, it would be ideal to begin the lessons during the summer. Before and after school is also an option. Consider your student's age, health, attention span, and time available when scheduling session times. An adult student typically can work for one to three hours at a stretch. A 12-year-old student usually can concentrate for 30 minutes to two hours. An elementary or kindergarten student might only be able to concentrate, initially, for 15 to 45 minutes (in which case it would be highly preferable to do several 10- or 15-minute lessons throughout the course of the day). Students almost always increase their ability to focus as they advance through the lessons.

Do I Begin with Lesson 1 or the Pre-Unit?   Start with Lesson 1 if your student knows the vowel and consonant sounds and reads the first list of words in Lesson 1 with ease. Otherwise, begin with the Pre-Unit starting on page 1. Completing the Pre-Unit will prepare your student to successfully handle Lesson 1. (Lesson E of the Pre-Unit and Lesson 1 of the main unit share the same words.) The launching point should be the lesson that best meets the needs and fits the ability of your student. (On the page following the supply list, you will find a subjective evaluation tool for assessing new reading students. The use of this tool is strictly optional.) We have found that adults, teens, and even straight-A students do not mind starting with Lesson A. Do not be fooled by the apparent simplicity of the words. Reading, like spelling, is a sequential process.

After your student has read a lesson, you will ask him if he would like to reread some or all of the words. We want students to master the material and be self-assured. As the learning progresses and the patterns increase in number, having that confidence will become more and more important. Every effort has been made with each successive lesson to use only words whose patterns have already been introduced or are now being introduced. This selectivity helps students be successful.

Final Advice for the Instructor.   If you follow the instructions faithfully, you will succeed. We believe that you will enjoy teaching this curriculum. We will remind you from time to time to be positive and encouraging. Your student *will* learn to read and spell!

Ready, Set, Go!   Find a suitable learning spot, gather the few needed supplies (see supply list), and pre-view the list of words in Lesson 1 (or Lesson A). Also, take a few minutes to scan the headings on the instruction pages to see what lies ahead. Remember, you don't have to know all of the patterns or be an expert. You just need to be able to read a list of words. If your student asks a question for which you do not have an answer, tell him that you will see if you can find the answer. The information will most likely be found somewhere in this book. So, relax . . . you can do this!

SUPPLIES NEEDED

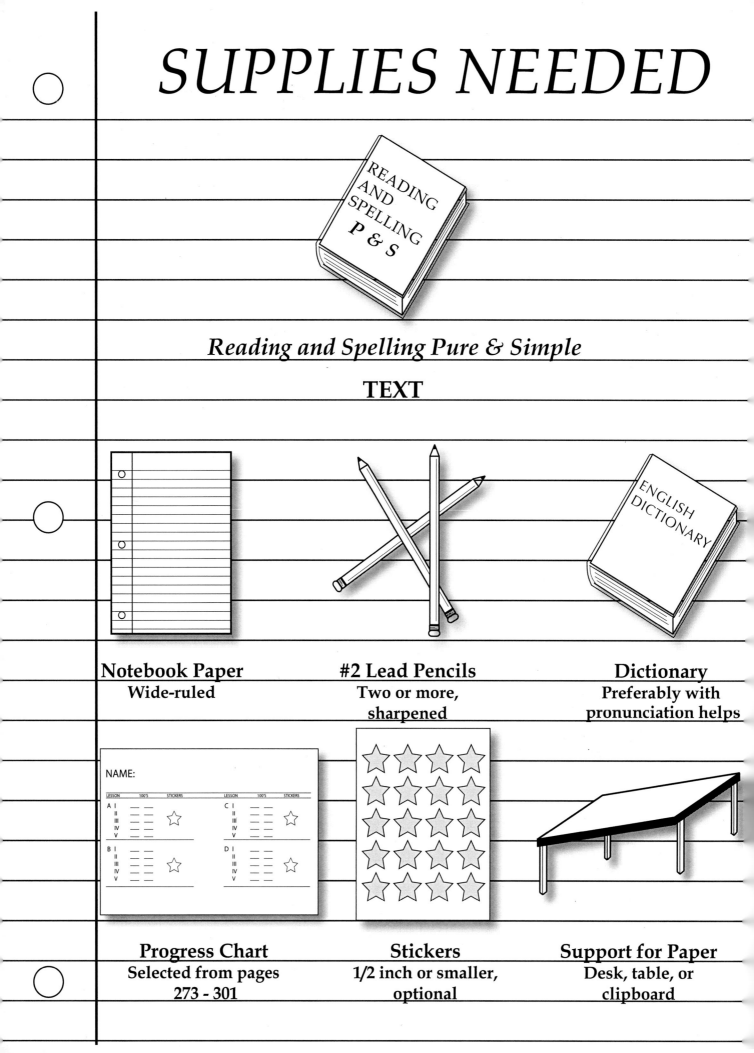

Reading and Spelling Pure & Simple

TEXT

Notebook Paper
Wide-ruled

#2 Lead Pencils
Two or more, sharpened

Dictionary
Preferably with pronunciation helps

NAME:

LESSON	100'S	STICKERS	LESSON	100'S	STICKERS
A I			C I		
II			II		
III		☆	III		☆
IV			IV		
V			V		
B I			D I		
II			II		
III		☆	III		☆
IV			IV		
V			V		

Progress Chart
Selected from pages 273 - 301

Stickers
1/2 inch or smaller, optional

Support for Paper
Desk, table, or clipboard

Ideas for Quickly Evaluating a New Reading Student

If your student is an inexperienced reader or a reader who needs remedial work, you may wish to do a reading evaluation. This section provides a subjective tool to assess reading issues. If you choose to do an evaluation (whether at the start of the lessons, mid-way through, or after completion), you will be asking your student to read a short text.

▶ Preparation.

Find a reading passage that is approximately 100 (or 150) words in length and appropriate for your student. Choose something that he has not read before.
You can select this text from the many pre-packaged grade-level evaluation tools.
You may also use one of your student's textbooks, a magazine of interest to your adult learner, a newspaper, or a book, *so long as there are no illustrations supporting the passage.* Make two copies of the sample text, one for the student and one for you.
You will mark on your copy.

▶ Direct your student to read the passage out loud. Make no comments, just listen.

While your student is reading the text, you will, on your copy . . .

- Jot down any words your student did not know, added, or mispronounced.
- Cross out (line through) any words your student skipped.
- Write an "H" over a word that your student hesitated to pronounce.
- Write a "C" over a word that he mishandled but then corrected.

Sample Evaluation (notice how the instructor marked her copy of the text)

                    rod   *af*
John and his younger sister, Susan, were standing on a ~~road~~ just after
       tal   *off*
school. John was a ~~tall~~ boy ~~of~~ about fourteen years of age. Susan was a smaller girl
                   H   *H C*
who was twelve years old. Susan stood quietly for a while in the cold, late afternoon.
   bock   *H breathing C*
When she broke her silence, she said, "Look! See my breath comes out as smoke!"
    stem   *told*
"That's ~~steam~~ not smoke," John ~~corrected~~ her. Susan rolled her eyes, then said,
     went   *at*   *chose*   *eat/eating at*
"I'm cold, I ~~want~~ to ~~eat~~." "Well, we can ~~choose~~ between ~~either~~ the deli," John said,
                           wole
"or taking the bus home. If we eat out, we will have to walk the ~~whole~~ way home at
  nig   *tack*   *form her*   *rid*
~~night~~. I would rather ~~take~~ the bus ~~from here~~ and ~~ride~~ home." "Can't we do both?"
                   H(skip)   kas
Susan asked. John shook his head and said, "No. I don't have ~~enough cash~~ for both."
   H H   skip skip skip   *said*
Susan ~~thought for a minute before saying~~, "Let's take the bus. Mom's dinners are

better anyway."   **[This passage is 157 words long.]**

▶ Ask comprehension questions.

After your student has read the passage, ask him a question or two from each of the following categories to see if he understood what he read.

- Fact questions ask **who, what,** and **where.**
- Sequencing questions ask the student to tell about events in chronological order or to tell about **when, after, before, then, next, yesterday,** or **tomorrow.**
- Opinion questions ask **why** or **how.**
- Inference questions ask **what might be true,** even though it is not directly stated within the passage. Ask what might have happened before the story began or after it ended.

Comprehension is the activity of paying attention, understanding, remembering, and being able to communicate what has been read.

If comprehension is the only concern you have about your student, there are two simple activities that usually will help. (1) Tell your student to silently read a sentence or two. Now cover the text and ask some questions. If your student is not providing satisfactory answers, have him reread the passage. Use this repeat reading process as often as needed to break the *"not listening to what is being read"* habit of the brain. It's almost as if the brain eventually wakes up after repeated querying and says to itself, *"Do I have to read this again?! I guess I'd better pay attention."* (2) To maintain focus, have your student use his finger or a pencil to point at the words as he reads across a line.

▶ Evaluate Pace.

Pay attention to the pace at which your student reads.

- Does he read too slowly?
- Does he read too fast?
- Does he read without pausing for commas or stopping at periods?

If your student reads too rapidly or fails to pause at commas or stop at periods, do him a favor and demonstrate correct reading tempo and punctuation manners. Also, have your student reread sentences until he succeeds in slowing himself down. Encourage him to give appropriate inflection at question and exclamation marks. One instructor we know encourages her students to pretend that reading is "a slow song." She taps her finger to set the tempo while her students are reading. One of her students once commented, "My brain likes to read to a slow song!"

A plodding or erratic pace may indicate that your student lacks a basic understanding of the words. He will benefit from the strong emphasis placed on comprehension in this book.

Q & A with Deede Cauley
Answers to Seventeen Often Asked Questions

1. What's so important about reading and spelling?

2. Why does this curriculum teach reading and spelling at the same time?

3. Why do we insist on comprehension?

4. Why are sentences and pictures absent from this curriculum?

5. When does the student begin to read sentences and stories?

6. Does a student need to know the alphabet in order?

7. Does the student need to know which letters are vowels and which letters are consonants?

8. Why is so much emphasis placed on reading "from left to right"?

9. What is meant by an "automatic" reading response?

10. Can these one-on-one lessons have an impact on a teacher's classroom?

11. Should allowances be made for regional pronunciations?

12. Will a "straight A" or "A / B" student benefit from this reading program?

13. Will these lessons work for students who have been diagnosed with dyslexia, A.D.D., A.D.H.D., or autism?

14. Are these lessons serviceable for students for whom English is a second language (ESL)?

15. Has "whole word" reading been discredited?

16. Are there age factors to consider in teaching reading?
    - Working with teens and adults
    - Working with elementary students
    - Working with preschoolers

17. Any special advice for moms and dads?

Q & A with Deede Cauley

When I give my reading workshops, tutor students, and work alongside other instructors, I am often asked certain questions. This chapter provides the answers to the seventeen most commonly raised questions.

1. What's so important about reading and spelling?

Reading is the foundational skill. We learn to read in order to understand the printed word. We learn to spell so that we can use the written word to communicate with others. Basically, the ability to read and spell helps us access information and enjoy life.

Does your student understand the importance of learning to read? If not, spend a few minutes discussing the benefits of reading. Here are some thoughts:

If you can read, you can...
• understand a prescription label (and take your medicines safely)
• pass a driver's test
• read a restaurant menu
• heed warning signs
• follow an instruction manual
• appreciate billboard messages
• read letters, newspapers, magazines, and books.

See if your student can come up with more benefits of knowing how to read. Encourage him to think ahead about how reading will help him in life.

2. Why does this curriculum teach reading and spelling at the same time?

Reading and spelling are related skills. Learning to read and spell at the same time is like the proverbial killing of two birds with one stone. It is the most efficient use of your and your student's time.

Spelling should never be considered as somehow less important than reading. It deserves equal time and attention. The value of being a good, accurate speller will become more apparent as your student gets older. The time will come when he will fill out a job application, respond to a boss's memo, compose a letter, write a report, or simply send an e-mail or "tweet" to a friend. Being a good speller is part of being well educated.

The mental and physical processes of becoming a reader are somewhat complex. For example, reading involves processing information from **eye** to **brain** during silent reading and from **eye** to **brain** to **mouth** during oral reading. Spelling is even more complicated, involving participation by the **ear, brain,** and **eyes** (hearing a word + writing or typing it + recognizing the way the word should look). Spelling also entails processing information from **brain** to **mouth,** as when a student spells out loud, and from **brain** to **hand as when a student** writes or types words on paper. Some students will be better readers than spellers, and vice versa. That's okay. Just be sure your student is faithful in reading all of the words in the lessons and doing all of the spelling exercises.

3. Why do we insist on comprehension?

Reading is pointless if a reader does not understand the meaning of words. This is why we emphasize the importance of reading for comprehension beginning with the very first word in Lesson 1. By spending time discussing the meaning of words, you will help your student develop the habit of automatically looking for meaning while reading. Understanding what the words signify will make reading interesting, satisfying, and useful.

4. Why are sentences and pictures absent from this curriculum?

The absence of pictures and sentences is intentional. It has been our observation that many students habitually guess at words. They have not learned that words are identifiable by the sounds that the individual letters of the words make. It is so much better to know and apply the sound patterns than to guess at words. Why guess if you can know?

Pictures provide context clues that may actually impede the reading process. To break dependency on clues, we have chosen not to provide illustrations. (We do, however, provide illustrated sound charts to help the instructor explain and model the sounds of the alphabet letters.) Likewise, the lessons do not present sentences, just word lists. Again, this is intentional. The reading of full sentences will come quite naturally in time, after your student has mastered the groundwork. Do students miss having sentences and stories as they work through these lessons? Our experience has been that they don't miss them one bit. In fact, if you introduce sentences or a story too early, your student will probably ask you, with some bewilderment, what happened to the word lists.

5. When does the student begin to read sentences and stories?

After your student completes the 90th lesson, he will segue into reading sentences and whole stories. It is amazing how ready and primed your student will be for this new venture. He will quickly discover that the task is almost effortless. As you and your student read a book aloud, ask comprehension questions. At first, some students will hesitate to answer questions. Supply the answers for those who look stressed. This is simply a confidence problem, not a reading problem. You and your student are getting ready to "reap what you have sown" and will now be able to enjoy the fruits of your labor.

You and your student can take turns reading out loud. Encourage your student to read with meaning. This is not to be treated as a race. Take your time and enjoy the story. Expect that your student might need to be coached about how to treat commas (a comma indicates a pause), periods (a period indicates a stop), and other punctuation marks (raise the tone into a question when the sentence ends with a question mark and show excitement, increased volume, or intensity, as appropriate, when the sentence ends with an exclamation mark).

At least a week before you complete the 90th lesson, you will need to start looking for a book that will interest your student, because after the final lesson, you and he will begin a reading project together. My students are especially fond of reading *Gifted Hands* by the renowned black neurosurgeon, Dr. Ben Carson.

6. Does a student need to know the alphabet in order?

Yes! It is imperative that a student know the alphabet in order. To use a dictionary or a telephone book, for example, a person needs to know alphabetical order. The most effective way to learn the alphabet is to memorize "The Alphabet Song." The melody for "The Alphabet Song" is the same as the melody for "Twinkle, Twinkle, Little Star."

"a b c d e f g, h i j k l m n o p, q r s, t u v, w x, y and z.

Now I've said my **A B C**'s . . . Next time won't you say them with me?"

7. Does the student need to know which letters are vowels and which letters are consonants?

Yes! Words are formed by putting letters of the alphabet into certain patterns. For example, every word has at least one vowel. The five vowels—**a**, **e**, **i**, **o**, and **u**—are absolutely key to pronouncing words. The twenty-one consonants—**b**, **c**, **d**, **f**, **g**, **h**, **j**, **k**, **l**, **m**, **n**, **p**, **q**, **r**, **s**, **t**, **v**, **w**, **x**, **y**, **z**—are fairly predictable as to the sounds they make, with the exception of **y** and **w**, which sometimes function as vowels.

Some letters make more than one sound. This is an important point. So let's repeat it: Some letters have more than one sound. The **s** in **Sis**, for example, says |s|, but the **s** in **his** says |z|. In all, there are 48 sounds and some 250 spelling patterns associated with the 26 letters in the English alphabet. This is not too many to learn.

8. Why is so much emphasis placed on reading "from left to right"?

There really is no other way to read and spell! English words are meant to be read and spelled from left to right. Shockingly, many reading programs do not teach this fundamental left-to-right principle. Some teach a scanning method, telling the student to look for familiar letter shapes somewhere in the words. Others teach a "whole word" memorization method, sort of like hieroglyphics. Reading from left to right, by contrast, provides **predictability** and **logical direction**. "Left-to-right" is easy to remember. It is dependable. It is a one-way street that prevents a wrong turn. Students who have begun the reading journey but not developed the left-to-right habit may need constant reminders and gentle encouragement. It is essential that beginning readers develop this necessary routine. Cursive writing requires a student to write from left to right.

9. What is meant by an "automatic" reading response?

An automatic reading response is one that is smooth and without hesitation. A student who hesitates when pronouncing or spelling a pattern needs more practice. Sounding out words is important for beginning readers and spellers, and this will initially slow them down, but the goal is to practice until their reading response is fluid and immediate. When the response becomes automatic, the student can concentrate more on content and meaning.

10. Can these one-on-one lessons have an impact on a teacher's classroom?

Yes. Every student needs to know the principles taught in these lessons. These principles include reading and spelling from left to right; focusing on the alphabet letter sounds and spellings; and keeping the focus on comprehension as the habit of "pattern reading" is built. When these principles are followed, the impact in the teacher's classroom will be discernible. The best instruction comes from an adult teaching a student one-on-one, but small group teaching can also be effective. Classroom-tested ideas are included on pages 201-205.

11. Should allowances be made for regional pronunciations?

Let's consider the word **pecan**. A person from New York typically says |pē′ • kən|. A person from the state of Washington says |pē′ • kăn′|. A Texan, on the other hand, says |pə • kŏn′|. Now consider the word **pencil**. An Oklahoman would say |pĭn′ • səl|, but a Minnesotan would say |pĕn′ • sĭl|. And when it comes to **wh**, as in **which** and **when**, a person from Kansas says |hwĭch| and |hwĕn|, but a person from Texas or Oklahoma says |wĭch| or |wĭn|. We recommend using the classic pronunciation as   shown in a dictionary, but feel free to adjust for regional differences. Sometimes you have to pick your battles.

12. Will a "straight A" or "A/B" student benefit from this reading program?

Do not be surprised if a "straight A" or "A/B" student is enthusiastic about these lessons. These students may be high achievers because they are excellent memorizers and can usually determine word meanings based on context or pictures. These same students might initially have trouble when faced with our lessons, though, as our material is bereft of context clues. In the long run, all students are better served by learning true phonics and the left-to-right pattern for sounding out words than by learning to memorize.

13. Will these lessons work for students who have been diagnosed with dyslexia, A.D.D., A.D.H.D., or autism?

We know of a young man, diagnosed with autism, who refused to do any school work. When the classroom aide tried these lessons with him, to everyone's surprise, the student worked with intensity. When the instructor used sentences to illustrate the meanings of the words, the student balked, but the next day he began making up his own sentences to show he understood. The instructional team was thrilled. We believe this autistic student responded well to the lessons because of two factors: (1) the uncomplicated nature of the lessons, and (2) the organized manner in which the teacher used a pencil to point to the beginning of each word on our lists. This helped the student to focus. Other students diagnosed with dyslexia, A.D.D. or A.D.H.D with whom we have worked have had similar good results.

14. Are these lessons serviceable for students for whom English is a second language (ESL)?

Learning English can be overwhelming for ESL students. To complicate matters, English has homophones, homonyms, homographs, idioms, and irregular phrases. If you have an ESL student, simply work through each lesson methodically and in order. ESL students tend to do well with this curriculum. Vocabulary building is one of our program's strong suits. As students learn to pronounce, spell, and understand the meaning of words, and as the instructor uses sentences to describe the words, the students will become more comfortable with the language.

Students often think in their original language and translate into English before speaking or writing words. Allow adequate time for them to do this mental processing. Answer your student's questions but keep discussion (your words) to a minimum. Some students have found it helpful to take notes during a session or to spend a few minutes between sessions studying or memorizing words. However, there is no need for this, as everything can be reinforced through review during the regular sessions. Work as quickly as the ESL student is able. Relax and smile. Allow your student to learn the lessons at his own pace. Review when needed.

15. Has "whole word" reading been discredited?

For years we have been told that people read by looking at the whole word. New laser technology has enabled researchers to follow readers' eye movements, and we now know that good readers actually look at every letter in a word. The key to overcoming deficiencies ("guess" reading and the inaccuracies it produces) is to train students to see and read each letter. That is what this book is designed to do.

Different parts of the brain appear to be involved in phonics-based reading than in guess-based or memorization-based reading. These findings are from magnetic imaging studies. Students who guess at words are busy trying to remember where they previously have seen a word. They glance at pictures for context clues or try to match a word to the perceived story line. This approach is fatiguing and is not what real reading is about. Real reading is linear and accurate.

16. Are there age factors to consider in teaching reading?

Yes. The age of a student usually is an important variable in how we approach the teaching of reading. Age affects everything from "desk time" and attention span to the reasons the student is learning to read. It even will affect the degree to which your student initially applies the newly acquired patterns and skills to outside reading.

• Working with teens and adults

Older students are sometimes fearful that they cannot learn to read. Encourage your student to just try these lessons. Start with Lesson A or Lesson 1, depending on the readiness of your student. An adult or teen can work for two or three hours and not lose concentration. Work as long, as quickly, and as often as you and your student have time and energy. Daily lessons are always better than weekly.

Adults and teens are different from younger students. Once an older student gets enthused about learning, in most cases, the new information will be applied to anything and everything that student is doing. Older students, unlike younger students, seem to be less compartmentalized when learning to read.

Older students are more prone to quitting before the lessons are complete. There are several reasons for this. First, they never thought that reading was an option for them, but now that they can read words and road signs nearly everywhere they go, they are satisfied. Second, older students might entertain the notion that this newfound reading ability obligates them to do more than they are accustomed to doing. This makes them anxious. For example, a young adult male might think that he has to go to college since he no longer has the excuse that he can't read. Assure these adults that being able to read opens doors, but it's their choice whether or not to walk through those doors.

If a teen or adult quits before the lessons are complete, it is probably not the tutor or teacher's fault. The student might be quitting because, strangely enough, the instruction was successful: The student now can read well enough to do what he set out to do. Perhaps his goal was to test for a driver's license, pass the GED, or take a civil service exam so he can become a police officer or public employee. Would it be best if he completed all of the lessons? Absolutely! Just do what you can to encourage him to cross the finish line of the 90th and final lesson.

• **Working with elementary students**

Elementary students who have little or no reading experience may easily succeed with our curriculum. Children are eager to learn, and having a good reading program makes all the difference. Reading proficiency is usually achievable before the end of first grade.

I have worked with students (even as young as kindergarten and first grade) who already have an intensely ingrained habit of guessing at words. These elementary students, as they work through the lessons, will not necessarily show immediate improvement in school, as they tend not to apply what they are learning in reading to their other classroom work. There are several reasons for this. Guessing entails calling out the first word that comes to mind. Switching gears to engage in real reading requires effort. Also, children do not usually have the maturity to see the value that real reading will have in their lives. They don't yet understand the bigger picture.

Children sometimes will need to complete up to at least Lesson 50 before their reading improvement begins to become apparent to others. You, the instructor, will need to continue working through the lessons till your student masters each pattern. By the time he has made it three-fourths of the way through the curriculum, he may become one of the best readers in the class. If you take your time and work consistently, your student will become an accomplished reader and speller.

It is especially important for elementary students to have daily lessons. Daily lessons produce the best results. If that is not an option, then study at least weekly. Weekly is better than having no lessons at all. Students who work all the way through these lessons during the summer may find that they have surpassed their peers.

Please, as much as possible, limit your elementary student's exposure to outside reading materials while this curriculum is being taught. It is not a good idea to switch back and forth between the structure of this program and the relative lack of structure characteristic of outside reading activities. If other reading is required, attempt to do these word lists before any other reading is done. For more insight on this, see Lesson 50 (page 102).

- ## Working with preschoolers

It is possible for preschoolers to learn to read, but do not insist on it. Create pleasant times by reading wonderful books to them. Encourage your child to draw and color, as these activities will enhance hand/eye coordination and help in the writing of alphabet letters in the future.

Before using these lessons with a young student, be sure that he:

Can recite the letters of the alphabet in order.

Knows that letters have sounds and that these sounds can be learned.

It isn't important that all of the sounds of the letters are known, just that the preschooler understands that each letter has a special sound that he can learn to recognize and say.

Is able to write the letters of the alphabet.

Test your student by asking questions.

> *"Can you write on paper the letter **M**?"*
> *"Can you write the letter that makes the |**m**| sound?"*
> *"What is the first sound you hear in the word **mat**?"*
> *"Can you write the first letter that you hear when I say '**mat**'?"*
> *"What is the last sound you hear in the word '**am**'?"*
> *"Can you write on paper the last letter you hear in the word '**am**'?"*

Children usually learn to print upper-case letters [A, B, C] before they learn the lower-case equivalent [a, b, c]. Sometimes you will see an inconsistent mix. Use your judgment about requiring one style over the other. As you go through the lessons, you will have opportunities to tutor your student about penmanship and letter cases.

17. Any special advice for moms and dads?

If you are teaching this curriculum to your own child, be intentional about being patient. The words **am** and **at** in Lesson A seem like such simple words. We tend to forget that it takes a lot of doing to launch a new skill. Be patient with your child! DO NOT CRITICIZE OR BERATE. Let your youngster have fun and enjoy the journey.

About the Author

Deede Hinckley Cauley (M. Ed., LPC, LMFT) has an impressive family heritage of service in the public schools. Collectively, her family has devoted more than 185 years (and counting) to the teaching profession. She herself has taught at nearly every level of instruction (university, college, high school, and middle school) in such subjects as reading, English, American history, social studies, psychology, and human growth and development. She holds lifetime certificates in Texas, one as a secondary-level teacher, and the other as an all-levels public school counselor. In addition, Mrs. Cauley is a licensed professional counselor and licensed marriage and family therapist. Mrs. Cauley earned her bachelor of arts degree from Southern Methodist University and a master's degree in education, personnel, and guidance counseling from the University of North Texas in Denton.

Mrs. Cauley served, also, as a Special Agent with the Federal Bureau of Investigation. The training she received in investigative methodology and research at the FBI Academy in Quantico, Virginia, and later in the Dallas field office has benefited the development of this book.

Mrs. Cauley has been involved in teaching reading to adults, teens, and children for nearly thirty years. She has experience as a special education (lab) instructor in reading and English and is a charter member of an adult learn-to-read organization. She has had the privilege of home schooling her son for two years. Currently, Mrs. Cauley is president of The Real Reading Company. She devotes much of her time to writing, giving reading workshops, and tutoring students.

Mrs. Cauley lives in Big Spring, Texas, with Dr. Richard Cauley, a wonderful husband, father, friend, and excellent dentist by profession. Grayson Cauley, their son, gave time tutoring, designed the logo for the company, and designed the covers for this book series. He also illustrated the supply list and sound charts. As this book goes to press, he is in college at Texas Tech University in Lubbock, Texas.

Pre-Unit

Preparing for Lesson 1
with
Lessons A – E

Preparing for Lesson 1
with Lessons A Through E

Does your student know the letters of the alphabet and the order in which they appear? If not, now is the time to learn the alphabet. Popular ways to learn the English alphabet are to (1) memorize and practice "The Alphabet Song"; (2) practice writing the alphabet letters in order; and (3) use a set of flash cards to drill through the letters.

This Pre-Unit, consisting of Lessons A through E, is not needed by every student. Some students already recognize the letters of the alphabet and know the sounds associated with them. If this is the case with your student, you may proceed to Lesson 1 on page 23.

Lessons A through E contain valuable teaching tips for beginning instructors. Experienced teachers may also benefit from the observations and insights presented here.

Lesson A   introduces: *a, m, t, b*

Lesson B   introduces: *l, p, n*
                    Reviews: *a, m, t, b*

Lesson C   introduces: *s, g, r, f*
                    Reviews: *a, m, t, b, l, p, n*

Lesson D   introduces: *h, w, v, j*
                    Reviews: *a, m, t, b, l, p, n, s, g, r, f*

Lesson E   introduces: *x, y, z*
                    Reviews: *a, m, t, b, l, p, n, s, g, r, f, h, w, v, j*

Teachers: You will find these lessons easier to teach if you familiarize yourself with the information found on pages **xiii** (general information), **xv** (procedure), **xvi** (teacher prep), and **xviii** (supply list).

Sound Chart for the Pre-Unit

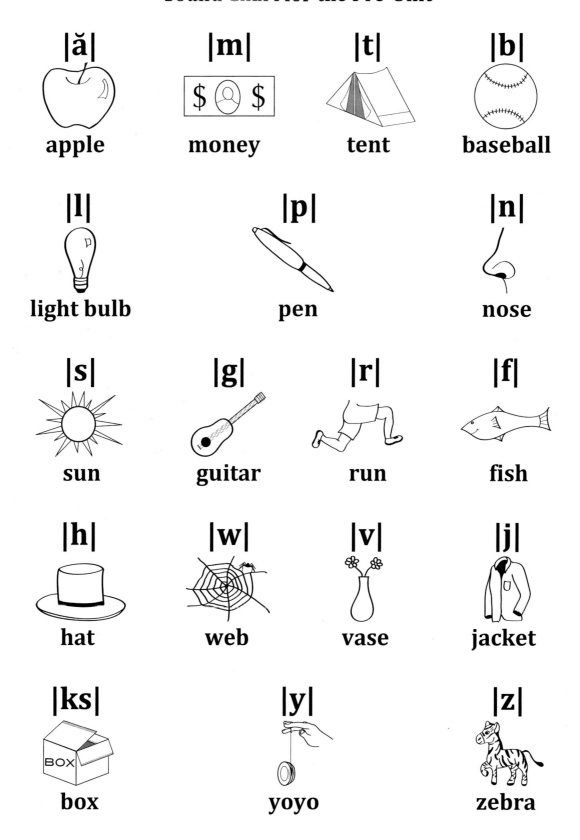

|ă|
apple

|m|
money

|t|
tent

|b|
baseball

|l|
light bulb

|p|
pen

|n|
nose

|s|
sun

|g|
guitar

|r|
run

|f|
fish

|h|
hat

|w|
web

|v|
vase

|j|
jacket

|ks|
box

|y|
yoyo

|z|
zebra

Overview of Lessons A Through E

"Do you know what this letter is?
*"That's right. It's **a**.*
*"Did you know that **a** makes a special sound? It says |ă|, as in **apple**.*
*"Let's say it together: |ă|, |ă|, |ă| . . . |ă| as in **apple**."*

Being introduced to a character of the alphabet and learning the sound that it makes is to take one's first step as a reader! We start with one letter, and once your student has mastered it, it will be time to introduce another letter, and another, and so forth. It is important for your student to realize that there is a connection between written letters and spoken sounds. (We'll discuss the fact later that some letters are capable of making more than one sound.) Recognizing the correlation between written letters and sounds is essential for real reading.

Reading is based on recognizable patterns. We prefer to explain reading concepts in terms of "patterns" rather than "rules." Students find patterns far less intimidating than rules. Being able to recognize letters and express their associated sounds enables students to read a huge array of words. There is no need to memorize words if one knows how to apply the patterns. Students who have received true phonics instruction will not guess at words, nor will they be dependent on other people to know what a word is or how to pronounce it.

Learning to spell is an integral part of this program. After your student has read several words, he will write the words on notebook paper. The act of writing by hand helps students remember words and creates "muscle memory." Writing also instills confidence and promotes mastery. We want students to know not only how to read but also how to write effectively. Don't skip the spelling process!

This Pre-Unit covers one vowel and seventeen consonants. After finishing Lesson E, your student will advance to Lesson 1. Lessons A through E are not needed by every student, as some pupils already have a good grasp of vowels and consonants. If your student hesitates over the words in Lesson 1, we advise you to start instead with Lesson A. (The last lesson in the Pre-Unit and the first lesson of the main unit intentionally cover the same one vowel and 17 consonants to make for a seamless transition.)

If you decide to skip the Pre-Unit, take a few minutes to skim through the helpful teaching tips and techniques found on pages 6, 8, 10, 12, and 14.

Watch your student's eyes! If he has a guessing habit, often he will look at you or at the ceiling instead of at the words printed on the page. Such a student usually is skilled at reading facial expressions to determine if a guessed-at word is correct. *Reading and Spelling* is designed to thwart the guessing habit. Undoing any habit takes time, so you may need to remind your student to pay attention to every letter in every word and to read (and spell) FROM LEFT TO RIGHT.

Instructions for Lesson A

> **Introduce the pronunciation and spelling pattern for the short sound of the vowel letter a. Also introduce the consonants m, t, and b.**

General Instructions

► **Point with a sharpened pencil to each of the large black letters listed across the top of the page: A a, M m, T t, and B b.** Ask your student to say each letter's sound: **a** says |ă|; **m** says |m| (not |ŭmŭh|); **t** says |t| (not |tŭh|); and **b** says |b| (not |bŭŭŭh|). The letter **b** has a clipped-off sound. References: Sound Chart (page 4) and List of 48 Sounds (page xiv).

► **At Roman numeral I, point to the left side of the first word: am. Ask your student to read this word out loud.** Discuss the meaning of **am** (am is a word that indicates existence) and give an example of this word in a sentence. *"I **am** reading with you."* Next, have your student read the second word **at** and also discuss its meaning (**at** is a location word). Example: *"I am **at** school."* Relax and take your time. Your student must train his brain and eyes to recognize letters, a process which accomplished readers tend to take for granted. Allow time for practicing until your student reads each word without hesitation. After your student has successfully read both words in Roman numeral I, mark the Pre-Unit Completion Chart (found on p. 283) with a 100 beside Roman numeral I, in the column marked **R** (R is for reading).

Teen and adult students usually do not need to have a completion chart until Lesson 1.

► **Next, say (call out) each word in Roman numeral I and have your student spell it on notebook paper.** Use the words in sentences. Allow time for your student to think about how to write the words. [You might ask, *"What letter makes the first sound you hear in **at**?"* (|ă| . . . **a**). *"What letter makes the second* sound *you hear?* (|t| . . . **t**). After your student has correctly spelled both words, mark the completion chart with a 100 beside the **S** (S is for spelling).

► **Now, have your student read and spell all of the rest of the words in Lesson A. Discuss the meanings of these words.** Keep a dictionary handy to look up unfamiliar or difficult-to-define words. Mark the completion (progress) chart.

II   **PRACTICE mat** and **tam.** *"There is a **mat** on the floor." "A **tam** is a hat."*

III   **PRACTICE tat** and **tab.** *"Megan and Kimberly's grandmother might teach them how to **tat** lace." "A **tab** in the notebook helps us find our place."* [You might point to a **tab** in a notebook.]

IV   **PRACTICE bat.** Note: B is pronounced |b|, not |bŭŭŭh|. Shorten or clip off the |ŭh| sound as much as possible. Direct your student to blend the first letter **b** with the second letter **a** to get |bă|, then add the last letter sound **t**: |bă| . . . |t| → |băt|. Words with multiple meanings, like **bat**, are easily understood in context. *"Jarod went to **bat** in the first inning of the game using his own baseball **bat**." "Mattias tried to **bat** away the black **bat** as it flew around his head."*

V & VI   **REVIEW** the reading and spelling of all seven words. Be sure that your student understands the word meanings. Ask for a definition or for a word to be used in a sentence or ask your student to act out a word. Mark the completion chart and let your student place a sticker in the space provided.

Lesson A

A a

M m   T t   B b

I.	am	at
II.	mat	tam
III.	tat	tab
IV.	bat	

Review

V.	bat	mat	tam	at
VI.	tab	am	tat	

Instructions for Lesson B

> **Introduce the pronunciation and spelling patterns for the consonant letters l, p, and n and continue with the sound of the short-vowel letter** a.

General Instructions

▶ Point with a sharpened pencil to each of the large black letters listed across the top of the page: **L l, P p,** and **N n.** Ask your student to say each letter's sound: **l** says |l|; **p** says |p| (not |pŭh|); **n** says |n| (not |nŭh|).

▶ Now, point to the first word in Roman numeral I and have your student read the word out loud: **lab.** Discuss the meaning of the word **lab.** (A **lab** is a room used for doing science experiments.) *"Nate did the experiment in the science lab."* Read, discuss the meaning of, and spell the next word: **Al.** *"Do you know my neighbor, Al?"* **Remind your student that we always read the letters of a word from LEFT to RIGHT.** When your student can confidently read and spell these two words, note this on the completion chart with a 100. For RTI requirements, use the Progress Monitoring Table (page 277).

Use your judgment about whether or not to insist on capitalization of the name **Al.** Capitalization will need to be addressed at some point. If you think this is the time to mention that people's names and other proper nouns start with a capital letter, do so. The same exercise of judgment is called for regarding the importance of penmanship.

▶ Have your student read, discuss the meaning of, and spell all of the words in rows II and III. As each set of words is correctly completed, record this on his completion chart.

II   PRACTICE pat, pal, map, tap, and **lap.** *"Charla will **pat** the puppy."* *"I have a **pal** named Dustin."* Ask your student whom he considers to be his friend or **pal.** *"The **map** will guide Maegan home."* *"Austin will **tap** you on the shoulder when it is your turn."* Possibly, show meaning through action. You might gently **tap** the table. Words with multiple meanings, like **lap,** will be understood in context. *"T. J. decided to run one **lap** before baseball practice."* *"The baby sat in her mother's **lap.**"* The near similarity of the spelling of **lab** and **lap** underscores the importance of paying attention to each letter in a word.

III   PRACTICE nap, pan, ban, man, and **tan.** *"Our dog, Doxy, took a **nap.**"* *"Shelleyn will boil eggs in a **pan.**"* *"We will **ban** Caleb from the room until we finish decorating for his surprise party."* *"Asher is growing into a fine **man.**"* *"Lexi and Benny rode to the beach for a **tan** in a **tan**-colored van."*

Be sure your student can read and spell all of the words confidently and without hesitation before beginning the next list or lesson. Discuss the meaning of the words.

IV   REVIEW pan, bat, lap, pat, and **mat.**
V   REVIEW ban, map, an, nap, and **tan.**
VI   REVIEW am, lab, man, tap, and **pal.**

Fill in your student's chart and allow him to place a sticker in the space provided.

Importance of Pointing

Point to the **left side** (not the top, bottom, or right) of each word with a sharpened pencil to help your student focus on the word. Your pointing helps him develop the habit of moving his eyes from left to right and through a word to the last letter. Pencil pointing gives effective control of the lesson and supports comprehension.

Lesson B

L l   P p   N n

I.   lab   Al

II.   pat   pal   map   tap   lap

III.   nap   pan   ban   man   tan

Review

IV.   pan   bat   lap   pat   mat

V.   ban   map   an   nap   tan

VI.   am   lab   man   tap   pal

Instructions for Lesson C

> **Introduce the pronunciation and spelling patterns for the consonants s, g, r, and f and continue with the short sound of the vowel a.**

General Instructions

▶ Point with a sharpened pencil to each of the large black letters listed across the top of the page: **S s**, **G g**, **R r**, and **F f**. Ask your student to say each letter's sound: **s** says |s|; **g** says |g| (not |gŭŭŭh|) (shorten the |ŭh| sound as much as possible); **r** says |r|; **f** says |f| (not |fŭh|).

▶ Have your student read the four words in row I (**Sam**, **sat**, **mass**, and **pass**). Discuss each word's meaning. *"Sam sat in my class."* *"The cafeteria has a mass of spaghetti."* *"Did you pass James in the hall today?"* *"Please pass the papers to the front of the row."* *"Did you pass the test?"* When your student has correctly read all four words, mark the completion chart.

▶ Call out (dictate) the four words at Roman numeral I and have your student spell them on notebook paper. Discuss the meaning of these words. Remind your student that we always spell from LEFT to RIGHT. Two of the words end with double consonants (**mass**, **pass**). **Often, the letter s is doubled at the end of short-vowel words.** (One word in Roman numeral II is spelled with one **s**: **gas**.) When your student has spelled all four words correctly, mark his chart.

▶ Have your student read, discuss the meaning of, and spell all of the words in rows II and III. As each set of words is correctly completed, record this on the progress chart.

II **PRACTICE gas, gab, gal, gap, gag, bag, lag, rag, sag, and tag.** Be sure your student shortens the |ŭh| sound in **g** as much as possible. Inexact pronunciation is a common student error that can hinder understanding of the meaning of words. Encourage your student to blend the first two letters of **gas**, |gă|, then pronounce the last letter in the word, as such: |gă| ... |s| → |găs|. Illustrate the other words in sentences. *"Did Joey fill the car with gas?"* *"Cade loves to gab about sports."* *"Marianne is a sweet, smart gal."* *"Did Kolt go outside to see the gap the earthquake caused in the pavement?"* *"Oh my, did you gag?"* *"We left the bag in the car."* *"Hurry, hurry, don't lag behind!"* *"Please get a rag and clean up this spill."* *"Did you see the sag in the old wooden floor?"* *"A sad day may cause one's spirits to sag."* *"Look at the tag and see how much the shirt costs."* *"Tag! You're it!"* **Tag** can function as a noun (price tag) or a verb (tag that person). The meaning depends on what the writer or speaker intends, and the sentence will provide context clues. This is another reason it is important to discuss the meaning of words.

III **PRACTICE ram, rat, ran, and rag.** The letter **r** can be difficult for some students to pronounce. The sound of **r** is sometimes described as a growl, like a puppy makes |rrr|. Now is not the time to be a perfectionist about speech, however. Relax. Just be sure your student recognizes the letter and can say and write it. *"A ram is a male sheep."* *"Let's ram the castle gate!"* *"The rat ran into the hole with a rag."*

      PRACTICE fan and fat. The sound of **f** is |f|, not |fŭh|. Do not say |ŭh|. *"It's hot. Please turn on the fan."* *"Isaac is a fan of that baseball team."* *"Cody cut the fat off of the steak."*

Review

IV   REVIEW pal, gap, sat, lap, sag, mat, tag, gal, tan, at.
V   REVIEW bag, map, ram, pat, nap, pan, fan, lab, man, tat.
VI   REVIEW rag, fat, am, lag, gas, ran, tab, mass, pat, pass.

▶ Mark the progress chart with a 100 and record the date this lesson is completed.

10

Lesson C

S s G g R r F f

I.   Sam   sat   pass   mass

II.   gas   gab   gal   gap   gag

      bag   lag   rag   sag   tag

III. ram   rat   ran   rag

      fan   fat

Review

IV.   pal   gap   sat   lap   sag

      mat   tag   gal   tan   at

V.   bag   map   ram   pat   nap

      pan   fan   lab   man   tat

VI.   rag   fat   am   lag   gas

      ran   tab   mass   pat   pass

Instructions for Lesson D

> **Introduce the pronunciation and spelling patterns for the consonants h, w, v, and j and continue with the short sound of the letter a.**

General Instructions

▶ Point with a sharpened pencil to each of the large black letters listed across the top of the page: **H h, W w, V v,** and **J j.** Ask your student to say each letter's sound: **h** says |h| (not |hŭh|); **w** says |w|; **v** says |v|; **j** says |j|.

▶ Point at the left side of the words at Roman numeral I. Remind your student to focus on reading the letters from left to right. Be sure he pronounces the letter **h** with no |ŭh| sound (just breath or air), and that he limits (clips or snips) the sound of |ŭh| in **w, v,** and **j.** Discuss the meaning of the words and illustrate the words in sentences. *"It's cold outside. Please put on your **hat**." "At Easter, Brittany and Parker like to eat **ham**." "Ivan likes to make jokes in class—he is a real **ham**." "Our dog, Lily, loves to **wag** her tail." "Hilario and Jesse will ride in a **van** to school today." "I have a friend named **Val**." "The toy factory has a **vat** filled with plastic for making toys." "**Jan** likes to eat **jam**." "Chelsea and Kenzie were almost late due to a major traffic **jam** this morning on the way to school." "Did you **jab** your finger into the banana pudding?" "We will jig and **jag** as we run."*

Ham and **jam** differ by one letter. Each letter is vital to the meaning. It is critical that you help your student understand the importance of paying attention to each letter. After your student has correctly read these ten words, mark the completion chart accordingly. If more documentation or detail of student progress is needed (as is usually required of RTI instructors), consider using the progress monitoring table found on page 222.

▶ Call out and have your student spell on notebook paper all of the words at Roman numeral I. Use the words again in sentences and mark the progress chart.

Review

Direct your student to read, discuss the meaning of, and spell all of the words at rows II, III, IV, V, and VI. Notice that in Roman numeral III, **mass** is spelled with a double **s**. This pattern is common for short-vowel words that end in **s**. This doubling is also usually true for words ending in **f, l,** or **z**. However, there are a few exceptions to this pattern. For example, **gas** ends with only one **s**.

Mark the date on the completion chart and reward your student with a 100. Most students like to accumulate 100s on their completion charts. Placing a sticker can also be motivating but may or may not be suitable for all. Ask your student, or use your judgment, about the use of stickers as motivators.

Equivalent Letters

It might help you and your student to know that there are a number of so-called *equivalent letters*. These are letters pronounced exactly the same with only one difference—one letter is voiced (as with **b**), while the other letter is voiceless (as with **p**). A list of equivalent letters is found on page 208. [For a definition of *voiced* and *voiceless* letters, see Basic Terms on page 212.]

Lesson D

H h W w V v J j

I. hat   ham

wag

van   Val   vat

jam   jab   jag   Jan

Review

II.   ban   wag   gap   am   sat   jam   lap

III.   mass   bat   van   fan   bag   nap   vat

IV.   map   ham   pat   an   lab   pan   tat

V.   gag   jag   sag   fat   rag   hat   tap

VI.   gas   rat   tag   at   tan   ran   ram

Instructions for Lesson E

**Introduce the pronunciation and spelling patterns for the consonants
x, y, and z and continue with the sound of the vowel letter a.**

General Instructions

▶ Point with a sharpened pencil to each of the large black letters listed across the top of the page: **X x, Y y,** and **Z z**. Ask your student to say each letter's sound: **x** says |ks|; **y** says |y|; **z** says |z|.

▶ Point to the words at Roman numeral I and ask your student to read them. The letter **x** is pronounced by combining the sounds usually associated with **k** and **s**— |ks|, as in **ax** |ăks| and **tax** |tăks|. Again, note that you must pronounce this single letter with two sounds. The letter **z** sounds like the vibration noise that bees make, |zz|. Discuss the meaning of all of the words and use them in sentences. *"Paul Bunyan chops wood with an **ax**." "John, please send this **fax** to the office." "Do not be **lax** in paying the **tax** on the candle **wax**." "Maggie is not crazy about eating this **yam** recipe!" "Our dog, Buddy, has a determined **yap** that warns us of danger." "Be careful! The electricity might **zap** you!" "The off-key **jazz** singer received some **razz** from the crowd."* After your student correctly reads these ten words, mark the completion chart.

▶ Recite (call out) the words at Roman numeral I and have your student spell them on notebook paper. A few words have double consonants (**jazz, razz**). As mentioned before, short-vowel words that end in **f, l, s,** or **z** almost always end with these consonants doubled. When your student correctly spells all ten words, mark the completion chart.

▶ Have your student read, discuss the meaning of, and spell the words at rows II, III, IV, V, and VI. Mark the progress chart and allow your student to place a sticker in the space provided for Lesson E.

Mark the bottom right corner of the progress chart with the date on which Lesson E is completed. Your student's next lesson will be Lesson 1 at the start of the main unit.

Left-to-Right Reading Direction and Syllable Patterns

Initially, students may have difficulty seeing and hearing words. Pointing to the left side of words as you and your student encounter them will help him remember that all reading is done from left to right.

Words are structured according to patterns. All words consist of syllables that are read and spelled from left to right. There are no true "sight words" in English, as all words have at least one identifiable pattern. Your goal is to help train your student's brain and eyes to quickly recognize letters and express their sounds. This is a skill that takes time to develop, but once this skill is established, you will have created a reader! Allow your student sufficient time to practice until he reads and spells without hesitation. Watch your student's eyes. You will know that you are advancing towards your goal when you see him truly focus on the letters in the words. Comprehension will be reflected in the confidence you hear in his voice and see in his writing. Relax and smile! Now that the words in the Pre-Unit have been mastered, it's time to move on to Lesson 1.

Lesson E

X x   Y y   Z z

I.   ax   fax   lax   tax   wax

yam   yap

zap   jazz   razz

Review

II.	tax	at	bass	wag	pan
	hat	lap	van	gag	ran
III.	ram	yam	tan	bat	fan
	wax	jazz	nap	jam	tap
IV.	jag	gal	ham	pat	an
	lab	gas	tat	gap	sat
V.	lag	mat	bag	sag	fat
	am	jab	nag	vat	fax
VI.	ban	razz	man	tag	tab
	nab	rag	lass	mass	pass

15

Unit 1

Short-Vowel Words

Lessons 1 – 32

The 4 Steps of Teaching Every Lesson

Lesson 1 is designed to be easy. If your student hesitates or struggles over the words in Lesson 1, discontinue this lesson and begin instead with Lesson A of the Pre-Unit. The Pre-Unit provides coaching in the sounds that letters make. The teaching protocol is the same for all of the lessons in this book. The procedure consists of four steps:

Step 1: Read. The first step involves having your student read aloud all of the words in a word list, starting with Roman numeral I. Be sure your student understands that, in English, WE ALWAYS READ FROM LEFT TO RIGHT! Point a sharpened pencil at the left side of each word and keep the pencil tip there until your student has read the word correctly. Pencil pointing is a non-verbal, positive way of prompting focus, controlling the pace of the lesson, and diplomatically signaling when a pronunciation must be corrected. You have the option of pointing the pencil tip at any letter or letters that your student is misreading. For example, if your student reads **ran** but the printed word is **ram**, you may want to position the pencil tip at the **m**. Certainly, offer verbal guidance when necessary, but do keep in mind that learners need time to process information and make their own corrections.

Step 2: Discuss word meanings. Check to be sure that your student knows the meaning of each word. Try these suggestions to test for comprehension:

- **Ask what the word means**   *"What does the word **tat** mean?"*
- **Use the word in a sentence**   *"One way to make lace is to **tat**."*
- **Tell the meaning**   *"If one wants to make lace, one usually learns to **tat**.*
- **Point to an object**   *"This is lace made by someone who knows how to **tat**."*
- **Illustrate with action**   *"See how I am making this lace? It's called **tat**ting."*
- **Look it up in a dictionary**   *"One way of forming thread into lace is to **tat**."*

Establish the habit of reading for meaning. Comprehension must be insisted upon, beginning with the very first word.

Step 3: Spell. Dictate (call out) the words of a word list and have your student spell them on notebook paper. Be sure that he writes from left to right. (Cursive writing allows no other direction.) You have the option of testing your pupil per word, at the end of every list, or at the end of the full lesson. Allow him adequate time to correct a misspelled word before you move to the next spelling word. This spares your student from later having to unlearn an error. Don't move on to the next list or lesson until your student knows how to accurately spell each word.

Step 4: Mark the completion chart. At the commencement of these lessons, you will have selected a progress (completion) chart from the options starting on page 273. You will use the chart to track lessons. Be sure to update the chart before you leave your session.

Teachers: You will have an easier time teaching these lessons if you familiarize yourself with the information found on pages **xiii** (general information), **xv** (procedure), **xvi** (teacher prep), and **xviii** (supply list).

Sound Chart
for Lesson 1 of Unit 1

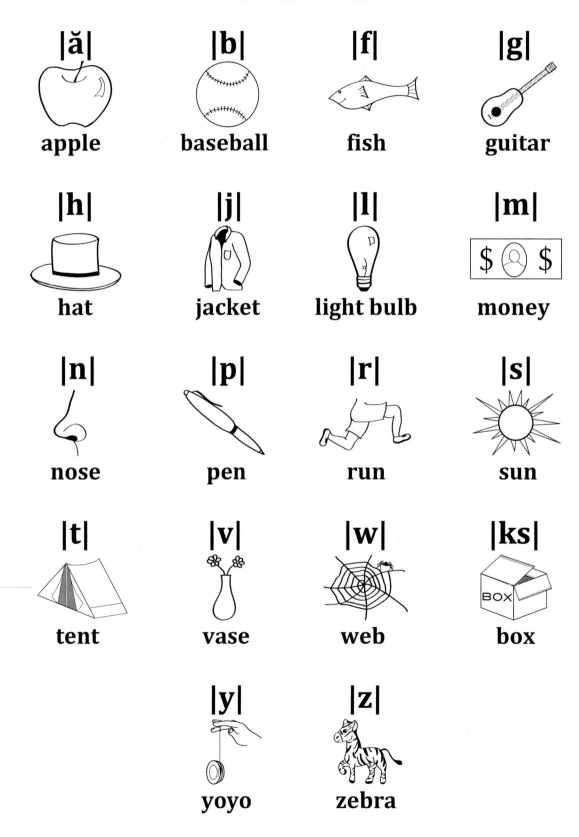

|ă|
apple

|b|
baseball

|f|
fish

|g|
guitar

|h|
hat

|j|
jacket

|l|
light bulb

|m|
money

|n|
nose

|p|
pen

|r|
run

|s|
sun

|t|
tent

|v|
vase

|w|
web

|ks|
box

|y|
yoyo

|z|
zebra

Sound Chart
for Lessons 2 through 32 of Unit 1

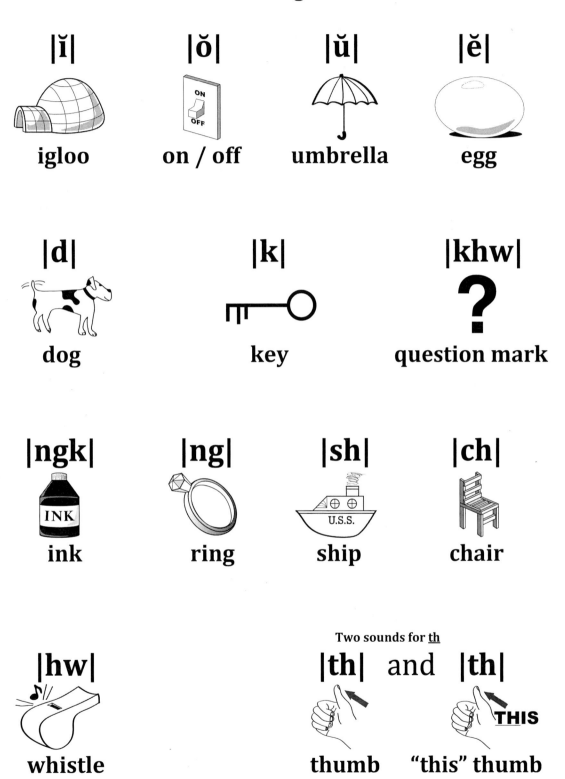

|ĭ|
igloo

|ŏ|
on / off

|ŭ|
umbrella

|ĕ|
egg

|d|
dog

|k|
key

|khw|
?
question mark

|ngk|
ink

|ng|
ring

|sh|
ship

|ch|
chair

|hw|
whistle

Two sounds for th
|th| and |th|
thumb   "this" thumb

Instructions for Lesson 1

If your student has any difficulty with this lesson, begin instead with the Pre-Unit.

Introduce the pronunciation and spelling patterns for the short sound of the letter a. **Also introduce seventeen consonants.**

A a	|ă|	am, at, apple	L l	|l|	lab, lit, pal, bell	T t	|t|	tat, top, set
B b	|b|	bat, rob, ebb	M m	|m|	mat, man, hem	V v	|v|	van, vat, vet
F f	|f|	fan, off	N n	|n|	nap, net, pan	W w	|w|	wag, win, wet
G g	|g|	gas, gag, egg	P p	|p|	pat, tip, hop	X x	|ks|	ax, box, fix
H h	|h|	hat, hop	R r	|r|	ram, rib	Y y	|y|	yam, yes, yell
J j	|j|	jam, Jill	S s	|s|	sat, bus, pass, toss	Z z	|z|	zap, zip, jazz

PROCEDURE FOR TEACHING THE LESSON(S)

Step 1: To begin the lesson, point with a sharpened pencil to the left side of the first word in Roman numeral I. Ask your student to read the word aloud. He must sound out the letters, in order, FROM LEFT TO RIGHT. [If your student does not recall the sounds of the letters, you will need to start him in the Pre-Unit.]

Step 2: Discuss the meaning of the word.

Step 3: Call out (recite) the word and have your student write it on notebook paper.

Follow this procedure (steps 1, 2, & 3) for the other words in Roman numeral I.

Step 4: Mark the completion (progress) chart with a 100 after your student has read and spelled every word in Roman numeral I correctly. (Completion charts are found starting on page 273.)

Follow this same procedure (read + comprehend + spell) for all of the words in the remaining rows. Mark the chart.

To help your student understand the meaning of the words, give a simple definition or point to an object that illustrates the word. Use the word in a sentence. Unusual words like **tat** are included that can't generally be guessed at. Words like **bat** provide the opportunity to illustrate that sometimes a word has more than one meaning. A **bat** is a flying mammal; it is a tool used by a baseball team; and it is an action, as in *"**Bat** that wasp away!"*

• Pronounce the sounds of the letters **b**, **g**, and **j** with as little \|ŭh\| sound as possible.

• The letters **f**, **h**, **p**, and **t** are pronounced with no \|ŭh\| sound: \|f\|, \|h\|, \|p\|, \|t\|.

• The consonants **f**, **l**, **s**, and **z** typically are doubled at the end of a short-vowel syllable or word, as in **off**, **ill**, **pass**, and **fuzz**.

• The letter **x** is pronounced by combining the two sounds \|k\| and \|s\|: \|ks\|, as in **ax**.

• Since some students confuse the letters **b** and **d**, the letter **d** will not be introduced until Lesson 10. Roman numeral VI provides additional practice for the letter **b**.

These lessons are designed to be handled with ease. Students should feel a sense of accomplishment and look forward to the next lesson. The lessons will build into more complex words, so spend time practicing. Ask your student if he would like to reread or respell some or all of the words. Stay on a lesson until he is confident and is reading effortlessly. Have your student read, understand, and spell the challenge word!

Lesson 1

|ă|

**B b   F f   G g   H h   J j   L l   M m   N n
P p   R r   S s   T t   V v   W w   X x   Y y   Z z**

I.	am	mat	wag	at	map
	bat	nap	yam	an	pan
II.	fan	pat	zap	tap	Al
	gas	ram	sag	vat	gag
III.	bag	sat	man	nag	ban
	hat	Sam	lap	tab	rat
IV.	jam	tat	ham	jab	tan
	lab	van	fat	lax	tax
V.	jazz	ax	fax	sax	wax
	pass	mass	sass	bass	lass

Review: B b

VI.	lab	bass	bam	tab
	bag	bat	ban	jab

Challenge Word:	Batman
[two-syllable word]	[Bat • man]

Instructions for Lesson 2

**Introduce the short-vowel pronunciation and spelling pattern
for the vowel letter** i.

Review patterns for the seventeen consonants introduced in Lesson 1.

Read and Spell Every Word

Each lesson has been carefully designed to be easy for most students. You might be tempted to skip words because your student appears to be handling everything effortlessly. Remember, though, that students need to practice reading out loud what they **see**, and practice spelling on paper what they **hear**. It is important that they get all the "run time" that the lessons afford. Roman numerals IV and V include words that rhyme, like **mill** and **fill**; **in** and **bin**; and **Jim** and **rim**. Words rhyme when they have the same vowel sounds and ending consonant sounds.

Introduce the Concept of Syllables

Tell your student that all words consist of one or more syllables. A *syllable* is the next bigger sound than a basic speech sound. A syllable may consist of one vowel or a vowel team known as a *digraph*, or it may consist of a vowel paired with a consonant either before or after it. A speaker's chin almost always drops when he says a syllable.

- WRITE on notebook paper this twelve-syllable word: **antidisestablishmentarianism**.
- ASK your student if he would like to read this word.
- READ through the word, placing a slash mark after each syllable as it is read aloud.

an / ti / dis / e / stab / lish / men / tar / i / an / is / m

We teach syllable patterns so that students can read and spell even twelve-syllable words by the end of the program.

Lessons 1 through 27 have only one-syllable words, all of them featuring a short vowel. For a vowel in a one-syllable word to take the short sound, the syllable must end with at least one consonant [**bat, razz**]. A syllable that ends with a consonant is said to be a *closed syllable*, as the vowel is closed off by the consonant. Challenge words are provided at the end of most lessons, starting with Lesson 1, to give students a chance to practice multi-syllable words. From Lesson 28 onward, your student will start encountering two-syllable words.

To Explain or Not to Explain a Pattern

Every student is different. For some, too much information about patterns might result in sensory overload. Just relax and concentrate on the actual exercises—reading, spelling, and learning the meaning of the words. Automatic response to the patterns is the priority for your student, not having him expound or quote rules. One convention your student does need to know is that names (proper nouns) begin with a capital letter. (We did not make a point of this in the Pre-Unit but do so now.) Some of the word lists contain names. In Lesson 2 we see **Jim** and **Jill**. Such capitalization is important.

Lesson 2

|ĭ|

I.	if	tip	big	rib	wig
	bit	lit	sit	wit	lip

II.	six	jig	fig	rip	fib
	bib	pit	hit	gig	fix

III.	hip	fit	pig	mix	sip
	it	rig	zip	miss	fizz

IV.	mill	fill	pill	will	gill
	ill	bill	hill	Jill	sill

V.	in	bin	fin	sin	win
	Jim	pin	tin	rim	him

Review: B b

VI.	bit	rib	bill	fib	big	bin	bib

Challenge Word:	**zigzag**
[two-syllable word]	[*zig • zag*]

Instructions for Lesson 3

> Review the short-vowel patterns introduced in Lessons 1 and 2: |ă| and |ĭ|.
> Also review the seventeen consonants studied in Lesson 1.

Correcting Reading Errors

Students who have difficulty handling Lesson 3 will need practice and persistence. Some will see a word like **gab** and guess that the word is the more familiar word **grab**. This tendency to misread will be dealt with by your using a sharpened pencil to point at the left side of a word to focus your student's eyes on the first letter. Then, remind him to SOUND OUT THE LETTERS FROM LEFT TO RIGHT. If you haven't worked with below-normal or non-readers, you may not be aware that there are a great many students who do not track from left to right. Forming this new habit is difficult for some students, but it is critical to reading success.

Keep the pencil pointed at the **left side** of a word that a student has mispronounced until he gets it right. This nonverbal technique avoids the need for you, the teacher, to use negative correction words like *"no"* or *"wrong."* If more assistance is needed, then point the pencil at the mispronounced letter or letters. For example, if your student is pronouncing the word **gab** as **grab**, point between the letters **g** and **a**. Be silent, and give your student a chance to figure out for himself that there is no **r**. This pointing technique will provide a more positive experience for you and your student as you work through the lessons.

If hints are needed, you might say

- *"Look at the word again."*
- *"Do you see the letter **r** in this word?"*
- *"Remember, there are words in this lesson that you may not have seen before or may seldom use."*
- *"Trust your eyes and read only what you see."*
- *"Blend the first two letters together. This will help you read the word."*

If more specific hints are needed, consider saying

1. *"What is the first letter you see?"* **g**
2. *"What sound does this letter make?"* |g|
3. *"What is the next letter?"* **a**
4. *"What is its sound?"* |ă|
5. *"Pronounce these two letters together."* |gă|
6. *"What is the last letter in this word?"* **b**
7. *"What sound does this letter make?"* |b|
8. *"Now, blend the sounds."* |gă|–|b|, |găb|
9. *"What does the word **gab** mean?"*
10. *"Can you use this word in a sentence?"*
11. *"Let's look it up in the dictionary."*

Challenge Words

Included in a box at the bottom of most lesson pages is at least one challenge word. All of these words consist of syllable patterns that were taught in the current lesson or a previous lesson. We want your student to appreciate that sometimes a simple word can be combined with another simple word to form an entirely new word, also known as a *compound word*. For example, **book** + **worm** = **bookworm**. Students tend to love these challenge words!

Lesson 3

Review

|ă| |ĭ|

I.

lab	mix	it	an	gill	wax	pit
sit	hip	sax	will	tip	miss	bill

II.

ban	in	fat	hat	pal	vat	pat
mill	at	rim	lip	pan	fig	Tim

III.

tag	ham	big	man	rib	wag	mat
mass	if	ran	ill	bat	wig	hill

IV.

am	nag	fit	pass	nap	rat	fix
jazz	pill	gag	fizz	rig	sin	rag

V.

lag	tan	him	fill	tab	win	map
hit	fax	bag	lap	sat	pin	sag

Review: B b

VI.

bit	bass	bag	gab	rib	lab	bill
tab	bib	jab	bat	fib	big	bin

Challenge Word	**rabbit**
[two-syllable word]	[rab • bit]

Instructions for Lesson 4

> **Introduce the pronunciation and spelling patterns for the short-vowel sound of the letter** o.

Special Note: Some dictionaries no longer use the ŏ pronunciation symbol for short-vowel **o** and instead use **ä** or **ô**. The difference in pronunciation for these is barely perceptible. The lesson page for this lesson provides all three symbols.

The capitalized proper noun **Sox** found at Roman numeral III denotes the name of baseball teams (Red Sox, White Sox). The consonant **x** is pronounced with a melding of two sounds, |k| and |s|, |ks|, as in **ox**. [Lesson 14 will cover **cks**, pronounced |ks|.]

Redirect Your Student's Eyes If Necessary

Remind your student to read all words from LEFT to RIGHT, sound to sound, all the way through to the end of the word. When some students guess at words, they may telegraph this by looking at your face, hoping for assistance or a clue, or by looking at the ceiling, trying to recall from memory. Guessers typically tune in on only a few letters to identify a word. They do not trust their eyes to give them all the information needed to actually read words. Always direct your student's attention to the page. Use the sharpened pencil to steer your student's eyes to the first letter of every word. Don't lift or move the pencil from a word until your pupil has read the word correctly.

The Word List Format Removes the Option of Guessing

These lessons consist of word listings. There are no pictures or illustrations (except for sound charts for reference), because they would provide visual clues that might aid in guessing. *Reading and Spelling Pure & Simple* teaches spelling and pronunciation patterns in an orderly fashion, with no guessing allowed. The use of a pointer, the emphasis on learning patterns, and the requirement that your student spell words and discuss word meanings are critical in equipping your student to become a reader.

Correcting Spelling Errors

If you say |sit| but your student writes **set**, ask him the following types of questions:

Instructor: *"Will you read out loud to me the word that you wrote?"*
Student: *"Yes . . . |sĕt|."*
Instructor: *"Is that the word that I said? Listen closely: |sĭ|–|t|, |sĭt|. Please **sit** in the chair."*

If you ask your student to spell |ram|, but he writes **ran**, tell him to look at your mouth while you say the word **ram**:

Instructor: *"Look at my mouth: 'ram.' A **ram** has horns. Is **ram** what you wrote?"*
Student: *"I wrote 'ran.'"*
Instructor: *"Ok, now write 'ram.'"*

Most students will be able to figure out their mistakes and make corrections. If your pupil is unsure about the sound or spelling of a letter, take time to review words that have that particular letter or sound. Allow your student to think and make his own corrections. Be very patient. This is a many-faceted learning process and more complicated than it appears. Relax, smile, and take your time.

28

Lesson 4

|ŏ|

I. |ŏ| or |ä|

pop	lot	mop	sop	hot
not	bon	pot	lob	tot

II. |ŏ| or |ä|

job	rob	hop	rot	sob
got	mob	bop	mom	gob

III. |ŏ| or |ä|

bob	top	jot	Tom	Ron
box	Sox	pox	fox	ox

IV. |ŏ| or |ô|

off	boss	loss	moss

V. |ŏ|, |ô| or |ä|

on	hog	log	bog
	fog	toss	

Review: B b

VI.

bob	boss	bog	job	bop
mob	rob	bon	box	sob

Challenge Word:	**bonbon**
	[bon • bon]

Instructions for Lesson 5

"Reading" by Picking Out a Few Letters

This page may help you understand why some students struggle at reading. I have had more than one student look at the word **give**, randomly select the letters **v** and **e** from the word, and guess that the word was the more familiar word **very**! I also have had students who, when reading the word **maybe**, cherry picked the letters **m** and **e** and guessed that the word was **me**. Guessers pick out letters and hope for the best. Keep guess-prone students away from picture books while they are learning to read, or else they may be tempted to "read" by interpreting what they see in the pictures. One of my students glanced at a picture, realized the context of the story, and said "*father*" for the printed word **daddy**.

Overcoming a Left-to-Right Orientation Deficit

Your using a sharpened pencil to point to the first letter of each word helps students who have difficulty remembering to read from left to right. It helps them stay focused and lessens the inclination to skip letters. Some students will have to work harder than others to overcome old habits. Until the left-to-right reading habit is well ingrained, try to limit your student's outside reading as much as possible. (We know you probably can't avoid outside reading all together.) Outside reading likely will have spelling and pronunciation patterns unfamiliar to your student. We'd rather he wait and learn the patterns and not be put in the position of having to guess at words.

Helping Students Stay Focused

Some students have difficulty staying focused. An instructor can help by pointing a pencil to the letter or word that the instructor wants the student to see. As students gain confidence in their ability to handle the lessons, they will have less difficulty staying on task.

Exactness in Spelling and Pronunciation

Be insistent about having your student spell and pronounce each word properly before moving on to the next word. Allow your student to make his own corrections. Your pausing, being silent, and not moving the pencil to the next word in line will signal to the student that there is an issue. Again, as much as possible, let your student figure out what needs to be fixed. Take time to read or spell the words as many times as is necessary for your student to reach proficiency. Some pupils will benefit at the beginning of each lesson from a quick review of words from one or two previous lessons. If your student hesitates with a specific letter or pattern, review this pattern until he has mastered it.

Notice that the syllable break for the challenge word **robin** is between the **b** and the **i**. The break occurs here in order to preserve the short-vowel sound in the first syllable, **rob**. The syllable break for **bobbin** is between the double consonants, **b** and **b**.

Lesson 5

Review

|ă| |ĭ| |ŏ|

I.   ram   on   big   off   gill   gap   miss
    job   tag   got   him   loss   will   hog

II. mill   pat   toss   fog   fax   mob   bin
    not   box   fig   rip   ham   bat   sob

III. fib   rig   fit   pig   fat   lot   zap
    am   pal   hot   pit   moss   van   boss

IV. at   zip   sit   wig   bag   tip   pass
    hit   rob   fan   jog   ox   yam   fox

V.   jam   six   wag   bit   pin   hop   mix
    if   pot   mop   pill   an   win   lap

Review: B b

VI. bob   bag   box   ban   fib   rib   bog   tab
    bill boss bat   bit   bib   lab   big   rob

Challenge Word:	**robin**	**bobbin**
	[rob • in]	[bob • bin]

Instructions for Lesson 6

Introduce the pronunciation and spelling pattern for the short sound of the vowel u.

Comprehension with Confidence

All of the words in every list are meant to be not only read but understood. Make it a point to comment about words or ask your student what the words mean. Use humor when you can. Find ways to enjoy a lesson. Never make fun of your student's answers or efforts to learn.

I - IV   NEW PATTERN. Now we will learn the pronunciation and spelling pattern for the short vowel **u**, |ŭ|, as in **up** and **run**. As a general rule, short-vowel words ending in **f** or **s** or **z** have a double (twin) consonant at the end (e.g., **huff, fuss, buzz**). But note that the words **us** and **bus** (in Roman numeral IV) are spelled with only one **s**.

A few dictionaries have replaced the short-vowel **u** symbol, ŭ, with the schwa symbol, ə. In this book, we will continue using the symbol **ŭ** for short-vowel **u**. The schwa sound and its symbol are explained in detail in Lessons 66 and 67. Roman numeral IV includes some words that rhyme, such as **huff** and **puff**, **buzz** and **fuzz**, and **fuss** and **bus**. As we have mentioned before, does your student know what rhyming words are? Be sure to explain this concept. Words rhyme when they have the same vowel sounds and ending consonant sounds. Most students enjoy encountering rhyming words.

V   NEW PATTERN. Here we will learn the sound that the short-vowel **u** makes in syllables that end with the **ll** spelling pattern (**hull, gull**). The sound is a wee bit different from the usual sound of short-vowel **u**. As noted briefly above, some dictionaries depict the **u** sound in the **ll** words with a schwa (ə). The schwa essentially represents a *shortened* short-vowel **u** sound and is frequently found in the unstressed syllables of multi-syllable words. (Again, see Lessons 66 and 67 for more information about the schwa.) Some students will not be aware of the very slight sound difference between |ŭ| and |ə|, but others will detect the difference and might get confused. It is excellent if you have a student who listens closely and detects nuances. If you think your student needs an explanation here, by all means give it.

Review

VI   REVIEW the pattern for the short-vowel **u**. Additional practice is provided for the letter **b**.

Can Your Student See and Hear?

If your student is still having difficulty reading and spelling words at this point in the lessons, consider that your student's eyes and ears may need to be professionally tested. Screening in schools is general in nature and does not always catch every problem.

Lesson 6

|ŭ|

|ŭ|
I. up hut mum sun pun
run sub hub pub sum

|ŭ|
II. rug rut gum fun tug
jug gun yum pup but

|ŭ|
III. bug rub nut sup gut
hug jut mug lug tux

|ŭ|
IV. huff puff buff muff us
buzz fuzz fuss buss bus

Note: The |ŭ| sound is shorter than usual in words or syllables ending in **ull**.

|ŭ| or |ə|
V. hull gull mull null lull

Review: B b

VI. bug sub bus rub
hub bun tub buff

Challenge Word:	**muffin**
	[muff • in]

Instructions for Lesson 7

> **Review the short-vowel sounds |ă|, |ĭ|, |ŏ|, and |ŭ| and the seventeen consonants that were introduced in Lesson 1.**

More Ideas on How to Thwart the Guessing Habit

Through the years I've dealt with students who, at least initially, seemed genuinely unable to stop guessing at words. They eventually overcame the problem, but I watched, studied, and puzzled over their struggles. I told students that we were now changing the way their brains process information. I often became aware of what I called "the brain switch"—the moment in time when students began to truly focus and *see* words on a page and recognize patterns. It was an intriguing phenomenon.

I've heard teachers say that some students can't learn by using phonics. I've been mystified by this statement. It dawned on me finally that a "brain switch" must occur— that is, in each student, the necessary brain processes must be activated.

Recent research based on magnetic imaging reveals the parts of the brain that light up when a student reads. One study showed that a dyslexic student's brain lit up only on the top right side, whereas a skilled reader's brain lit up in the upper back portion of the head, on both the left and right sides. Other research shows that phonics instruction done for 45 minutes every morning over the span of one school year will change the area of the brain that lights up from the unskilled area to the skilled area.

Guessing involves one or more of the following strategies:

(1) use the context of a story to help figure out the words;
(2) look at the pictures on the page for clues;
(3) think and remember when or where a word has been seen in the past;
(4) key on certain letters in a word but ignore the others; or
(5) memorize new words one word at a time.

Guessing, initially, is easier for a student than pattern reading, as the student just says the first word that comes to mind. But guessing is hit and miss, misleads, and actually (ironically) requires more concentration. Once pattern reading is established, your student will find reading much easier and definitely more enjoyable. Pattern reading with emphasis on comprehension is by far superior to guessing or memorizing.

At this point, your student might have only a little pattern knowledge and might be struggling to be a disciplined, left-to-right reader. While he is working through our pattern-intensive, very structured curriculum, it is a good idea to limit or reduce his outside reading, lest he slip back into old guessing habits when he encounters patterns he hasn't yet learned. Eliminating outside reading may be unrealistic, but do what you can to keep him centered on the need to read, not guess. As previously mentioned, if outside reading is unavoidable, at least organize your day or schedule so that our lessons come first or are at a time significantly separated from the other reading.

The habit of guessing can be replaced with the skill of real reading. Doing the lessons on a daily basis will speed up the process.

Lesson 7
Review
|ă| |ĭ| |ŏ| |ŭ|

I.	ban	yam	moss	fig	nap
	top	lap	jot	on	hum
	ill	pat	non	pill	nut

II.	bus	rum	tub	map	sat
	hop	fox	him	gum	off
	man	gag	mom	tin	sag

III.	am	hug	six	ax	bit
	if	nag	bob	rat	ox
	bag	bill	mug	fat	huff

IV.	job	gas	pop	rib	mop
	at	big	jut	sap	lull
	fix	mob	Jill	fog	sum

V.	rug	fun	buzz	vat	pot
	in	wig	rub	bug	rim
	mass	not	zip	fill	box

Review: B b

VI.	bus	bat	fib	rub	jab	boss	bag
	sob	tub	big	bill	box	lab	bin
	ban	sub	job	rob	tab	buzz	bib

Challenge Word:	laptop
	[lap • top]

Instructions for Lesson 8

Introduce the short-vowel pronunciation and spelling patterns for the vowel e.

I - IV   NEW PATTERN. The letter **e** is the last of the short vowels. This vowel is presented last because it is usually the most difficult to master. At this point in the program, your student will have had at least seven lessons practicing the basic consonant sounds and spellings and the four other short vowels. Perhaps your student will surprise you and handle the letter **e** with ease.

Note: In some regions of the country, people pronounce the short-vowel **e** more like the short-vowel letter **i**, saying |tĭn| for **ten**. Try to teach the classical pronunciation found in dictionaries.

V   NEW PATTERN. Observe that a slight change occurs in the sound of |ĕ| when it appears in syllables or words ending in **m** or **n**. Notice this with **hem** and **ten**. This effect may be caused in part by how the mouth transitions from the vowel to the consonant. The **m** and **n** are somewhat nasal. [This nasal tone is also true with the letter **a**, as in **ham** and **tan**.] Most students will not detect the difference in pronunciation, but a few students will hear it. Commend them for being observant. Regional differences may account for some of what your student is inclined to say and even hear.

VI   REVIEW words spelled and pronounced with the short-vowel **e** sound, |ĕ|, and the (sometimes confusing) consonant letter **b**. Sample words are **bell** and **ebb**.

Your student may notice that some of the words in Lesson 8 rhyme. This is true for **bell** and **sell**, **less** and **mess**, **beg** and **egg**, and **pet** and **met**. Roman numeral V has six words that rhyme. Note: It is the *sounds* in **beg** and **egg**, not their spellings, that make them rhyme.

Focus, Focus, Focus!

ARE YOU POINTING with a sharpened pencil to the left side of each word as you go from word to word to help your student develop better eye/brain coordination? Be mindful of your student's eyes. Are his eyes trained on the word to which you are pointing or is he looking elsewhere? By zeroing in on each letter in proper sequence (from left to right), your student is helping his brain to trust what his eyes see on the page. If your student is outpacing the pencil, you will need to pick up the pencil's pace. It will be a positive experience for your student if you silently use the pencil to do the "correcting" as much as possible.

Lesson 8

|ĕ|

I.   net   yes   web   let   peg   vet   get

II.   bet   jet   pet   beg   wet   pep   yet

III.   met   set   vex   ebb   less   mess   Bess

IV.   egg   bell   sell   yell   tell   fell   well

Note: The **e** sound changes slightly when the syllable in which it appears ends in **m** or **n**.

V.   hem   ten   pen   men   hen   yen   Ben

Review: B b

VI.   bet   bell   web   beg   ebb

Challenge Words:	setup	bellhop
	[set • up]	[bell • hop]

Instructions for Lesson 9

Past reading experience may cause a student to become easily discouraged. Be positive and encouraging. It's worth the effort. Your student will learn to read and spell.

> **Review the previously introduced five short vowels and seventeen consonants.**

As your student reads and spells through future lessons, you may find that Lesson 9 is a good lesson to revisit. A Lesson 9 review is especially helpful if your student:

- Has missed several weeks or months of instruction (spring break, illness, schedule conflicts, etc.);
- Cannot seem to focus on the letters in the words and instead relies on guessing;
- Is struggling to read, to define, or to spell the words on his current lesson and needs a boost in confidence; or
- Would benefit from refreshing his knowledge of the patterns.

Isolate Problems and Instill Confidence Through Review

It is common for students to confuse the letters **b** and **d**. Words containing the letter **b** have been provided at Roman numeral VI of this lesson. For other letters or letter patterns for which your student needs practice, look for words in the word lists that feature these letters and have your student read and spell them. Practice makes perfect, and review builds confidence.

Your student should reread and respell words until he knows them perfectly. If he has to stop at times and slowly sound out the individual letters in a word (for example, "|r| - |ă| - |m|" or "|ră| - |m|," rather than "|răm|," this should be considered a word read with hesitation. Practice until your student reads words automatically, without any hesitation whatsoever.

Differentiating the Sounds of Short-Vowel e and i

Short-vowel **e** is pronounced with more of an open mouth than is short-vowel **i**. If your student is confusing these two sounds, do the following exercise. Have him touch his index finger to his front teeth and say |ĕ|. Tell him to notice that his lips and teeth are configured in such a way that he can slide his finger into his mouth. Next, have him pronounce the short-vowel sound |ĭ| and mention that with this sound his finger cannot pass beyond his teeth because his teeth are too close together.

With this lesson your student will have been introduced to all five short vowels. Half of the words in the English language are pronounced with these short-vowel sounds. He also has been introduced to 17 of the 21 consonants. These vowels and consonants will appear on almost every page that your student will read, now and in the future. Be a stickler about helping your student overcome troublesome words. Mastery (complete automaticity) is a higher priority than speed. (We will keep reminding you of this!)

The Letter g

For now, your student knows that the letter **g** says |g|. The additional sounds of **g** will be introduced in Lesson 71.

Lesson 9
Review
|ă| |ĭ| |ŏ| |ŭ| |ĕ|

I.	ram	mix	nut	max	fun
	gas	pat	boss	pen	tag
	if	rig	jazz	an	fell

II.	bet	sob	ten	Tim	tax
	huff	pan	jug	lull	hot
	yet	rob	rib	ill	off

III.	fan	us	but	fin	mess
	am	in	run	bus	hem
	on	ebb	mom	sun	will

IV.	toss	pun	wit	egg	jab
	sit	rag	bell	hum	bit
	at	jet	tin	loss	rug

V.	yes	men	box	vat	pit
	jog	nap	it	up	lag
	hat	sin	net	not	mug

Review: B b

VI.	bus	bug	big	lab	beg	sob	bit	sub
	bog	bag	rub	bin	tub	rob	bill	lob
	bass	fib	jab	box	bet	mob	rib	web
	boss	bib	bat	buzz	job	bell	tab	hub

Instructions for Lesson 10

> ## Introduce the letter d.

> **TELL YOUR STUDENT!** The letter **d** will be introduced in this lesson.

Your student might get confused if you don't inform him that the letter **d** is being introduced in this lesson. We tell our students to consider **d** the "new" or "different" letter ("it is not the same as the letter **b**"). Every word in Lesson 10 is spelled with at least one **d**. Inform your student that both **b** and **d** appear in five of the words in this lesson.

I   **LEARN** the letter **d** paired with |ă|, as in **ad**.

II   **LEARN** the letter **d** paired with |ĭ|, as in **did**.

III   **LEARN** the letter **d** paired with |ŏ|, as in **odd**.

IV   **LEARN** the letter **d** paired with |ŭ|, as in **dug**.

V   **LEARN** the letter **d** paired with |ĕ|, as in **red**.

Over the next few lessons we will practice the consonants **b** and **d**. If your student is still confused by **b** and **d**, take time to review the words at Roman numeral VI of Lesson 9 until he is proficient. For additional practice, also review Lessons 1 – 8, as they feature many words that contain a **b**. When you see that your student is handling words with **b** and words with **d** on an individual basis successfully, then it's time to mix it up and alternate between words containing **b** and **d**.

Instructions for Lesson 11

> ## Review the pronunciation and spelling pattern for the letter d.

Know the Meaning of the Words

Does your student know the meaning of words like **dell**, **dill**, and **den**? Encourage him to ask you about unfamiliar words. Comprehension is an essential part of becoming an authentic reader. Take time to explain the difference, for example, between **ad** and **add**. By using the dictionary often with your student, you will reinforce the concept that when it comes to words, dictionaries have all the answers.

Lesson 10

D d

> **TELL YOUR STUDENT!**
> The letter **D d,** pronounced |d|, is introduced in this lesson.

I. ad	pad	mad	sad	dad
add	fad	had	lad	tad
II. hid	lid	mid	rid	did
dig	dip	dim	din	dill
III. nod	pod	sod	rod	odd
mod	dog	dot	doll	doff
IV. mud	dug	dud	dull	rudd
V. red	led	wed	fed	dell

Lesson 11

Review: D d

I. ad	pad	hid	sad	bad
led	fed	pod	dig	bud
II. mud	dot	wed	rudd	nod
dim	odd	dug	did	dab
III. add	dull	lad	dog	bid
red	den	dip	sod	dub
IV. had	dud	rid	doll	bed
dell	mid	doff	tad	dad
V. dill	lid	rod	odd	mad
Deb	Ted	Ed	Todd	Judd

Challenge Word:	madman
	[mad • man]

41

Instructions for Lesson 12

Be positive and encouraging!

> **Review the pronunciation and spelling patterns for the consonants** b **and** d.

If your student shows any hesitation over the letters **b** and **d**, more review is in order! Please do not proceed to the next lessons until these letters are clear in your pupil's mind. Go over the word lists again (and again, as often as needed), having your student read and spell words that feature **b** and **d**.

Let Your Student Do the Mental Work

Learners should be allowed time to think through pronunciations and spellings and correct themselves if necessary. Be patient! Let your student do this mental work! If he fails to detect an error, don't advance the pencil to the next word on the list until he makes a correction. Make a tiny pencil mark next to the problematic word or make a mental note to yourself to revisit that word soon. Reviewing words before introducing a new pattern generally is helpful to your student.

Reviewing the previous lists will usually take your student only a few minutes. If it takes longer than that, more practice on earlier lessons may be in order. Sometimes a student is having a bad day; other times he just needs to review more intently. Mastery of each lesson is a critical precursor to the lessons that follow. From this point forward the lessons will involve less review. You will have to use your judgment to decide whether or not to take a step back and spend more time reviewing.

Effective Pencil Use

If your student reads a word incorrectly, keep your pencil pointed at the word. Do not move the pencil to the next word until he has made a correction. If your student continues reading and ignoring your pencil cue, just relax and wait. Eventually, he may ask you why you are still pointing at the word. Explain that he needs to look at the word again. After he accurately reads the word, move the pencil to the next word on the list. He may initially fuss about this method, but once he understands that errors are going to be corrected at the time they are made, he will get on board. He will know to stop and make corrections, as needed, when needed. Don't waver on this! It will pay huge dividends later. Directing-by-pencil is a nonconfrontational technique that not only provides positive reinforcement and nonverbal correction for the student but ultimately makes the lessons a pleasant experience for everyone involved.

Equivalent Letters

If you have a student who is confusing the letters **b** and **p** or **d** and **t**, please refer to the discussion on equivalent letters on page 208. The information on voiced and voiceless letters may also be of help (see page 212).

Lesson 12

Review: B b D d

I. bad   fed   boss   dull   ban   dig   nod
rob   dill   bat   hid   did   wed   box

II. buff   bed   bus   ebb   sod   fad   din
add   doll   tab   dab   had   Dan   hub

III. red   bud   bun   rub   dim   lab   mud
ad   bog   mod   dog   beg   mad   bit

IV. tub   jab   dad   buzz   odd   bet   bid
led   bob   mid   dip   bill   pub   web

V. bag   dell   bib   lid   God   dug   pod
dot   rib   job   sub   big   but   sad

VI. sob   dub   lad   bell   rid   Ed   nub
bin   den   bug   pad   mob   fib   rod

Challenge Word: **hidden**
[hid • den]

Instructions for Lesson 13

> ## Introduce the pronunciation and spelling patterns for the consonants c, k, and q.

When pronouncing **k**, say |k|, not |kŭh|. **K** is pronounced without an |ŭ| sound.

I   **NEW PATTERN.** Introduce the most common spelling pattern for the |k| sound, **k**, as in **kit**. The **k** almost always is paired with the vowels **e** or **i**, as in **keg** and **kit**, and hardly ever with any of the other vowels.

II   **NEW PATTERN.** Introduce the **c** spelling pattern for the |k| sound, as in **cat**. The letter **c** with the |k| sound almost always appears paired with the vowels **a, o,** or **u**, as in **cat, cot,** and **cut**. This is a steadfast rule. Knowing this pattern can help us remember how to spell certain words.

III   **NEW PATTERN.** Introduce the **qu** spelling pattern pronounced |khw|, as in **quiz**. Words in the English language with the |khw| sound are spelled **qu**. Mention to your student that the letter **q** rarely appears by itself—it is almost always paired with the letter **u**.

A few English words have **qu** but are pronounced with the relatively sharper |k| sound, as heard in **mosquito**. Foreign words (mostly Asian and African derived) are the only words that have a |khw| sound but are spelled **kw**. Examples are **Tae Kwon-Do** and **Kwanza**. Proper names do not necessarily follow a regular pattern. A case in point is **Iraq**, which is spelled with a **q** but without the **u**. As with all proper names, the originator can direct what the spelling and pronunciation of the name will be. [See Lesson 89]

IV   **REVIEW** the three spelling patterns that make a |k| or |khw| sound, as in **cat**, **kit**, and **quiz**.

Instructions for Lesson 14

> ### Introduce a fourth spelling pattern that exhibits a |k| sound: ck
> **(as in** pack **and** dock**). We also will learn** cks (|ks|), **as in** rocks **and** ducks.

I - IV   **NEW PATTERN.** Learn the fourth spelling pattern that has the |k| sound, **ck**, as in **back** and **lock**. Most short-vowel words and syllables that *end* with a |k| sound are written using the **ck** spelling pattern (**back, duck**).

V & VI   **NEW PATTERN.** Learn the **cks** spelling pattern that has the |k| plus |s| sounds, |ks|, as in **rocks** and **ducks**. An **s** is added to a noun to indicate that there is more than one item (two **rocks** instead of one **rock**). An **s** is added to a third-person singular verb to denote present action ("*Frances **rocks** the baby to sleep.*")

Remember to read, spell, and discuss the meaning of the challenge words.

Lesson 13

c or k = |k| qu = |khw|

k = |k|

I. kit   kiss   kin   kill   kid   Kim   keg

c = |k|

II. cat   cut   cab   cod   can   con   cup
      cot   cop   cub   cap   cuff   cob   cull

qu = |khw|

III. quiz   quid   quip   quill   quit   Quinn   quell

Review: c k qu

IV. cat   kill   quiz   cuff   quip   kin   cup
      quill   cull   cog   kit   cap   kiss   cab
      cod   cuss   cud   cot   cut   kid   con
                       keg   cub   quell

Review: b d

V. quid   cub   cod   cad   kid   cud   cab

Lesson 14
ck cks

ck = |k|

I.   back   sick   lack   kick   sock   quick

II. lock   buck   deck   luck   tick   rack

III. pack   jock   tack   wick   sack   mock

IV. duck   rock   dock   lick   pick   quack

cks = |ks|

V.   rocks   decks   mocks   picks   bucks   ticks

VI. ducks   wicks   backs   socks   lacks   packs

Challenge Words:	napkin	catnip	duckbill
	[nap • kin]	[cat • nip]	[duck • bill]

45

Instructions for Lesson 15

Review the spelling patterns x **and** cks, **pronounced** |ks|.

Two Spellings for One Sound

Instructor, please take note: This lesson introduces two possible consonant spellings for the sound of |ks|—cks and x. In other words, your student will need to select the appropriate spelling from several choices. Spelling choices in this lesson and future lessons will be introduced and mastered one at a time. Focus on today's lesson.

I   REVIEW the **x** spelling pattern with the |ks| sound, as in **six**.

II   REVIEW the **cks** spelling pattern with the |ks| sound, as in **rocks**.

III & IV   REVIEW the **x** and **cks** spelling patterns with the |ks| sound, as in **box** and **ducks**.

As was discussed in Lesson 14, if a word ending with **cks** is a noun, the **s** indicates that the noun is plural (more than one), as in the sentence: *"Gavin is putting five basalt **rocks** in Carolynn's flower bed."* The **s** ending on a verb, however, shows that a certain action is occurring now, in the *present tense* (e.g., *"Allen's band really **rocks**"*).

Better Reader or Better Speller?

Some students find reading the patterns easier than spelling them; others find spelling easier than reading. Both skills must be mastered in every lesson! A third skill that is essential for real reading is *comprehending the meaning of the words*. If your student can pronounce a word but does not know what it means, what has he gained? Sometimes a student will glean a word's meaning from context, or perhaps he will find the meaning by asking you for a definition or by consulting a dictionary. However the meaning is obtained, it is crucial that your student understand the words. This is a practice to be nurtured.

We require your student to spell all of the words in each lesson on paper. The activity of writing words establishes a pathway between your student's brain and hand, and research indicates that the act of writing does increase learning. The spelling of every word initially may seem to slow down the learning process but it is absolutely essential.

Your student's handwriting probably will improve (with some encouragement from you) as he spells through the lessons. Penmanship is important, and so as your student gains confidence as a reader, you might aim for improvements in his penmanship one letter at a time. For example, if he is not closing the letter **o**, making it look like the letter **u**, explain to him that until he finishes his **o**'s, you will not be able to count words as being spelled correctly. At a minimum, insist that he write his words legibly.

Frequency of Lessons

Students benefit enormously from daily lessons. This frequency spurs progress and helps speed elimination of the difficult-to-break habit of guess reading.

Lesson 15

x or cks = |ks|

x = |ks|

I. six   mix   sax   fix   fox   wax   tux

     box   tax   vex   fax   ax   ox   pox

cks = |ks|

II. rocks   packs   backs   locks   licks   docks   lacks

     ducks   bucks   sacks   kicks   socks   decks   quacks

Review: |ks|

III. wax   bucks   rocks   fox   lacks   socks   tax

      locks   fix   docks   picks   max   ducks   packs

IV. fax   pecks   vex   sacks   box   kicks   backs

     decks   mix   licks   ax   six   lax   quacks

Challenge Words:	caplet	kickback	backpack
	[cap • let]	[kick • back]	[back • pack]

Instructions for Lesson 16

Review five pronunciation and spelling patterns for the |k| sound.

This lesson **REVIEWS** five of the six spelling patterns for the **|k|** sound: **c, k, ck(s), x,** and **qu,** as in **cat, kit, back, rocks, fox,** and **quiz.** [A sixth pattern, **ch,** is found in the words **ache, chasm,** and **Christmas** and will be handled in Lesson 79.] All six spelling patterns for the **|k|** sound will be reviewed again in Lesson 80.

Instructions for Lesson 17

Introduce the second sound for the letter s (|z|), **as in** is **and** has.

I   **NEW PATTERN.** Introduce the **s** spelling that has a soft **|z|** sound, as in **is** and **has.**

II   **REVIEW** the **s** and **ss** spellings that say **|s|,** as in **bus** and **miss.**

III   **REVIEW** the **z** and **zz** spellings that say **|z|,** as in **zip** and **jazz.** Note: The word **quiz** ends with a single **z.** Your student should pronounce the two **d**'s in **Zudd**™ with one **d** sound, **|zŭd|.**

IV & V   **REVIEW** the **s** and **ss** spellings that have either a **|s|** or **|z|** sound, as in **bus, fuss,** and **is,** and the **z** and **zz** spellings with the **|z|** sound, as in **zip** and **jazz.** The letter **z** is usually pronounced **|z|.** The **tz** letter combination has a **|ts|** sound, as in **pretzel, quartz, waltz,** and **Ritz**™. [See Lesson 89]

Strive for Full Confidence in Each New Lesson

If your student hesitates over words, it is a sign that he needs more practice. Reviewing can consist of reading and spelling a whole lesson, one particular Roman numeral list, or a sampling of words from one or more lists. Continue reviewing until his confidence is clearly established.

Don't Be Afraid to Do a "Start Over"

Even this late in the lessons, there have been times that I have started a student over at Lesson 1. In fact, I have required a few students to go back to the early lessons more than once. Mastery of the early lessons cannot be emphasized enough.

If you believe that your student really isn't up to successfully tackling future lessons, please do the courageous thing and go back and start over. You decide how far back to go for a re-set and how many sessions are needed to achieve mastery. The times that I have asked students to begin again with Lesson 1 (or 9 or 24 or whatever I think best), I have seen relief in their eyes. Moving too quickly can leave some students feeling stressed. One way to diplomatically broach the subject is to ask your student, *"Would you like to go back to Lesson X and get this word pattern really solid?"* The answer, almost always, is yes. Again, I emphasize that these early lessons are powerful when mastered—don't miss this power because you are in a hurry. Patience will pay off for you and your student.

Lesson 16
|k|

c = |k|

I. cat	cut	cap	cod	con	cull

k = |k|

II. kit	kid	kin	kiss	kill	keg

ck = |k| **cks = |ks|**

III. back	pack	mock	sock	luck	quick
rocks	socks	picks	lacks	decks	ducks

x = |ks|

IV. ax	wax	vex	six	fox	tux

qu = |khw|

V. quiz	quill	quip	quit	quid	quell

Review: |k| |ks| |khw|

VI. kit	cull	quick	ox	quiz	packs
duck	quell	locks	keg	six	cab

Lesson 17
|s| or |z|

s = |z|

I. is	has	as	his

s and ss = |s|

II. bus	gas	sass	moss	loss	lass
miss	buss	fuss	toss	kiss	hiss

z and zz = |z|

III. zap	zip	Zen	zig	Zudd™	zag
jazz	buzz	razz	fizz	fuzz	quiz

Review: s z

IV. has	fuss	rocks	packs	backs	mix
bus	picks	jazz	six	boss	quacks
V. is	fizz	his	razz	as	fox
decks	wax	gas	quiz	less	wicks

Challenge Words:	**luckless**	**cobwebs**
	[luck • less]	[cob • webs]

Instructions for Lesson 18

> **Review all of the short-vowel patterns from the first seventeen lessons.**

This lesson **REVIEWS** all five short-vowel pronunciation patterns. All of the consonants are reviewed also, as are certain patterns for the |k| sound, namely **c**, **k**, **x**, **ck**, and **cks**. The letter **q** is almost always paired with **u** and usually pronounced |kw|. We also review the second sound for the letter **s**: |z|, as in **his**.

a, b, c, (ck[s]), d, **e**, f, g, h, **i**, j, k, l, m, n, **o**, p, q(u), r, s (|s| and |z|), t, **u**, v, w, x, y, z

How Is Your Student Doing?

A student typically begins a lesson by sounding out individual letters and syllables. This can be a slow process. As your student works through the lists, he might still pronounce some of the words haltingly. Continue practicing until he can read every word without hesitation. Your goal for every lesson is for your pupil to read every word accurately, confidently, and knowledgeably. This goal is true for spelling, too. Your student should practice writing words until he can spell each word effortlessly. These lessons are building a tool box of syllables that can be used to pronounce and spell practically all of the words in the English language. Future lessons will prove difficult if these beginning, basic patterns have not been mastered.

The Student's Pace

I've had enthusiastic students who were able to handle four consecutive lessons in one sitting. (And by handle, I mean they earned a 100 on everything) The norm, however, for adults, teens, and above-average elementary students is two lessons per session. A few learners will struggle to complete and master a single Roman numeral list, an exercise which may leave them exhausted (but pleased with their success). **Relax and give your student the freedom to progress at his own pace.** As he gains self-assurance, he will not only pick up the pace naturally but often will increase his ability to focus for longer periods of time.

It is always a good idea to ask your student if he would like to read or spell any words again. He may have appeared to be confident, efficient, and quick with the assignment, but that may not be the way he is actually feeling. Adults, teens, and pre-teens are willing to tell you if they need to repeat a lesson or a particular set of words. A younger student will not usually volunteer this information. Ask the younger student, but always use your judgment. If hesitation surfaces later, just return to that pattern and do extra review. For example, reread or respell one or more of these lessons if you notice that your student seems to hesitate on specific vowel sounds (or spellings): Lesson 1 for |ă|; Lesson 2 for |ĭ|; Lesson 4 for |ŏ|; Lesson 6 for |ŭ|; and Lesson 8 for |ĕ|. Lessons 9 and 18 are good places to have your student practice all five short vowels.

Lesson 18

Review: Short Vowels

I.	back	rim	moss	fig	nap
	top	bus	pack	on	hum
	bat	jot	hit	rub	yam
II.	dill	buff	sell	sob	pet
	bet	add	doll	wed	rid
	cull	ox	quip	miss	cup
III.	quell	sick	red	luck	rocks
	tax	cot	kiss	wax	dug
	rock	quiz	hat	cuff	fox
IV.	ten	cog	God	mess	mad
	puff	kick	wet	nut	fell
	tip	dot	men	pill	ham
V.	off	fix	tab	ebb	mob
	quit	lip	six	set	bag
	job	it	run	cut	sock
VI.	leg	cub	ax	quick	loss
	quill	had	kid	cop	ducks
	mass	packs	bed	bad	box

Challenge Words:	**hatless**	**cutback**
	[hat • less]	[cut • back]

Instructions for Lesson 19

> **Introduce consonant blends. Each consonant in these blends is sounded (pronounced).**
>
> **Introduce words that end with the consonant blends**
> ps, ts, pt, ld, nt, nd, lt, mp, sk, st, lk, **and** ft.

If you are using the detailed completion chart, it is time for the next card. [Page 295]

Consonant blends at the end of a word (so-called *ending blends* or *end blends*) are easier for most students to learn than consonant blends that appear at the beginning of a word. That is why ending blends are introduced first.

I 　　**NEW PATTERN.** Learn words that end with the consonant blends **ps** and **ts**, as in **gaps** and **pets**. A few of the words can function as nouns or verbs. As indicated in Lesson 15, an **s** at the end of a noun means the noun is plural (more than one). An **s** at the end of a verb indicates present tense (cuts, jots) (*"The florist **cuts** flower stems"*; *"The newspaper reporter **jots** interview notes"*).

Note: The word **apps** is spelled with two **p**'s.

II 　　**LEARN** words that end with the consonant blends **lt**, **ld**, and **pt**, as in **melt**, **held**, and **kept**.

III 　　**LEARN** words that end with the consonant blends **gs** and **nd**, as in **legs** and **land**.

IV 　　**LEARN** words that end with the consonant blends **nd**, **nt**, and **mp**, as in **send**, **rent**, and **jump**.

V 　　**LEARN** words that end with the consonant blends **sk** and **st**, as in **ask** and **best**.

VI 　　**LEARN** words that end with the consonant blends **st**, **ft**, and **lk**, as in **last**, **gift**, and **milk**.

Difficulty Pronouncing "ulk"

If your student is having difficulty reading words with the **ulk** ending (**sulk**, **bulk**, **hulk**), have him reread the five words listed in Lesson 6 at Roman numeral V: **hull**, **gull**, **mull**, **null**, and **lull**. With a pencil, write the letter **k** beside the word **hull** [**hull** 　 **k**]. Several times in a row, have your student read **hull**, then add the sound of |k|: |**hull**| – |**k**|, |**hull**| – |**k**|, |**hull**| – |**k**|. If your student still has trouble, don't get bogged down. When you begin the next session, do a review of any word that was earlier problematic. Often, it will be easily read this time around.

Lesson 19
Ending Consonant Blends

I. | gaps | mops | yaps | quips | cups | zips |
|---|---|---|---|---|---|
| apps | hops | tips | jets | its | vets |
| pets | tats | huts | wits | cuts | jots |

II. | melt | belt | felt | pelt | wilt | jilt |
|---|---|---|---|---|---|
| tilt | silt | cult | quilt | weld | meld |
| held | kept | apt | wept | rapt | opt |

III. | legs | begs | sags | bogs | rags | tugs |
|---|---|---|---|---|---|
| rigs | pigs | digs | mugs | bugs | rugs |
| land | fund | and | hand | pond | sand |

IV. | send | band | end | lend | bond | bend |
|---|---|---|---|---|---|
| rent | hint | ant | hunt | sent | went |
| jump | camp | romp | limp | pump | amp |

V. | ask | risk | desk | mask | dusk | task |
|---|---|---|---|---|---|
| bask | cask | tusk | west | lost | nest |
| best | list | test | must | cost | past |

VI. | last | fast | rest | just | zest | cast |
|---|---|---|---|---|---|
| gift | tuft | raft | sift | soft | left |
| milk | silk | elk | sulk | bulk | hulk |

Instructions for Lesson 20

Review several ending consonant blends.
Each consonant is pronounced (sounded) in these short-vowel words.

Introduce words that end with the consonant blends
ct, lm, lp, xt, cks, cts, lts, lms, lds, xts, lps, mps, nts, nds, nk, nks, ng, and ngs.

Also, introduce words with a variant sound for the letters n and g
when n and g are in the consonant blends nk |ngk| and ng |ng|.

I - IV   **LEARN** more *ending* consonant blends. Remind your student that, as always, we sound out the letters in a word from left to right.

IV   **NEW PATTERN.** Here we learn the **nds** ending consonant blend. When we pronounce **nd**, the letter **d** is clearly enunciated, as in **land** and **mend**. However, when **s** is added to form **nds** at the end of a word or syllable, the tongue goes to the place where **d** is pronounced but the sound for **d** is not clearly made. Rather, the **d** is mostly silent because the tongue stays on the roof of the mouth. Illustrate this by saying the word **lands**. Now say the word **mends**. Notice how the **d** sound almost dissolves or disappears.

V & VI   **NEW PATTERN.** We now will learn the second sound for the letter **n**. This sound is manifested in words ending in **nk**, **nks**, **ng**, or **ngs**, as in **bunk**, **bunks**, **song**, and **songs**. The **n** in **nk(s)** and **ng(s)** is not pronounced like the basic sound for the letter **n**. A lone **n** is pronounced with a nasal hum that creates vibration and involves the tongue touching the top of the mouth just behind and above the top teeth. The letter **n** in the consonant blends **nk** and **ng** [bunk, song] is pronounced farther back, more in the center or back of the roof of the mouth. Have your student pronounce the word **run**, emphasizing the **n** |rŭn|. Then have him say the words **bunk** |bŭngk| and **song** |sŏng|, paying attention to the difference in the sound of the letter **n**. The **n** sound in both of these words is nasal and voiced. Have him touch his throat with his finger tips and feel the vibration that occurs when he says |n|, |ng|, and |ngk|. It can be quite helpful to explain these differences.

VI   **NEW PATTERN.** There is a second sound for the letter **g**, as it appears in the ending consonant blends **ng** and **ngs**, as in **song** and **lungs**. Here the **g** is pronounced without a |gŭh| sound. First, have your student say the word **bag**, emphasizing the letter **g**, and notice the slight |gŭh| sound, |bă gŭh|. Then have him say the word **lung** and remark that the sound of the letter **g** is shortened and pronounced without the |gŭh| sound. Likewise, we say |sŏng|, not |sŏng gŭh|.

Lesson 20
Ending Consonant Blends

ct, lm, lp, and xt

I.

act	fact	pact	sect	duct
elm	film	help	text	next

cks and cts

II.

sacks	decks	picks	locks	bucks
acts	sects	facts	ducts	pacts

lts, lms, lds, and xts

III.

belts	lilts	melts	wilts	quilts	tilts
films	elms	helms	welds	melds	texts

lps, mps, and nts

IV.

helps	camps	bumps	limps	jumps
hints	punts	hunts	rents	bunts

The letter d is almost silent in these words.

lands	mends	winds	hands	sends

The n sound changes in these words!

nk and nks

V.

bunk	junk	sunk	honk	dunk	hunk
bunks	dunks	hunks	punks	junks	honks

Both the n and g sounds change in these words!

ng and ngs

VI.

song	long	hung	rung	lung	sung
songs	rungs	lungs	longs	gongs	tongs

Instructions for Lesson 21

Review the patterns for ending consonant blends.

Blends: sks sts

I   **LEARN** the **sks** and **sts** end consonant blends, as in **asks** and **lists**. These words have two instances of the sound of **s**. This results in a slight tongue twisting effect. If your student struggles with these words, have him first pronounce the word without the **s** ending, then add the **s**. The progression is thus: |ask| + |s|, or |asks|.

II - IV   **REVIEW** end consonant blends.

Why So Much Review?

We review in order to integrate patterns, not to memorize words. Review exercises allow for practicing one, a few, or all of the previously introduced patterns. Sometimes new words are presented to help you assess whether or not your student is genuinely applying the patterns.

If your student continues to confuse any of the alphabet letters or syllable patterns, such as **j** and **g**, spend time reviewing words that have these patterns until your student becomes proficient. For example, first, read only words with the letter **j**, as in **jot**, until the words are mastered. Then review words having the other letter, **g**, as in **gal**. Finally, review words that have one or both of the letters **g** and **j** until these are easily handled (e.g., **jug, jig, jog, gill, jot, gal**).

Is your student having a difficult time spelling? Follow a routine of reading and spelling until mastery occurs.

Recognizing Improvement

At this point in the lessons, many common words have not been learned yet. For example, your student has not learned all of the patterns for pronouncing **begin, explain, choose, decide, turn, page, follow, multiply, divide, start, instruction, tiger, dinosaur**, and **directions**. The building blocks for acquiring these words are being put into place. So be patient!

Your student might be halfway through these lessons before the people in his life recognize that he is reading better. Most students themselves recognize immediately that their ability to read and spell and comprehend has improved.

Consider Spelling the Words First

We teach students how to pronounce a word, then have them practice how to spell it. In some cases, your student might be helped by spelling a word first, then learning how to pronounce it. You might try this reverse protocol if the typical approach is not working smoothly for your student. We trust you to decide if he will benefit from spelling, then reading. If you are teaching a new sound or spelling pattern in the lesson, mention this before you begin.

Lesson 21
Ending Consonant Blends

sk and **sks**

I.   ask   risk   desk   mask   task   bask

       asks   risks   desks   masks   tasks   basks

st and **sts**

       list   last   cost   west   best   rest

       lists   lasts   costs   rusts   casts   rests

Review: Ending Blends

II.
lamps	song	melts
belt	zips	lands
golf	gong	decks
font	apt	tusk

III.
texts	junk	hulk
band	jumps	films
locks	tact	next
bend	gift	zest

IV.
pump	sacks	honks
wits	lungs	quilt
cups	vast	lend
bunks	winds	sects

Challenge Words: **listless**   **bucket**

                                        [*list • less*]   [*buck • et*]

Instructions for Lesson 22

> Introduce the patterns for beginning consonant blends. Each consonant is individually pronounced (sounded) in these blends. The blends are bl, br, cl, cr, dr, fl, fr, gl, gr, pl, sc, sk, sl, sm, sn, sp, squ, st, tr, tw, scr, **and** str.

> The italicized words are helper words. Use them only if needed.

I - IV   NEW CONCEPT. In this lesson, we will learn *beginning* consonant blends. Beginning consonant blends are just slightly more difficult than the ending consonant blends that were previously introduced. In the short-vowel words on the lesson page, each consonant in the frontal blend is spoken. Have your student read (then spell) the main words in row I. The words underneath in italics are helper words (all of which were introduced in Lessons 1 through 21) and should be used only if your student needs a hint for succeeding with the main word. As always, remember the importance of reading and spelling each word from left to right. Before allowing your student to begin the next lesson, be sure that he can read and spell these newly introduced words without the use of helper words.

There are some end blends in the lesson words. These blends are **ss**, **nd**, **mp**, **st**, **ll**, and **nt**, as in **bless**, **stand**, **stamp**, **trust**, **twill**, and **squint**. (We saw these end blends previously in Lessons 19 through 21.)

The letter **c** pronounced |**k**| almost always appears with the vowels **a**, **o**, or **u** and whenever a |**k**|-sounding consonant blend is involved (**cat**, **cot**, **cut**, **class**, **crest**). The **c**-with-**a**-**o**-**u** pattern is quite consistent and may be considered a true spelling rule.

LEARN more beginning consonant blends. **REVIEW** end consonant blends. Here we will encounter the **ck** digraph. A *digraph* is a pairing of two letters that together make one sound.

VI   LEARN the **squ** spelling, pronounced |**skhw**|, as in **squid** and **squint**. The letter **q** is almost always paired with **u**. The short vowel pronounced in these words is the **i**. (See Lessons 13 and 16)

Help Wanted

One of The Real Reading Company's excellent instructors covers the helper words with a piece of paper. If her student is having difficulty pronouncing a new word, she slides the paper down to reveal the helper word. With this clue, her student is usually able to read the main word. Another instructor we know has a technique for getting students to focus. She tells her student to *"Get ready!"* She waits one second to allow the student time to focus, then has her student begin reading.

Spelling Pedagogy

During the spelling portion of this lesson, if your student is having difficulty spelling a particular word (**black**, for example), tell him the helper word (**lack**). These helper words have been encountered in previous lessons. Mention that you want him to write "Not the word |**lack**|, but |**b**| – |**lack**|, |**black**|."

Lesson 22
Beginning Consonant Blends

> **Use the words in italics ONLY as helper words and ONLY if needed.**

I.

blot	clip	clad	clap	fled	flap
lot	*lip*	*lad*	*lap*	*led*	*lap*
flag	pled	glad	glib	flit	slot
lag	*led*	*lad*	*lib*	*lit*	*lot*

II.

sled	slip	slit	brim	brag	bran
led	*lip*	*lit*	*rim*	*rag*	*ran*
brig	twin	drug	Fred	grim	grub
rig	*win*	*rug*	*red*	*rim*	*rub*

III.

trip	smug	trim	tram	crib	twig
rip	*mug*	*rim*	*ram*	*rib*	*wig*
scan	skit	snap	skin	snag	trap
can	*kit*	*nap*	*kin*	*nag*	*rap*

IV.

spin	stop	spun	span	spot	stub
pin	*top*	*pun*	*pan*	*pot*	*tub*
bless	block	blast	blend	bland	pluck
less	*lock*	*last*	*lend*	*land*	*luck*

V.

class	clock	click	clamp	floss	flock
lass	*lock*	*lick*	*lamp*	*loss*	*lock*
black	slack	slick	crest	crock	frock
lack	*lack*	*lick*	*rest*	*rock*	*rock*

VI.

stand	stamp	stuck	stack	smock	spill
and	*amp*	*tuck*	*tack*	*mock*	*pill*
trust	twill	scram	strut	squid	squint
rust	*will*	*cram*	*rut*	*quid*	*quint*

Challenge Words:	**spotless**	**backstop**	**bedrock**
	[*spot • less*]	[*back • stop*]	[*bed • rock*]

Instructions for Lesson 23

Review beginning consonant blends.

Review

Some students might read and spell through all of the words in one session, only to return to the "guess" habit in the next. It is normal for students to periodically return to old habits. It is very difficult for a few students to stop guessing. They are disinclined to see and process the printed words on the page. Gentle reminders from you will be in order if this occurs. Give your student plenty of time to do the mental work involved in making needed adjustments and becoming a disciplined reader.

Even More Ideas for Interrupting the Hard-to-Break Habit of Guessing

Remind your student that any ingrained habit is difficult to break, but it can be done!

- *"Trust Your Eyes"*   Tell your student to take a deep breath, exhale, relax, and read the word to which you are pointing. He must focus on what he sees and not rely on his memory. Say to him, "What do you see on the page? Trust your eyes. Look at the letters. Sound out the letters of the word." Many times a student will recognize a word when he hears himself speak it.

- *"One More Time"*   Explain a troublesome letter or syllable pattern one more time. (And again and again, if necessary!)

- *"Review Until Smooth"*   Review words from an earlier lesson. Drill with the student until his reading is quick and smooth.

- *"Push the Card"*   One reading interventionist that we know places a 3 x 5 index card on the left side of a word that her student will be reading. She then pushes the card across the word, left to right, as he reads it. The purpose of this is to cause her student to have to read quickly, without hesitation. You can draw an arrow on the right edge of your card (→)to prompt additional focus.

- *"Get Ready!"*   Say to your student, *"Get ready!"* Wait one second, then cue him to start reading an indicated word list.

- *"Close the Eyes Technique"*   Tell your student to close his eyes. Tell him that you are going to point to one word on the page. You want him to open his eyes when he is ready and to read the word. Then, continue to read through the list. This activity is designed to help students who can't seem to see what is printed on the page. As mentioned earlier, research indicates that the part of the brain used in pattern reading is different from the part of the brain used in working from memory. This "close the eyes" technique seems to help some students use the part of their brain that is geared for reading.

Be creative and trust your own ability to think of ways to help your student.

Lesson 23

Beginning Consonant Blends

I.	clam	smog	spill	smell
	fret	brass	slim	skip
	snug	bliss	clan	stamp

II.	truck	clamp	drop	speck
	bless	frog	scam	bluff
	snack	crops	stand	slat

III.	dress	stump	block	plan
	slum	twist	tram	brand
	bland	crest	cross	clock

IV.	brick	plus	stock	drill
	spend	crab	plum	swell
	spell	flat	drab	plant

V.	scram	snub	fluff	still
	track	stick	swim	plump
	sped	stomp	glass	snap

VI.	stop	span	clap	blond
	glad	stem	clip	trunk
	stunt	flag	trick	strong

Challenge Words:	**bandstand**	**droplet**
	[band • stand]	[drop • let]

Instructions for Lesson 24

> **Review the pronunciation and spelling patterns taught in Lessons 1 through 23.**

All of the review words contain a short vowel. Be aware that the words beginning in **qu** (**quips**, **quits**, **quilt**, **quack**) may cause some confusion. Remember that **q** is almost always paired with **u**. The short vowel that really drives these **qu** words is either an **i** or an **a**.

Instructions for Lesson 25

> **Introduce the digraph sh and the trigraph shr.**

I - IV   **NEW PATTERN.** The **sh** spelling pattern is pronounced |sh|, as in **dish** and **shop**.

V   **LEARN** the **sh** spelling pattern pronounced |sh|, as in **slush**.

NEW PATTERN. The **shr** spelling pattern is pronounced |shr|, as in **shred**.

Digraphs

A digraph consists of two letters that, when paired, have a special pronunciation. Examples of digraphs are **sh**, |sh|, as in **ship**, and **ch**, |ch|, as in **check**. The individual sounds of the consonant **s** and the consonant **h** are not preserved when their letters are combined in the digraph. Rather, they form a new sound entirely, as we see with |sh|, as in **cash** and **ship**.

The letters of a digraph are always found entirely in the same syllable. If the letters that look like they are a digraph are separated into different syllables, then these letters do not comprise a digraph. For example, the **th** in **pothole** is not a digraph. Why not? Because **pothole** has the **t** and **h** in separate syllables (pot • hole).

There are many digraphs and trigraphs not mentioned here that will be covered in upcoming lessons.

Lesson 24
Review: Lessons 1 - 23

I.	text	brick	wicks	legs	just	and
	cuts	twist	class	stop	spit	bat
	milks	damp	flick	black	fact	men

II.	quips	jazz	tact	kicks	tramp	laps
	blot	clan	crest	brag	elk	off
	up	track	husk	bluff	mast	rest

III.	quits	stand	fled	dress	run	click
	scram	amp	block	end	slack	on
	egg	stick	mats	brass	nap	fix

IV.	quilt	sped	juts	van	if	hand
	grass	pluck	drop	yes	ran	gifts
	quacks	plants	snub	wag	net	press

Lesson 25
|sh| |shr|

I.	dish	mash	gush	mush	rash
	cash	sash	wish	lash	Josh

II.	dash	fish	hush	gash	rush
	brush	crush	flash	clash	blush

III.	trash	swish	brash	stash	fresh
	slash	crash	slosh	plush	smash

IV.	shop	ship	sham	shall	shed
	shell	shun	shut	shod	shock

V.	slush	flesh	splash	squish	shrub
	shred	shrimp	shrill	shrunk	shrug

Challenge Words:	**mishmash**	**dishpan**	**backlash**
	[mish • mash]	[dish • pan]	[back • lash]

Instructions for Lesson 26

> **Introduce the spelling patterns** ch, nch, **and** tch.
> **The digraph ch, pronounced** |ch|, **is illustrated in** chop, much, **and** inch.
> **We also welcome the trigraph** tch, **which is pronounced** |ch|, **as in** catch.

I   **NEW PATTERN.** We are going to learn the **ch** digraph spelling pattern with the |ch| sound. This sound is found at the beginning of syllables and words, as in **chop**.

II   **LEARN** the **ch** spelling pattern with the |ch| sound found at the end of syllables or words, as in **much**.

III   **NEW PATTERN.** Here we will learn the **nch** spelling pattern with the |nch| sound, as in **inch**. This is a trigraph (consists of three letters constituting one sound). This would be an opportune time to use a dictionary to look up at least some of the lesson words. Students will benefit if they get in the habit of consulting a dictionary.

REVIEW the slight sound change that occurs in short vowels **i** and **e** when these letters are followed by the consonant **n**, as in **inch** and **bench**.

IV   **LEARN** the **tch** trigraph that makes the sound of |ch|, as in **match** and **itch**. Most short-vowel words ending in the |ch| sound are spelled with the silent letter **t** [tch] and are pronounced the same as the simple digraph **ch**, as in **stitch**. Only a few short-vowel words and syllables ending with the |ch| sound are spelled without the silent **t**. Roman numeral II lists three of the exceptions: **much, rich,** and **such**. Other exceptions are **which** (Lesson 27) and **touch** (Lesson 67). These five words may be the only exceptions to this short-vowel pattern.

Review: ch nch tch

V & VI   **REVIEW** the **ch, tch,** and **nch** spelling patterns for the |ch| and |nch| sounds, respectively.

The Sound for "ch" Is Quick

Vowels have a "continuous" sound because their sound can continue for as long as the speaker has breath and time. In contrast, the **ch** (|ch|) is a "quick" or "stop" sound. Telling your student about the "quick" sound of |ch| may help him pronounce it. To illustrate, ask your student to say |ch|, opening his mouth and dropping his tongue from the roof of the mouth and releasing a puff of air, fast. This motion will stop the sound.

Lesson 26
ch nch tch

ch

I.
chop	chill	chum	chap
check	chat	chimp	chess
chick	champ	chin	chaff

ch

II.
| much | rich | such |

nch

III.
inch	pinch	finch	ranch
bench	quench	French	branch
lunch	punch	crunch	brunch

tch

IV.
match	catch	etch	stitch
itch	crutch	patch	clutch
scotch	stretch	switch	scratch

Review

V.
chick	winch	crunch	chaff	quench	such
patch	stretch	chin	punch	twitch	check
finch	much	witch	rich	hunch	etch

VI.
chest	inch	chat	chess	catch	chip
pitch	fetch	chimp	batch	lunch	branch
bunch	stench	scratch	clutch	switch	notch

| Challenge Words: | **hunchback** | **chopstick** |
| | [hunch • back] | [chop • stick] |

Instructions for Lesson 27

> **Introduce the** wh **spelling pattern pronounced |hw| or |w|.**
> **Also introduce the** th **spelling pattern.**
>
> **Review the digraphs** ch **and** sh **and the trigraphs** nch, tch, **and** shr.

I   **NEW PATTERN.** Learn **wh**, which is pronounced either **|hw|** or **|w|**.
The **|hw|** generates air and no vocal cord vibration. When **|hw|** is used as the **wh** sound
in **which** and **when**, more "air time" is involved than if **|w|** is used. Compare **|hw|** to the
use of the voiced **|w|**; the latter involves vibration and less air. Modern dictionaries
indicate that both pronunciations are valid.

Notice when spelling **where** and **there** that these words end in a silent **e**. Some reading
teachers consider **ere** to be a recognized blend. Often, people pronounce these words
with more of a long-vowel **a** sound, **|ār|** or **|âr|**. The presence of **r** usually alters the
sound of a vowel that precedes it. Your student will not have difficulty with these
words.

II   **NEW PATTERN.** Learn the **th** spelling pattern, which has two
pronunciations: with vibration of the vocal cords, as in **this** and **that**, and without
vocal cord vibration, as in **thin** and **path**.

III - VI   **REVIEW** the digraph/trigraph spelling and pronunciation patterns **ch**, **tch**,
nch, **sh**, **shr**, **wh**, and **th** (the **th** and the **wh** blends are introduced with and without
vibration of the vocal cords).

The Difference between Voiced and Voiceless Sounds

Consider the words **thin** and **path**. The **th** in each of these words is *voiceless*, meaning
that the pronouncing of the **th** does not produce vibration in the speaker's throat.
The speaker does, however, expel air through his mouth. Place your hand in front
of your lips and feel the air that is expelled when you say the **th** sound in **thin** and **path**.
Now consider the words **which** and **when**. Put your hand on your throat and
pronounce these words. There should be no detectible vibration on the **wh**, meaning
that **wh** is not voiced.

In comparison, *voiced* sounds are pronounced with almost no air but with some
vibration. Touch your throat and say **this**. Notice what happens. You should feel some
vibration. Now try the same experiment with **that**. Again, you should feel some
vibration. With your hand in front of your lips, now say **then** and **that** and notice the
almost imperceptible amount of air.

The Second Sound for the wh Digraph

There is indeed another sound for the **wh** digraph, but it will not be introduced until
Lesson 51. This is the **wh** that appears in **who, whom, whose,** and **whole**. It is a
voiceless sound and is pronounced much like the letter **h**, **|h|**.

A Note About "There"

Roman numeral II presents the word **there**. **There** belongs to a trio of homophones;
its compatriots are **their** and **they're**. These words sound alike but mean quite
different things. Point out to your student that he should always be mindful of words
that sound alike but are spelled differently. [See Lesson 84]

Lesson 27
wh th

wh = |**hw**| or |**w**|

I.

which	whip	whack	whelp	whiff
when	whit	whim	whet	whop
	whisk	whiz	where*	

th (voiced)

II. this   that   than   thus   them   then   there*

th (voiceless)

thin	theft	thrill	thud	thump
thick	thatch	thrift	thrash	bath
path	moth	with	math	cloth

* **where** and **there** end with a silent **e**

Review: ch nch tch sh shr th wh

III.

when	hath	than	shell
thud	thrift	shaft	whip
which	brunch	chin	lunch

IV.

chill	bath	whisk	thus
thrill	thump	thrash	shrimp
whet	check	bench	ranch

V.

sixth	chop	flesh	latch
then	champ	whim	squish
fresh	punch	etch	hush

VI.

slash	gash	crutch	finch
this	quench	ditch	patch
tenth	splash	rich	craft

Challenge Words:	**thickness**	**whippet**
	[*thick • ness*]	[*whip • pet*]

Instructions for Lesson 28

Introduce the pronunciation and spelling patterns for compound, two-syllable, short-vowel words.

Use the italicized words only as helper words and only if needed.

This lesson's reading list features 50 words, each consisting of two syllables. Beneath each word are two italicized helper words. The components of the helper words will be familiar to your student, as they have been presented in one or more previous lessons.

Lesson 28 should be a rewarding one for your student. Tell him to read the main words in each row. Point to the helper words only if your student is having difficulty. Remind him, if necessary, that words are pronounced and spelled LEFT to RIGHT, syllable to syllable, sound to sound, spelling pattern to spelling pattern, to the end of each word. Review until your student does not need to rely on the helper words. This list might strike some learners as being a whole slate of challenge words.

Counting Syllables

One easy way to identify the number of syllables in a word is to count the number of times your chin drops when you say the word. For example, when you pronounce |**Bat • man**|, your chin drops twice. Thus, this word has two syllables. (You also can clap your hands to the syllables.)

Helper Words

Initially, you might want to cover the italicized helper words with a piece of paper. If your student has trouble reading the main word, slide the paper down to reveal the helper words. Have him read the helper words out loud. Often, this process assists your student in reading the compound word found above it. A *compound word* is one which consists of two or more individual words combined to make a new word. (Did you know that the accent in nouns is usually on the first syllable?) Work with your student until he can read without using helper words.

Spelling Hints

Direct your student to spell the compound words on paper. If he has trouble, use the helper word as a hint.

Say something like:

> *"The first syllable is **back**; the second syllable is **pack**, |backpack|."*
> *"The first syllable is **drum**; the second syllable is **stick**, |drumstick|."*

If your student writes **address** with only one **d** or one **s** (**adres**), say:

> *"Does the word **address** have one **d** or two **d's**?" [dd]*
> *"Does the word **address** have one **s** or two **s's**?" [ss]*

Lesson 28

Two-Syllable Words

> **Use the italicized words only as helper words and only if needed.**

I.

address	backpack	eggnog	dustpan	backhand
ad · dress	*back · pack*	*egg · nog*	*dust · pan*	*back · hand*
drumstick	backlog	backlash	backstop	dockhand
drum · stick	*back · log*	*back · lash*	*back · stop*	*dock · hand*

II.

backup	dishpan	bandit	bandstand	lapdog
back · up	*dish · pan*	*band · it*	*band · stand*	*lap · dog*
bedbug	bedrock	bellhop	listless	gumdrop
bed · bug	*bed · rock*	*bell · hop*	*list · less*	*gum · drop*

III.

blastoff	bobcat	bathtub	buckskin	candid
blast · off	*bob · cat*	*bath · tub*	*buck · skin*	*can · did*
cannot	clamshell	checkup	offhand	handcuff
can · not	*clam · shell*	*check · up*	*off · hand*	*hand · cuff*

IV.

cobweb	cockpit	cabin	insect	hunchback
cob · web	*cock · pit*	*cab · in*	*in · sect*	*hunch · back*
caplet	castoff	catfish	blacktop	hilltop
cap · let	*cast · off*	*cat · fish*	*black · top*	*hill · top*

V.

crabgrass	inlet	eggplant	himself	cutback
crab · grass	*in · let*	*egg · plant*	*him · self*	*cut · back*
cutoff	intend	desktop	chopstick	handspring
cut · off	*in · tend*	*desk · top*	*chop · stick*	*hand · spring*

Instructions for Lesson 29

> **Review the pronunciation and spelling patterns for compound, two-syllable, short-vowel words.**

A *noun* is a word that refers to a person, place, or thing. A *verb* is a word that indicates action or a state of being. Hint: If the compound word is a noun, its first syllable is accented. If it is a verb, the second syllable is accented. Notice this with **address** (a noun: a place someone lives) and **address** (a verb: to give a speech).

Instructions for Lesson 30

> **Introduces the pattern for two-syllable words ending in -es or -ed.**

I - III   **NEW CONCEPT.** Here we introduce the -**es** spelling pattern that ends many words.[1] The **es** has either a short-vowel **e** sound |ĕ| or the schwa sound |ə|, as in **boxes** and **rushes**. (The schwa is discussed below.) The |s| and |z| sounds of **s** are practiced in these lists.

IV - VI   **NEW CONCEPT.** Now we will learn the -**ed** spelling pattern that ends a fair number of words.[2] The -**ed** has either a short-vowel **e** sound |ĕd| or the schwa's *shortened* short-vowel **u** sound |əd| (examples are **tested** and **ended**). Base words that end with a **t** or **d** (like the words **test** and **add**) are pronounced with the -**ed** syllable being separate, as in **tested** and **added**. Roman numerals IV and V introduce base words that end with **t** and add **ed**, as in **tested**. Roman numeral VI introduces base words that end with **d** and add **ed**, as in **added**.

The Schwa Sound: ə

If a student struggles with the ending syllables of these words, tell him that words ending with -**es** and -**ed** can be pronounced with either the short-vowel **e** sound, |ĕ|, or with a *shortened* short-vowel **u** sound, |ŭ|. This special sound, known as a *schwa*, is shown in dictionaries as an upside-down e: ə. The schwa is quite common in English and is found in most multi-syllable words. The schwa (|ə|) is usually easier to say than the short-vowel **e** (|ĕ|).

Additional information about the schwa sound is provided in Lessons 65, 66, and 67.

If your student likes challenge words, he will be delighted with this lesson.

---

[1] When -**es** is added to a verb (a word indicating action or a state of being), it denotes present tense (*"Mike **blesses** us with his music."*) When -**es** is added to a noun, it indicates that the word is plural. (*"Mrs. Dillard was sad when all of her **classes** were dismissed for the summer."*) Some words are nouns and verbs. For example, *"Cora **dresses** in her best clothes for church"* (here, **dresses** is a verb). *"Ainsley and Shelby like to wear their frilly **dresses**"* (here, **dresses** is a plural noun).

[2] The -**ed** ending changes a word from the present tense to the past tense. For example, *"Jeff will **mend** the fence"* denotes future tense, but *"Chris **mended** the fence"* denotes past tense.

Lesson 29
Two-Syllable Words

I.	inlet	setup	laptop	shellfish	spotless
	flashback	flatbed	upon	pillbox	sandbag
II.	freshman	kickoff	cabin	triplet	standup
	handbag	pigskin	matchless	subplot	within
III.	liftoff	fishnet	upset	tablet	offset
	itself	helpless	sunset	quicksand	uplift
IV.	nutshell	windmill	pumpkin	puppet	suntan
	inkblot	hubcap	grassland	landmass	inland
V.	napkin	wingspan	bandstand	offspring	robin
	address	lipstick	tomcat	chipmunk	potluck

Lesson 30
-es

I.	boxes	rushes	snatches	messes	dashes	benches
	box	*rush*	*snatch*	*mess*	*dash*	*bench*
	brushes	crunches	crutches	ashes	flinches	twitches
II.	classes	gushes	quenches	taxes	bunches	latches
	dresses	hushes	itches	smashes	flosses	etches
III.	glasses	trashes	notches	faxes	punches	sketches
	blesses	branches	inches	clutches	sixes	stretches

-ed

IV.	tested	dusted	wilted	rented	listed	belted
	test	*dust*	*wilt*	*rent*	*list*	*belt*
	acted	rusted	punted	quilted	rafted	lasted
V.	opted	stunted	printed	hinted	crested	minted
	planted	twisted	trusted	granted	lifted	shifted
VI.	added	banded	funded	handed	welded	sanded
	ended	landed	blended	bonded	mended	branded

Instructions for Lesson 31

Introduce the -ing spelling pattern.

I - IV   NEW PATTERN. This lesson introduces the spelling pattern for words that consist of a base word to which the suffix -**ing** has been added. The suffix -**ing** is a trigraph—three letters pronounced as one sound. It is pronounced |ĭng| or sometimes |ēng|. (The letter **i** sounds more like the long-vowel **e**, |ēng|, found in **boxing**.)

REVIEW the sound of **ng** (**boxing, packing**). If your student is having difficulty with these words, go back and review Lesson 20, Roman numeral VI.

Instructions for Lesson 32

Review the patterns that were introduced in Lessons 1 through 31.

Please be sure that your student is successful with all of the words in Lesson 32 before you leave this lesson. The next lesson is the start of a new unit.

Short-Vowel Patterns

If a syllable contains a short vowel, the syllable will end with one or more consonants (for example, **ăt, rĭb, tŏp, ŭs, ĕbb, răpt**). The consonant "closes" or seals the vowel into the syllable. Letters before a vowel seldom impact the sound that a vowel makes.

With the completion of this lesson, your student has become well versed with the pattern most commonly found in the English language, that being the short-vowel pattern.

After You Complete Lesson 32 . . .

Tell Your Student!

In Lesson 33 (the next lesson), your student will learn about a very different set of sounds for the five vowels.

Lesson 31
-ing

I.

boxing	crossing	hitching	fetching	resting
box • ing	*cross • ing*	*hitch • ing*	*fetch • ing*	*rest • ing*
packing	hunting	quacking	tossing	limping

II.

singing	docking	etching	stitching	buzzing
camping	trucking	fizzing	blocking	dashing

III.

ebbing	telling	brushing	flocking	lumping
tracking	crunching	glossing	stomping	inching

IV.

hinting	grasping	pumping	acting	ending
rocking	checking	itching	drinking	lacking

Lesson 32
Review: Lessons 1 – 31

I.

freshman	shocking	quenching	funds	dressing
drafted	dishcloth	nested	melted	quenches

II.

address	printed	candid	planted	lapdog
bunted	inset	himself	crafting	blessing

III.

helping	tested	bringing	chanted	sifted
trusted	crafted	pickax	blacktop	etching

IV.

quilted	kickoff	mocking	lasted	rested
landed	shellfish	chopsticks	cabin	flatbed

V.

acted	topnotch	quicken	backtrack	insects
glint	mixes	handspring	shrimp	yelling

Unit 2

Long-Vowel Words

Lessons 33 – 50

Sound Chart for Unit 2

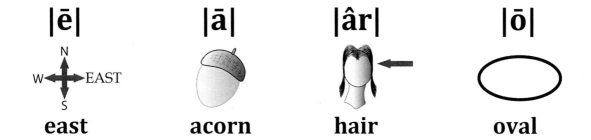

|ē| east

|ā| acorn

|âr| hair

|ō| oval

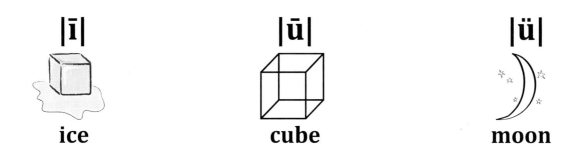

|ī| ice

|ū| cube

|ü| moon

Overview of Unit 2

Unit 2 presents several new reading concepts of major significance. Among the new concepts are long vowels, the function of "silent **e**," and the role of double vowels. The unit also teaches about homophones.

The eye and brain are quick, and once your student understands the patterns involved here, he will be able to move forward with his reading and spelling, and do so with ease. At first glance, the new ideas might seem daunting. Rest assured that the instructions for each lesson are designed to give clear, steady guidance to the instructor, who can then, in turn, provide direction for the student as needed.

Your student will now be learning a very different set of sounds for the five vowels. The sound of a long vowel is identical to the name of the vowel. The letters **a**, **e**, **i**, **o**, and **u**, when they function as *long vowels*, will say their own name! The **a** will say |ā|, as in **lake** or **pale**; **i** will say |ī|, as in **mile** or **quite**; **o** will say |ō|, as in **code** or **note**; **u** will say |ū|, as in **use** or **cute**; and **e** will say |ē|, as in **mete** or **Pete**. Lesson 33 introduces "silent **e**." The presence of the letter **e** at the end of a word ALMOST ALWAYS causes the vowel appearing earlier in the word to sound like its name.

The long sound of a vowel is indicated in dictionaries with a diacritical mark known as the *macron*—a little horizontal bar positioned directly over the vowel. Information about the macron is found in Lesson 67.

A Tip for Teaching Long Vowels

Relax and take your time with Lesson 33. This is challenging material for some people. By now your student is familiar with short-vowel words, such as **cap**. But, what if an **e** is found at the end of **cap**, and it is **cape**? This is a new word altogether. How is **cape** pronounced? The presence of the letter **e** at the end of a short-vowel word changes the first vowel from having a short-vowel sound to having a long-vowel sound. Furthermore, the **e** at the end of the word is not pronounced—it is silent.

It is important that your student understand this pattern. From now on, we will refer to this pattern as the "long-vowel, silent **e** pattern." A suggested dialog for teaching this concept is provided below. Marking vocabulary words with a pencil may help illustrate what the silent **e** does to a word.

TEACHER: *"We are going to learn a new pattern. Many words follow this pattern. You will be able to read hundreds of new words after you learn this pattern.* (Point to the word **cap** in Roman numeral I) *Let's have you read this word."*

STUDENT: *"Cap."*

TEACHER: *"That's right.* **Cap** *has the short-vowel* **a** *sound, /ă/. Now, what happens if I add the letter* **e** *to the end of the word?* (Point to the **e** in **cape**) *The letter* **e** *at the end of a word changes how we read it and makes it a brand new word. When you see a word that ends in* **e**, *you need to pronounce the vowel that is inside the word with its long-vowel sound. The vowels, as you know, are . . ."*

STUDENT: *"a, e, i, o, u."*

TEACHER: *"That's correct. Now, we know that the short vowels are pronounced /ă/, /ĕ/, /ĭ/, /ŏ/, and /ŭ/. But, today we're going to learn the long-vowel sounds for* **a, e, i, o,** *and* **u**. *A long vowel is very easy to remember—it says its own name. So, for example, the long vowel* **a** *says /ā/. See? It says its own name! The long-vowel sound for* **e** *is /ē/. The long vowel sound for* **i** *is /ī/. Do you see the pattern? What do you think the long-vowel sound for* **o** *says?* **O** *says . . ."*

STUDENT: *"/ō/"*

TEACHER: *"That's right! And the long vowel* **u** *says . . ."*

STUDENT: *"/ū/"*

TEACHER: *"Very good! Let's look at the word* **cape** *once more. Does this word end in* **e**?

STUDENT: *"Yes."*

TEACHER: *"That means that the* **a** *in* **cape** *will have a long-vowel sound. The long-vowel sound of* **a** *is /ā/. "But we're not finished yet. We need to remember that the* **e** *at the end of a word is silent. That means that we do not pronounce it. It's almost as if we pretend the* **e** *isn't there. To help us remember how to read a word that ends in* **e**, *I am going to use my pencil to mark the word. I'm going to draw a slash through the* **e** *to remind myself that the* **e** *is silent, and I'm going to draw a bar over the* **a** *to remind myself that the* **a** *says its long sound,* **cāpe̸**. *Now, let's have you practice on the next word."*

If your student struggles with reading these words, just keep practicing. You can have him spell and mark some words from Roman numeral I with a slash through the silent **e** and a bar (technically known as a *macron*) over the interior vowel. Do not, however, let him become reliant on physically marking the words. We want him to handle this mental process quickly.

One Note About Spelling: The silent **e** is not pronounced at the end of a word but must be included for accurate spelling.

Instructions for Lesson 33

Review the short-vowel spelling patterns taught in Lessons 1 through 32.

This lesson launches a new concept: the LONG VOWEL PATTERN.
The long vowel is triggered by the presence of the letter e at the end of a word.
Examples of "silent e" long-vowel words are lake, mete, bike, robe, and use.

BE SURE YOUR STUDENT KNOWS that the vowel sounds are going to be different in this lesson.

NEW CONCEPT. This lesson departs from the short-vowel pattern found in Lessons 1 through 32. Your student will discover that having an **e** at the end of what would otherwise be a short-vowel word changes the word to another word altogether. The new word has a *long-vowel* sound.

I - VI   **READ and SPELL** all of the words. The previous page provides some ideas for you to use if your student struggles with reading this lesson. It might be helpful, for example, to select a few words and have your student mark through the silent **e** and place a bar above the pronounced long vowel, as illustrated here: *cāpȩ*. Take your time and learn the word meanings.

There are many ways a teacher can explain the long-vowel pattern. Do keep the explanation as simple as possible.

Long- and Short-Vowel Sounds

Every one of the short-vowel words learned in Lesson 33 becomes a new word when an **e** is added at the end of the word. This final **e** is not pronounced. We say it is *silent*. By adding an **e** to **cap |kăp|**, for example, it becomes **cape |kāp|**.

Have your student practice until he can read and spell all of the words with ease. You can direct him to read words across the page, down each column, or skipping around the lists. Consider having the struggling student read and spell one short-vowel pattern at a time—Roman numeral I for |ă|; II for |ĭ| and then |ĕ|; III for |ŏ|; IV for |ŭ|; and V & VI for blends & digraphs. Be sure that he knows the meaning of every single word.

There are students who will breeze through Lesson 33, and there are other students who will struggle. If your student has trouble with the long-vowel pronunciation or spelling pattern, consider having him practice first on the short-vowel words. Then, have him read only the long-vowel words. Next, alternate between short- and long-vowel words. Reread and respell until your student masters everything in the lesson.

Lesson 33
Long Vowels and Silent e

TELL YOUR STUDENT!

Long-vowel sounds with silent e are introduced in this lesson. READ and SPELL all of these short- and long-vowel words.

Short-Vowel Words & Silent e Long-Vowel Words

a

I.
cap	cape	ban	bane	gap	gape	pan	pane
man	mane	fad	fade	pal	pale	rat	rate
tap	tape	van	vane	mat	mate	gal	gale
Sal	sale	Sam	same	can	cane	mad	made

i and **e**

II.
sit	site	hid	hide	fin	fine	dim	dime
rid	ride	kit	kite	pin	pine	bid	bide
bit	bite	rip	ripe	met	mete	pet	Pete

o

III.
not	note	cod	code	hop	hope	con	cone
dot	dote	rod	rode	mop	mope	rot	rote

u

IV.
us	use	cut	cute	cub	cube	tub	tube

consonant blends and **consonant digraphs**

V.
past	paste	slop	slope	slim	slime	slat	slate
spit	spite	spin	spine	twin	twine	plan	plane

VI.
glad	glade	glob	globe	grad	grade	grim	grime
quit	quite	shin	shine	bath	bathe	scrap	scrape

Challenge Words:	likeness	salesman
	[like • ness]	[sales • man]

Instructions for Lesson 34

> **Learn more about the "silent e" long-vowel spelling and pronunciation pattern.**

Long-Vowel Spelling Pattern with Silent e

I   **PRACTICE** more short- and long-vowel words. We learned in the previous lesson that the first vowel in a word is rendered long by the presence of a second vowel. The second vowel is treated as silent.

Observe the words **pile** and **mile**. They end in **e**, so the first vowel of each word will be treated as long, and the ending **e** will be treated as silent. Now observe the words **back** and **tack**. If a word ends in one, two, or three consonants, the enclosed vowel will be pronounced with the short sound.

Special Note: The word **bass** in list I is an unusual word in that it has two meanings and two pronunciations. A band student will likely read the word as |bās|, a musical instrument, but a student who fishes will likely say |băs|, a fish. Here, it is meant to be |băs|.

II - IV   **PRACTICE** more silent **e** long-vowel words.

V & VI   **REVIEW** silent **e** long-vowel words and short-vowel words.

> Here is the main pattern to remember: When there are two vowels in the same syllable, the first vowel is pronounced with the long-vowel sound, and the second vowel is silent.

Examples: In **game**, the **a** says |ā|, and the second vowel is silent.

In **bike**, the **i** says |ī|, and the second vowel is silent.

In **code**, the **o** says |ō|, and the second vowel is silent.

In **fuse**, the **u** says |ū|, and the second vowel is silent.

In **Pete**, the **e** says |ē|, and the second vowel is silent.

- Lesson 34 includes words exhibiting the two sounds of **s**: |s| and |z|. It also presents the spelling pattern **th**, which may be either voiced or voiceless, depending on the word in which it appears. These subjects were discussed in Lessons 17 and 27, respectively. Examples: **Skate** has the |s| sound but **fuse** has the |z| sound. The **th** in **those** is voiced (causing vibration), but the **th** in **theme** is voiceless (causing no vibration).

- The sound of a long vowel is slightly blunted when the vowel is followed by the letter **r**. These are sometimes referred to as *r-controlled words*. Notice this with the words **fire**, **here**, **cure**, **score**, and **fore**.

- Names of people start with a capital letter. Use your student's first and last names as examples.

Note: The word **live** will be pronounced with either |ī|, as in, *"Sabrina's show was broadcast **live** on TV"* or |ĭ|, as in *"LaMarcus and Lucy plan to **live** in Carlsbad."* Your student will be able to easily decide, based on the context of a sentence, which word is meant.

82

Lesson 34
Long Vowels with Silent e

I.	pill	pile	mull	mule	fill	file	till	tile
	mill	mile	bill	bile	fuss	fuse	bass	base
	back	bake	lick	like	sack	sake	pick	pike
	tack	take	stack	stake	smock	smoke	quack	quake

a i o u

II.	game	came	name	case	make	cave
	bike	nine	time	rise	dime	wife
	live	five	line	life	lone	vote
	code	bone	hole	pole	fuse	use

blends and **digraphs**

III.	taste	skate	blame	flake	cube	mute
	brave	grape	crate	brake	shape	chase
	quake	whale	tribe	bride	pride	while

IV.	drive	chime	froze	stone	spoke	chose
	smoke	quote	shone	these	Steve	store

r-controlled words

	fire	here	more	cure	score	fore

Review

V.	those	date	store	nose	pure
	theme	lane	bath	cod	twin
	fuse	spin	scale	fire	mule
	them	rope	fuss	waves	bit
	state	prize	glide	scrape	size

VI.	Pete	lick	shake	strive	glob
	white	trade	fin	mill	cure
	lime	wire	hose	gave	wave
	slack	lake	van	stack	grad
	met	rod	quite	tone	skate

Challenge Words:	sidelines	admire	makeup	campsite
	[side • lines]	[ad • mire]	[make • up]	[camp • site]

Instructions for Lesson 35

> Introduce another major new concept, that of *double vowels.*
> Double vowels are vowels that appear side by side (are contiguous).
> Examples are ee and eer. The ee and eer **spelling patterns have a
> long-vowel** e **sound, as in** free, bee, **and** deer.

I - IV   **NEW CONCEPT.** We will learn the **ee** spelling pattern, which has a long-vowel **e** sound |ē|, as in **free** and **bee**.

V   **LEARN** the slight change in pronunciation that occurs in words spelled with **ee** followed by the consonant **r**, as in **deer** and **cheer**. Some students easily detect the slight difference in pronunciation. If you are working with a student who hears the difference, commend him for having a good ear.

Instructions for Lesson 36

> Introduce the double vowel patterns of ea and ear.
> These double vowels say the long-vowel e, |ē|, as in teach, dream, and hear.
>
> Introduce the long-vowel sound of e, |ē|, when the letter e stands alone.
> An example of a stand-alone e is found in the words be and we.

I - IV   **NEW PATTERN.** Learn the **ea** spelling pattern that produces a long-vowel **e** sound, |ē|, as in **seat**. The pronunciation of this vowel pairing follows the very strong pattern that "THE FIRST VOWEL IS LONG, AND THE SECOND VOWEL IS SILENT." The words **leave** and **please** end in a silent **e.** Remind your student that the silent **e** must be included for proper spelling.

V   **LEARN** the slight change in pronunciation that occurs for the long-vowel **e** in syllables or words that are spelled **ea** and that end with the consonant letter **r**, as in **ear** and **hear**.

Roman numeral V includes the word **tear** |tēr|, meaning a drop of moisture from the eye. **Tear** |tēr| is pronounced differently from **tear** |tĕr|, meaning a rip (noun) or to rip (verb). These words remind us of the importance of reading for meaning. Consider this sentence: *"A **tear** fell when Cari saw that her newly designed dress had a **tear**."* Use this example to impress upon your student the importance of thinking about what words mean. We will learn more about the **ear** spelling and sound patterns in Lesson 77.

VI   **NEW PATTERN.** Learn the **e** spelling pattern with the stand-alone long-vowel **e** sound, |ē|, as in **be** and **we**.

In Lesson 61, we will again encounter the open and accented **the**, pronounced |thē|, and in Lesson 66, we will learn the unaccented **the**, pronounced |thə|.

Lesson 35
ee and eer = |ē|

I.	free	heel	Lee	see	feed
	bee	street	tee	week	heed
II.	feet	deep	teem	seen	keep
	green	peek	meek	leek	sweet
III.	teeth	need	speed	sweep	steel
	sheep	seeds	speech	seem	seek
IV.	three	eel	weed	screen	sheet
	sleep	steed	flee	tree	queen

eer = |ēr|

V.	deer	steer	seer	jeer	sheer
	cheer	veer	peer	cheers	steers

Lesson 36
ea, ear, and e = |ē|

I.	seat	zeal	team	heat	read
	beam	eat	weak	meal	leap
II.	neat	leak	reap	lean	sea
	east	each	tea	leaf	steam
III.	teach	yeast	cream	treat	preach
	stream	clean	reach	wheat	beast
IV.	dream	squeak	ease*	please*	leave*

ear = |ēr|

V.	ear	year	near	tear	gear
	hear	dear	smear	clear	spear

Open, Accented Syllable   e = |ē|

VI.	be	we	he	she	me	ye	the**

* **Ease, please,** and **leave** end with a silent **e**.   ** Lesson 66 will introduce "**the,**" pronounced |thə|.

Challenge Words:	**fifteen**	**weekend**	**sixteen**	**repeat**
	[*fif • teen*]	[*week • end*]	[*six • teen*]	[*re • peat*]

85

Instructions for Lesson 37

Review the short-vowel e spelling pattern pronounced |ĕ|,
as in **set** and **text**. We saw a great many of these short-vowel words in Unit 1.

This lesson also reviews the long-vowel spelling patterns **ea** and **ee** pronounced |ē|, **as in** neat **and** feed.

Words that are *homophones* are introduced in this lesson.
Students often enjoy learning homophones, as these words are fun and are a memorable aspect of our language.

If you are using the detailed completion chart, it is time for the next card. [See page 297]

e = |ĕ| e, ea, and ee = |ē|

I - III   REVIEW the SHORT vowel **e** spelling and pronunciation pattern |ĕ|, as in **set**.

REVIEW the LONG vowel **e** spelling pattern **ea** pronounced |ē|, as in **each**.

Homophones

IV   NEW CONCEPT. A significant number of English words are classified as homophones. *Homophones* are words that sound the same but have different meanings and spellings. [*Homo* means *same* and *phone* means *sound*; therefore, *same sound*.] **Meet** sounds like **meat** ("*Kurtus will **meet** us at the **meat** market*") but they are different, distinct words. The existence of homophones illustrates the importance of considering context to decide meaning and spelling. Keep a dictionary handy for definition support.

Occasionally, you can enhance your student's comprehension skills by using an object to illustrate a word. Roman numeral IV gives us the homophones **beet** and **beat**. You might use these in a sentence, as follows: "*A pickled **beet** is hard to **beat**,*" then offer your student a slice of one. Show-and-tell is often memorable.

Homophones might be viewed as difficult by a few students. However, most students find them easy and fun to learn.

Spelling continues to be important. When calling out these words for your student to spell, be sure that you give him a clear definition. This will allow him to be able to determine the word you intend for him to write on the paper. Take your time. Slow down if needed. Relax and enjoy the learning process.

Review: e ea

V   REVIEW the short-vowel **e** sound, as in **etch**, and the long-vowel **e** sound spelled **ea**, as in **each**.

Review: e ee

VI   REVIEW the short-vowel **e** sound, as in **help**, and the long-vowel **e** sound spelled **ee**, as in **weed**.

LOOKING AHEAD: Lesson 62 will introduce the |ē| sound spelled **y**, as in **lady** and **penny**. Lesson 74 will introduce the |ē| sound spelled **ie**, as in **field** and **babies**. Lesson 76 will introduce the |ē| sound spelled **ei** and **ey**, as in **seize**, **ceiling**, **key**, and **money**. We are learning one pattern at a time.

Lesson 37
e = |ĕ|
ea, ee, and e = |ē|

I. set   seat   sell   seal   bed   bead   led   lead

net   neat   best   beast   stem   steam   den   dean

II. pled   plead   whet   wheat   Ben   bean   etch   each

lest   least   speck   speak   dell   deal   men   mean

III. fed   feed   pep   peep   fell   feel   ten   teen

wed   weed   ref   reef   kept   keep   step   steep

HOMOPHONES are words that sound the same but have different meanings and spellings. Some of the words below are homophones. Can you spot them?

IV. met   meat   meet   peck   peek   peak

bet   beet   beat   pet   Pete   peat

Review of Short- and Long-Vowel e Words
e ea

V. bead   set   speak   bless   team   reach   near

hear   held   peach   heal   speck   least   glen

etch   leaf   treat   red   meal   crest   sheath

each   sleds   squeak   reap   ears   text   glean

e ee

VI. help   keep   elk   wheel   bets   Greek   theft

weed   dress   meek   be   stress   sweet   yes

whet   steep   sell   seek   pled   queen   stem

sheep   spell   sleek   eggs   speed   belt   meet

Instructions for Lesson 38

> Review the e, ee, and ea **spelling patterns that say** |ĕ| **and** |ē|,
> **as in** best, seem, seam, me, three, steam, deer, **and** dear.

Review: ee = |ē| ea = |ē|

I   **REVIEW** the **ee** and **ea** spelling patterns for homophones (words that sound the same but have different meanings and spellings), as in **seem** and **seam**. Consult the dictionary for definitions. The words in Roman numeral I remind us of the importance of developing the habit of reading for meaning. Comprehending the meaning of homophones usually is not difficult if the reader thinks about how the word is used in the sentence.

Review: ee = |ē| ea = |ē|

II - VI   **REVIEW** the **ee** and **ea** spelling patterns for |ē|, as in **three** and **east**.

        REVIEW the slight sound change that occurs in **e** words that end with an **r**, as in **steer** and **near**.

Instructions for Lesson 39

> **Introduce the long-vowel** a, **which says** |ā|, **as in** aim.
> **Also introduce** y **acting as a silent vowel in the** ay **spelling, as in** pray **and** day.

Although the lists appear more complex, we still are adding only one pattern at a time.

ai = |ā|

I & II   **NEW PATTERN.** The **ai** spelling pattern says |ā|, as in **rain**. Usually the **ai** is followed by at least one consonant, as in **aim** and **faith**. **Maine** has a silent **e**.

ay = |ā| y as a **vowel**

III   **NEW CONCEPT.** There is an **ay** spelling pattern with **y** serving as a vowel and having a long-vowel **a** sound |ā|, as in **day**. Most **ay** words have **ay** at the end of a word or syllable, as in **play** and **daytime** |dāy • tīmȩ|. When a syllable or word begins with the letter **y**, as in **yes** and **beyond** |bē • yǒnd|, the letter **y** is functioning as a consonant, not a vowel. (References: Lessons E and 1)

ank = |ā| ang = |ā|

IV   **LEARN** the **ank** and **ang** patterns. These are pronounced with the long-vowel **a** sound, |ā|, as in **bank** and **sang**. These words involve the so-called *second sound* for the consonants **n** and **g** (nk and ng). (Reference: Lesson 20)

air = |âr| are = |âr|

V   **LEARN** spelling patterns **air** and **are**, which have the long-vowel sound of |âr| with the slight **r** change (**hair** and **share**). The sound is usually represented in the dictionary with the symbol |âr|.

Lesson 38
Review: ee ea e

I.	seem	seam	meet	meat	steel	steal
	week	weak	peel	peal	peek	peak
	deer	dear	flee	flea	see	sea
II.	zeal	leap	feet	sheep	neat
	preach	shell	beach	she	fear
III.	three	be	wheel	reach	beam
	best	deal	heap	sweep	rent
IV.	steer	seek	weep	sweet	weed
	east	hear	teach	melts	yeast
V.	spell	reap	seed	need	seen
	near	week	free	squeak	ear
VI.	me	clear	tea	speech	leaf
	steam	keep	shred	speak	stream

Lesson 39
|ā| |âr|

I.	aim	wait	sail	pail	aid
	gain	main	hail	tail	mail
II.	rain	nail	vain	jail	gait
	faith	plain	braid	brain	claim
	Maine	chain	sprain	quail	drain
III.	day	say	bay	pay	hay
	way	gray	pray	stray	spray
	play	stay	tray	clay	May
IV.	bank	sank	yank	blank	thank
	sang	rang	gang	hang	pang
V.	hair	air	fair	pair	chair
	share	dare	rare	care	pare

* The **air** and **are** spellings have a slight sound change in long-vowel **a** words, |âr|, as in **hair** and **care**.

Challenge Words:	daytime	beyond	fairway
	[day • time]	[be • yond]	[fair • way]
nineteen	Sunday	railway	weekday
[nine • teen]	[Sun • day]	[rail • way]	[week • day]

Instructions for Lesson 40

Review the short- and long-vowel sounds of a.

Review nk and ng, as in bank and sang.

Review: |ă| |ā| |âr|

I – IV   REVIEW words spelled with the short- and long-vowel sounds of **a**.

We will learn additional patterns for the |ā| and |ă| sounds in future lessons, as follows: **a**, as in **basin** (Lesson 61); **ei** and **ey**, as in **veil** and **they** (Lesson 76); **ea**, as in **great** (Lesson 77); **eigh**, as in **eight** (Lesson 81); and **au**, as in **laugh** (Lesson 85). Relax and remember that these sounds and spellings will be learned and mastered one pattern at a time.

Instructions for Lesson 41

Introduce the long-vowel o sound |ō| found in the spelling patterns
oa, ou, oe, silent e, ore, oar, oor, and our,
as in coat, soul, toe, hope, more, oar, door, and four.

Does your student understand the words being taught? Some of these words are homophones, which tend to be intriguing to new readers. Examples of homophones are **sore** and **soar**.

oa = |ō|

I - III   LEARN the **oa** spelling pattern for the long-vowel **o** sound |ō|, as in **boat**.

ou and oe = |ō|

IV   LEARN the **ou** and **oe** spelling patterns for the long-vowel **o** sound |ō|, as in **soul** and **toe**.

silent e = |ō|

V   REVIEW the silent **e** spelling pattern for the long-vowel **o** sound |ō|, as in **hope**.

ore, oar, oor and our = |ōr|

VI   LEARN words like **more**, **oar**, **door**, and **four**. These words have the long-vowel **o** sound, but this sound is modified a bit by the presence of the letter **r**. These words are sometimes referred to as *r-controlled words*. Some students might pronounce the word **your** with more of a murmur diphthong sound |ər|.
We will learn more about the murmur diphthong and words spelled **our** in Lessons 69 and 86, respectively. Be sure that your student includes the silent **e** when he spells the last word in Roman numeral VI, **course**.

Lesson 40
Review: |ă| |ā| |â|

I.	play	snail	thank	gray	ranch	pale
	fact	claim	faith	clamp	quail	grade
II.	bank	game	rare	spray	flash	bran
	sang	fair	clam	spank	vain	quake
III.	care	stray	trade	quack	jail	sprain
	patch	gash	clash	stair	tame	baste
IV.	chain	rank	pray	train	tray	mail
	brass	shade	blank	day	paint	lake
V.	tale	sank	slap	shaft	square	name
	lands	dare	plane	catch	plan	wait
VI.	hair	splash	air	prank	chair	flame
	share	drain	vast	brain	brand	chase

Lesson 41
|ō|

I.	boat	toad	soap	foal	coal	hoax
	coat	oak	coast	road	soak	goad
II.	goat	loam	loan	oats	Joan	moat
	load	moan	goal	foam	float	groan
III.	loaf	oath	coach	throat	roast	cloak
	boast	toast	coax	broach	croak	poach
IV.	soul	toe	woe	doe	foe	roe
V.	hope	pole	rose	bone	woke	zone
	pose	joke	scope	stone	slope	quote
VI.	more	sore	lore	tore	bore	store
	oar	soar	board	hoard	door	floor
	four	your	pour	court	mourn	course

Instructions for Lessons 42

Review the short- and long-vowel sounds of o. **Spelling patterns include**
o, oa, oor, ou, **and silent** e, **as in** cost, coast, door, soul, **and** toe.

Review: |ŏ| |ō|

o = |ŏ| oa = |ō|

I   **REVIEW** words containing the short-vowel **o** (**cost, off**) and the long-vowel **oa** that says |ō| (**coast, oaf**).

Review: |ŏ| |ō|

II - V   **REVIEW** |ŏ| words like **off** and **stop**, and |ō| words like **road, soul, go,** and **toe**. We also look again at |ōr| words like **door, four,** and **horse**. Pay particular attention to **horse**, the last word in Roman numeral V. This word ends in a silent **e**.

The challenge words for this lesson include homophones. As mentioned in Lesson 37, homophones are words that sound the same but have different meanings and spellings. [*Homo* means *same* and *phone* means *sound*; therefore, *same sound*.] **Road** sounds like **rode**, yet these words have different meanings.

Take a moment to remind your student that words often are understood in context. Consider the context of the following sentences (the homophones are in bold print): "*The Queen of Hearts began her* **reign** *during a* **rain** *storm. When lightning struck, the royal guards had to* **rein** *in their skittish horses.*"

For practice, task your student with identifying the homophones in the following sentence: "*Annelise and Maely* **rode** *on their grandpa's horse down the bumpy* **road**." Talk about the meanings of these homophones.

Always read and spell the challenge words, including any homophones, that are listed at the end of the lessons.

Not in this lesson, but in a future one (number 77), we will talk about *homonyms*, which are different from homophones. [*Homo* means *same* and *nym* means *name*; therefore, *same name*.] The word **bat** is a homonym. There is a **bat** that is a piece of baseball equipment, for example, and there is a **bat** that is a flying mammal.

Another category of words is *homographs*. Homographs are words that are written the same. [*Homo* means *same* and *graph* means *writing*; therefore, *same writing*]. **Wind** and **wind** are examples of homographs. They are written exactly the same but have different meanings (one is a verb and one is a noun). Here the words will also be pronounced with different sounds, though they are written the same. "*Juan liked to listen to the* **wind** *at night as it would whistle and* **wind** *around the chimney.*" More homograph information can be found on pages 184, 185, and 209.

Lesson 42

Review: |ŏ| |ō|

I.

cost	coast	cot	coat	blot	bloat
crock	croak	got	goat	God	goad
off	oaf	rod	road	sock	soak
sop	soap	Todd	toad	clock	cloak

II.

stop	hope	boast	long	store
road	cost	flock	robe	mope
rode	gloat	strong	moan	vote

III.

off	cloak	toad	bones	sock
door	woke	smock	note	joke
stock	oak	coax	block	oats

IV.

soul	bloat	code	coach	zone
go	cone	cot	globe	poach
coast	mock	floor	soak	tone

V.

four	loan	rod	coat	groan
toe	soap	your	slope	lock
quote	clock	cope	doe	horse

Challenge Words:	**railroad**	**airport**	**tadpole**	
	[rail • road]	[air • port]	[tad • pole]	
Homophones:	road rode		morn mourn	
		ore oar or		

Instructions for Lesson 43

> Reviews the long-vowel |ō| that appears in the spelling patterns
> oa, **silent** e, oe, oo, **and** ou, **as in** coat, quote, toe, floor, **and** soul.
>
> **This lesson introduces the long-vowel |ō| that appears in**
> snow, hold, most, both, go, floor, **and** born.

*You might think, when looking at these lists, that they are more complex than previous ones. We are simplifying the learning process by introducing and mastering one pattern at a time. Keep in mind that all of these words are pronounced with one vowel sound (|ō|). Your student already knows all of the consonant letters, blends, and digraphs on this page. Roman numeral II adds one consonant, **w**, which acts as a vowel in these words. Your student will not find these words as difficult as you might think.*

|ō| |ōr|
oa oe ou silent e

I **REVIEW** the **oa**, silent **e**, **oe**, and **ou** spelling patterns for the long-vowel **o** sound |ō|, as in **soap**, **quote**, **toe**, and **soul** and the **our** in **four**.

ow

II **NEW PATTERN.** Learn the **ow** spelling pattern for the long-vowel **o**, as in **snow**. In these words, the **w** changes from acting as a consonant to acting as the second vowel in the word. Thus, the pattern holds that the second vowel is silent, and the first vowel says its name.

ol ost oth

III **NEW PATTERN.** Learn the **ol**, **ost**, and **oth** spelling patterns for the long-vowel **o** sound, |ō|, as in **hold**, **most**, and **both**.

o = |ō| oor and or = |ōr|

IV **LEARN** the **o** spelling pattern for the long-vowel **o** sound, |ō|, as in **go**.

LEARN the **oor** and **or** spelling patterns for the |ōr| sound, as in **floor** and **born**. Tell your student that the sound of long-vowel **o** changes a bit when **o** is followed by an **r**. Again, these are called *r-controlled words*.

Review: |ō| |ŏ|

V & VI **REVIEW** spelling patterns for both the long-vowel **o** and the short-vowel **o**.

The sounds of **ou** and **ow** have been or will be introduced as follows:

Lesson 41	ou our = |ō| and |ōr|	soul, four
Lesson 43	ow = |ō|	snow, bowl
Lesson 67	ou = |ŭ| or |ə|	touch, famous
Lesson 68	ou ow = the diphthong |ow|	out, owl
Lesson 69	our = |ər|	journey
Lesson 70	ou = |ü| and |ů|	soup and could
Lesson 85	ou = |ŭ| and |ŏ|	rough and cough
Lesson 86	Review of the ou sounds	

Lesson 43
|ō| |ōr|

|ō| and |ōr|

I.

soap	goal	float	coal	oath
soak	bloat	groan	coach	whoa
quote	pole	role	pose	note
toe	woe	soul	four	pour

ow

II.

snow	bow	row	tow	own
bowl	grow	flow	show	growth

ol ost oth

III.

hold	old	told	bolt	gold
cold	most	host	post	both

o and **r-controlled**

IV.

go	no	so	floor	poor
born	for	form	or	torn
worn	sort	corn	fort	storm
north	horn	shorn	sport	stork

Review: |ō| |ŏ|

V.

your	port	slow	hope	rod	toast	post
road	floor	born	bold	blown	hoard	loan
soak	woke	jolt	low	torn	toll	moth
toes	fourth	oath	drop	code	soul	rode

VI.

for	go	pour	shown	row	stop	fold
jog	four	rob	groan	hoe	no	coach
door	coat	woe	hold	float	short	scroll
so	form	crop	growth	tow	globe	cost

Challenge Words:	sleepless	concrete	coastline
	[sleep • less]	[con • crete]	[coast • line]
roadside	snowboard	fourteen	boatload
[road • side]	[snow • board]	[four • teen]	[boat • load]

95

Instructions for Lesson 44

> **Review the spelling and pronunciation patterns presented in the first 43 lessons.**

This is a good time to practice everything taught so far. Spend as much time as you need doing this review. Strive for total mastery of all of the sounds, spelling patterns, and word meanings.

Instructions for Lesson 45

> **Introduce the** y, ie, ind, silent e, ye, ire, yre, **and** ild **spelling patterns for the long-vowel i sound** |ī|, **as in** sky, pie, kind, time, style, bye, fire, lyre, **and** mild.

y = |ī|

I   **NEW PATTERN.** Here we learn the **y** spelling pattern that says |ī|, as in **sky** and **fly**. When **y** makes the long-vowel i sound, |ī|, it usually is an accented syllable.

ie   ind

II   **NEW PATTERN.** Learn the **ie** spelling pattern with the long-vowel sound |ī|, as in **pie** and **tie**. We change a **y** to an **i** whenever we add the suffixes -**es** or -**ed** to a word. This is illustrated with **fly** (→flies) and **try** (→tried).

NEW PATTERN. Learn the **ind** spelling pattern that has the long-vowel i sound, as in **kind**. When the word **wind** is a verb, it has a long-vowel i; when it is a noun, it has a short-vowel i. Ponder the following sentence: *"The **wind** would **wind** around Brian's chimney at night."* The intended meaning and also therefore the correct pronunciation can be determined from the context. Here, the second **wind** is pronounced with the |ī| sound.

silent e

III   **REVIEW** the role that silent **e** plays in making *i* say its long-vowel sound as, for example, in **time**.

ire   yre   ye

IV   **NEW PATTERN.** Learn the **ire** and **yre** spelling patterns for the long-vowel i sound |īr|, as in **fire** and **lyre**. Again, the letter **r** causes a slight sound variation which some students may notice. Be sure to discuss the meaning of unfamiliar words like **lyre**. Consult the dictionary. This section also covers the pattern for **bye** and **lye**.

ild   y with silent e

V   **NEW PATTERN.** Learn the **ild** and silent **e** spelling patterns that say |ī|, as in **mild** and **style**. Two notes: Capitalize the proper name **Pyle**. When spelling the word **rhyme**, be sure to include the silent **h**.

There are other long-vowel **i** spelling patterns. These will be taught later in connection with the silent letters **g** and **gh**, as in **sign** and **light** (Lesson 81). Inside the challenge word box in Lesson 84, we'll look at irregular words like **aisle** (it has three silent letters!—**a**, **s**, and **e**). **Aisle**, **isle**, and **I'll** are homophones.

96

Lesson 44
Review: Lessons 1 – 43

I. coach	queen	year	poor	street
dream	no	three	hold	squeak
II. hoax	ranch	foe	need	kept
sweep	quake	rate	bleak	sheep
III. leaf	board	groan	road	yeast
boats	peach	floor	green	door
IV. tree	store	seek	bath	quit
broach	heat	foam	host	meal
V. slide	feel	speak	plead	jolt
pay	coal	scream	roast	plain
VI. tube	wheat	plane	whet	gash
teeth	quite	faith	mule	pray

Lesson 45
|ī| |īr|

y

I. sky	my	try	dry	cry	fry	spy
fly	why	ply	by	shy	sly	spry

ie and **ind**

II. pie	tie	die	lie	lies	flies	tried
kind	wind	find	mind	bind	grind	blind

silent e with **i**

III. time	side	kite	mile	file	pine	site
slide	chime	shine	bike	smile	ride	gripe

ire, **yre**, and **ye**

IV. fire	tire	hire	mire	sire	wire	spire
lyre	pyre	bye	lye	rye	dye	stye

ild and **y** with **silent e**

V. mild	wild	child	type	style	styles	rhyme*

* Notice that the word **rhyme** is spelled with a silent **h**. See other silent **h** words in Lesson 81.

Challenge Words:	**wildlife**	**timeline**	**typecast**	**fireman**
	[*wild • life*]	[*time • line*]	[*type • cast*]	[*fire • man*]

Instructions for Lesson 46

This lesson reviews long-vowel |ī| and short-vowel |ĭ|.

Review: |ī| |ĭ|

I - V   **REVIEW.** This lesson has six columns of words that contain either a long or short vowel. Allow plenty of time for spelling practice. Mark the completion chart accordingly. Learning to spell strongly reinforces your student's reading skills.

Instructions for Lesson 47

Review spelling and pronunciation patterns taught in Lessons 1 through 46.

I - VI   **REVIEW** spelling and pronunciation patterns for all of the vowels, blends, digraphs, and trigraphs learned to date.

If your student struggles over reading or spelling a particular word, it is a good idea to practice more with the patterns that are present in that word. Emphasize that reading is based on the ability to recognize patterns. But, at the same time, reading is more than just being able to recognize and pronounce pattern-based words—it's also about making sense of what the words mean! So, discuss the meanings of words and make comprehension a priority. Spelling is an important activity that helps us be better writers, empowering us to say what we mean and mean what we say.

Lesson 46
Review: |ī| |ĭ|

I.	type	pie	dye	mist	my	bid
	lyre	kind	mire	tie	chin	kite
II.	try	wild	shy	spine	lie	hill
	mill	sly	pry	grime	spill	zip
III.	style	tire	child	smile	wide	fire
	quite	fly	shine	dim	quit	cry
IV.	fries	click	bind	why	twin	chime
	bye	find	twig	grind	pick	vim
V.	blind	rye	trip	sky	by	him
	mild	still	slime	twine	dire	print

Lesson 47
Review: Lessons 1 – 46

I.	brunch	vote	type	bold	bond
	blown	drain	tries	itch	teeth
II.	dream	ranch	check	scratch	cold
	spray	pinch	life	yeast	pay
III.	brass	growth	post	bank	quench
	strive	match	grape	joke	gear
IV.	green	plum	shown	peach	flow
	toast	claim	ditch	cure	theme
V.	stretch	stray	year	branch	scroll
	quail	brake	east	trash	latch
VI.	acts	quote	nose	blow	switch
	roll	kicks	scrape	quick	late

Challenge Words:	reptile	grapevine	pathway	grinding
	[rep • tile]	[grape • vine]	[path • way]	[grind • ing]

Instructions for Lesson 48

Introduce the long-vowel u sound found in such words
as cute, cue, pure, few, **and** feud.

Also introduce the |ü| sound that is variously spelled
oo, o, ue, **silent** e, u, ui, **and** ew, **as in** moon, do, blue, rule, flu, fruit, **and** new.

Is the **u** in a particular word pronounced |ū| or |ü|? Usually the answer lies in which sound is more naturally produced.

|ū| |ūr|

I   **REVIEW** silent e spelling patterns for the long-vowel **u** sounds |ū| and |ūr|, as in **cute**, **cue**, and **pure**. The long-vowel sound of **u** is the same as the name of the vowel. Note the long-vowel **u** sound in **use**. Learners will often detect the definite sound change of the long vowel **u** when **r** follows **u** (**pure** and **cure**).

NEW PATTERN. Learn the **ew** and **eu** spelling patterns for the long-vowel **u** sound, |ū|, as in **few** and **feud**.

|ü|

II   **LEARN** the **oo** and **o** spelling pattern with the |ü| sound, as in **moon**, **do**, and **lose**. Notice the spelling of **loose**, **choose**, and **snooze**; these words end in a silent **e**.

ue   u

III   **LEARN** the **ue** and silent e spelling patterns for the |ü| sound, as in **blue** and **rule**.

silent e   ui

IV   **LEARN** the **u** and **ui** spelling patterns for the |ü| sound, as in **flu**, **truth**, and **fruit**.

ew

V   **LEARN** the **ew** spelling pattern for the |ü| sound, as in **new** and **flew**.

Instructions for Lesson 49

Review the spelling patterns for the long-vowel |ū| and |ü| sounds.

Review: |ū| |ü|

I - VI   **REVIEW** the |ū| sound with the silent **e**, **ew**, and **ue** spelling patterns, as seen in **cube**, **cue**, **few**, and **feud**, and the |ü| sound spelled **oo**, **ue**, **u**, silent **e**, and **ew**, as present in **moon**, **blue**, **flu**, **rule**, and **new**.

The **oe** spelling pattern of **shoe** will be introduced in Lesson 70. Words like **beauty**, **view**, **milieu**, and **lieutenant** will be covered in Lesson 89. We are learning one pattern at a time.

Lesson 48
|ū| and |ü|

|ū|

silent e, **ew**, and **eu**

I.

cute	fume	cube	mute	fuse	mule
cue	hue			pure	cure
few	pew			feud	

|ü|

oo and **o**

II.

moon	too	room	stoop	boom	soon	bloom
loose	choose	snooze		do	to	lose

ue and **silent e**

III.

blue	due	true	sue	clue	flue	glue
rule	tube	rude	dues	sued	flute	plume

u and **ui**

IV.

flu	truth		fruit	suit

ew

V.

new	dew	stew	chew	blew	brew	crew
flew	grew	drew	shrew	threw	shrewd	strewn

Lesson 49
Review: |ū| |ü|

I. cube	feud	rule	flu	moon	Sue
II. cue	cure	mute	threw	due	rue
III. few	crew	pew	fuse	root	sued
IV. fruit	flew	glue	clue	stew	plume
V. new	hue	dew	drew	fume	suit
VI. blue	shrew	true	June	Tuesday	New York

Challenge Words:	**moonlit**	**newsroom**	**latitude**	**fumigate**
	[moon • lit]	[news • room]	[lat • i • tude]	[fu • mi • gate]

Instructions for Lesson 50

More review! This lesson provides a retrospective of Lessons 1 through 49.

Measuring Student Improvement
and Dealing with Skeptics

By this lesson, many students will demonstrate gains in their reading ability in the classroom or work environment. Just requiring a student to read and spell from left to right will greatly help. Many students will recognize the progress in themselves. This advancement is not always apparent to others, however. Comments from people who are skeptical of your student's progress may discourage you and your pupil. Rest assured that discernible, measurable improvement, if not already apparent, is just a few lessons away.

Your student has not yet been shown the phonics patterns for such everyday words as **helped, printed, open, story, point, boy, count, turn, first, word, percent, example,** and **put**. Nor has he acquired the tools for pronouncing **sign, hour, answer, science, half, money, they, learn, usual, telephone, decision,** or **book**. While some perceptive students might figure out these words without having been introduced to their patterns, most will not. This is why it is important to finish ALL of the lessons in this book! Missing a few patterns can handicap a student. You are currently more than halfway through the program. Thus far, this curriculum has covered only the short- and long-vowel syllable patterns that appear in a great many English words. Stay with us—the best is yet to come!

Some students will still try to "guess" read. The bouncing back and forth between these tightly controlled lessons (with their strong insistence on patterns) and outside reading assignments (with no such controls and many patterns not yet learned) can derail your student's progress as a pattern reader. Here are some strategies for compensating:

1. Remind your student—every time you start your lesson work—to read from left to right and apply the patterns he has learned. Encourage him to concentrate on the letters in the words in order.

2. Try to make one of our lessons the first activity of the day or of the reading instruction period. Do our lessons before any other reading is done. If your student must encounter outside reading, consider having the teacher read the outside material to him. We don't want your student having to switch between words whose patterns he knows and words whose patterns he has not yet learned. We want to keep him in the part of the brain that involves pattern reading.

3. Always support your student, no matter what he is reading. When he encounters patterns he has not yet learned, either tell him what the pattern is or mention that he will be learning it soon.

4. Strive to have at least one lesson a day.

I - VI PRACTICE all of the words. Read, comprehend, and spell. Mark the chart.

Lesson 50

Review: Lessons 1 – 49

I. coach   storm   glue   bind   yeast

     fruit   dry   plain   flew   by

II. twine   fail   boot   stream   torn

     gray   boast   mild   boost   sky

III. chime   preach   shaft   why   gold

     rule   hue   lunch   food   floor

IV. shine   shrew   ply   squeak   snooze

     child   game   scold   true   find

V. room   volt   new   hoax   cube

     time   clue   shoot   chain   float

VI. news   grime   my   blue   cure

     coast   smile   roar   cost   style

Challenge Words:	**skyline**	**doorstop**	**wasteland**
	[*sky • line*]	[*door • stop*]	[*waste • land*]

Unit 3

More Vowel and Consonant Variations

Lessons 51 – 72

Sound Chart for Unit 3

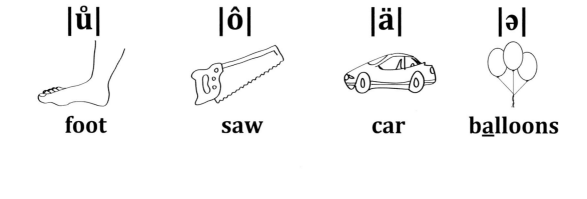

|ŭ| |ô| |ä| |ə|

foot   saw   car   b<u>a</u>lloons

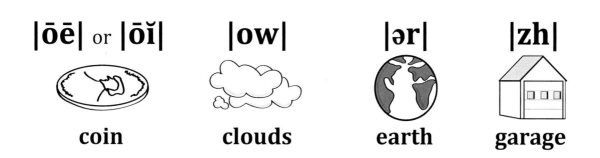

|ōē| or |ōĭ| |ow| |ər| |zh|

coin   clouds   earth   garage

Instructions for Lesson 51

Be positive and encouraging. It's worth the effort; your student is progressing nicely.

> **Introduce the oo spelling pattern that has four different sounds,
> as featured in** moon, book, flood, **and** door.

o and oo = |ü|

I – III   **NEW PATTERN.** Learn the **o** and **oo** spelling patterns that have the |ü| sound, as in **do, too, moon, loose, lose,** and **choose**.

wh = |h|

III   **NEW PATTERN.** Learn the second **wh** spelling pattern pronounced like the letter **h**, |h|, as in **who, whom,** and **whose**. Both the |hw| and |h| pronunciations for the **wh** spelling pattern are voiceless (produce no vocal cord vibration). The **wh** spelling is also pronounced |w| (with the voiced sound of **w**). The dictionary is your final authority on pronunciation and spelling.

Keep a dictionary handy for looking up words like **loose**, an adjective that has the **s** sound |lüs| (*"Chaim has a **loose** tooth"*). Compare this to **lose**, a transitive verb that has the **z** sound |lüz| (*"James was excited that his basketball team did not **lose** the game"*).

oo = |ů|

IV   **NEW PATTERN.** Learn the **oo** spelling pattern pronounced with the |ů| sound, as in **book** and **good**.

oo = |ŭ|

V   **NEW PATTERN.** Learn the **oo** spelling pattern pronounced with the short-vowel **u** sound |ŭ|, as in **blood**.

oor = |ōr|

REVIEW the **oor** spelling pattern pronounced with the long-vowel **o** sound, |ōr|, as in **door**. An **r, m,** or **n** following a vowel or vowels often works a slight sound change in the vowel. Some students are aware of this variation, while others will not detect it.

> Remember!
> Read. Know the meanings of the words. Spell.
> Mark the completion chart.

Lesson 51
o and oo
wh = |hw|

o and **oo** = |ü|

I.
do	to	too	zoo	moo	boo	goo
moon	pool	boom	tool	zoom	tooth	boost

oo = |ü|

II.
room	booth	proof	spoon	cool	scoop	troop
broom	droop	stoop	brood	snoop	loop	smooth

oo and **o** = |ü|

III.
loose	bloom	hoop	food	noon	boot	soon

wh = |h|

lose	choose	snooze	ooze	who	whom	whose

oo = |u̇|

IV.
book	look	foot	took	wood	cook	hoof
good	hood	soot	wool	hook	stood	brook

oo = |ŭ| **oor** = |ōr|

V.
blood	flood	door	boor	poor	floor	moor

Challenge Words: **broomstick** **cooking** **textbook**
[broom • stick] [cook • ing] [text • book]

Instructions for Lesson 52

> Review the oo spelling pattern that is in moon, book, flood, and door.
> The oo spelling has four different pronunciations.

Review: oo

I - IV   **REVIEW** four sounds for **oo**. Ask your student to read the words in the lesson. Ask him to define the words. Then have him spell them. Is your student reading and spelling all of the words without hesitation? Do you sense that he is confident? If you have even the slightest doubt, take time for more review and practice.

Each new lesson includes previously learned patterns. Spelling will help to cement the reading skill. Ask your student if he would like to reread or respell any of the words. Often, a brief time of reading through a list (up, down, across, skipping around) will boost confidence. Pay attention to the words that cause hesitation. If a specific pattern is troublesome, return to Lesson 51 and select the appropriate Roman numeral word list to practice on (for example, I – III for |ü|, IV for |ů|, and V for |ŭ| or |ōr|).

Mastery of each pattern prepares your student for success in the next lessons. When he has gained an easy familiarity with the pronunciation patterns, he can concentrate even more on comprehension. In some cases, as with homophones and compound words, your student will have to determine which pronunciation has the most fitting meaning.

Reading Mechanics

Use your judgment to decide how much of the mechanics of reading and spelling to explain. Some students benefit from supplemental information, while others only get confused or panicked by it. An adult working through Lesson 1 froze up when her instructor mentioned that the vowel **a** has more than one sound. At that point in time, this student was not ready for this revelation. A few weeks later, her instructor happened to mention that the |k| sound has six spellings. The student wanted to know all six spellings! (She had been trying to locate a mechanic in the phone book and was receptive to learning that **ch** sometimes makes a |k| sound.) If your student asks questions, do provide answers. The instructions for each lesson will help you with most questions that may arise.

One young mother was having trouble explaining to her son about when to double a consonant. She asked me for advice. I said, *"Tell him that you have to double the final consonant when adding -ed or -ing if you want to keep the vowel sound of the word short. For example, hop becomes hopped, not hoped."* She passed on this explanation to her son. He looked at her for a minute, looked at the list of words, and said, "OK, that makes sense."

This curriculum is designed to teach the basics of reading and spelling and word meaning. Grammar and punctuation and certain language mechanics are best handled after the student has learned the basic reading and spelling patterns. Some students will benefit from a discussion about nouns, verbs, sentence structure, order of words, punctuation, verb tense, etc. Others simply will be overwhelmed. Use your judgment. There are some excellent grammar books and online websites that can be used as resources.

110

Lesson 52

Review: oo

I.

book	brood	room	hoof
drool	good	stoop	spoon
cook	proof	hook	zoom

II.

too	wool	tooth	look
brook	root	wood	scoop
moon	bloom	hoop	roof

III.

foot	zoo	crook	noon
smooth	soot	boost	door
door	mood	loose	blood

IV.

flood	troop	stood	ooze
do	spoof	tools	booth
who	hood	floor	choose

Challenge Words:	**goodness**	**midline**	**grapefruit**
	[good • ness]	[mid • line]	[grape • fruit]

Instructions for Lesson 53

> **Practice two-syllable words.**

Compound Words

I - V   **PRACTICE** more two-syllable words. Remind your student to read and spell these words FROM LEFT TO RIGHT, blending the sounds, syllable to syllable. Each word in Lesson 53 can also be described as a *compound word*. A *compound word* is a word consisting of two words, each of which has a certain meaning apart from the word that results from the combination of the words. **Playback** is an example of a compound word (**play** + **back**). Many of the words on this page might seem like challenge words to your student.

For the first row of compound words in Lesson 53, we have indicated the syllable divisions. Draw attention to the helper words only if your student needs assistance reading the compound word.

Instructions for Lesson 54

> **Review multiple-syllable and compound words.**
> **This lesson also provides practice for the patterns learned in Lessons 1 – 53.**

Multiple-Syllable and Compound Words

I - IV   **PRACTICE** even more multiple-syllable and compound words. Have your student read and spell these words and discuss their meanings. If necessary, remind your student that all words are ordered (written, read, and spelled) FROM LEFT TO RIGHT. Some of the words in Lesson 54 have more than two syllables, and some are simple compound words. All of the patterns in this list have been introduced in previous lessons.

Lesson 53
Compound Words

I.	playback	fireside	dateline	flashback	coastline
	play • back	*fire • side*	*date • line*	*flash • back*	*coast • line*
II.	roadway	lineup	airway	hemline	freeway
	grassland	holdup	nameless	byline	makeup
III.	runway	wireless	homeless	shakeup	offspring
	stainless	beeline	ringside	checkup	pathway
IV.	inside	sleepless	cleanup	driveway	hillside
	streamline	pipeline	helpless	tasteless	seaside
V.	roadside	cordless	sideline	aimless	wayside
	tireless	stateside	skyline	playroom	useless

Lesson 54
Review of Lessons 1 – 53

I.	weekday	follow	wasteland	treatment	eliminate
	maybe	fourteen	basement	excludes	concrete
	leaflet	seaside	goodness	absentee	hairbrush
II.	candid	subject	skateboard	homeland	sixteen
	praying	Sunday	Tuesday	increase	molding
	yellow	complex	clipboard	weekend	mainland
III.	reading	imply	seventeen	doomsday	obscure
	offshore	basket	blackboard	doorway	window
	seating	mailbox	handcrafted	elbowroom	blockade
IV.	value	object	publishing	instruct	salesman
	product	begin	represented	seasickness	following
	noontime	obsess	distributing	lunchroom	thankless

Instructions for Lesson 55

Introduce the |ô| pronunciation used in al, aw, au, **and** qua,
as found in such words as ball, law, fault, **and** squall.

Also introduce the |ä| pronunciation used in al, wa, qua, **and** ar,
as found in the words calm, watts, quad, **and** star.

Introduce words pronounced |ä|, |ô|, **or** |ō| **as in** want, quash, ma, **and** war.

If you are using the detailed completion chart, it is time for the next card. [See page 299]

|ô| |ä|

LEARN the |ô| and |ä| sounds of **a**. These two sounds are quite similar and often pronounced the same. Note that they resemble the short sound for the letter **o** |ŏ|, as in **on** and **off**. Some readers will detect the nuances of these sounds.

|ô|

I   LEARN the |ô| sound spelled **al**, as in **ball** and **salt**.

LEARN the |ô| sound spelled **aw** and **wa**, as in **law** and **wall**. The **aw** spelling is usually found at the end (final) or middle (medial) position of a word, as in **law** and **dawn**.

LEARN the |ô| sound spelled **au** and **qua**, as in **fault** and **quart**. The **au** spelling is usually found at the beginning (initial) position or in the medial position of a word, as in **aught** and **haul**. The **qua** is usually in the initial position in a syllable. The words **warm** and **ward**, though not spelled with an **au**, also have the |ô| sound.

We have enough pattern knowledge as of this lesson to learn the word **fault**. **Fault** has two meanings: *"It's not Lyla's **fault** that her twin sisters are not easy to tell apart"* and *"The earthquake revealed a previously unrecognized **fault** under the parking lot."*

|ä|

II   LEARN the |ä| sound spelled **al**, **qua**, **wa**, and **ar**, as in **calm**, **quad**, and **star**. Note: When **ar** is the unaccented syllable, the sound is usually pronounced |ər|, as in **polar** and **molar**. This particular sound will be covered in Lesson 69.

|ä| |ô| |ō|

III   LEARN the sounds |ä|, |ô|, and |ō| and the spellings **wa**, **qua**, and **a**, as in **want**, **quash**, and **ma**. The dictionary indicates that either |ä| or |ô| can be used with these words.

LEARN the sounds |ô| or |ō| with words like **war** and **quart**.

Review: |ô| |ä| |ō|

IV & V   REVIEW the |ô| and |ä| sounds found in words like **ball**, **law**, **fault**, **quad**, **star**, **want**, **ma**, **war**, and **quart**

Your student does not yet know all of the patterns found in **aught**. While **au** is introduced in this lesson, the silent **gh** will not be introduced until Lesson 81.

Lesson 55
|ô| |ä| |ō|

al, **aw**, **au**, and **qua** = |ô|

I.

ball	all	call	gall	stall
salt	balk	palm	raw	saw
law	dawn	draw	straw	drawl
maul	haul	laud	fraud	launch
fault	taunt	vault	squawk	squall

al, **qua**, **wa**, and **ar** = |ä|

II.

calm	balm	watts	swamps	qualm
quad	squad	squat	squab	squalid
star	yard	ark	far	park
car	mark	sharp	bark	part
spark	dark	start	Mars	march

wa, **qua**, and **a** = |ä| and |ô|

III.

want	watch	wash	wasp	walrus
			ar = |ô| or |ō|	
quash	squash	ma	war	quart

Review: |ô| |ä|

IV.

farm	marsh	fallen	ball	charm	dawn
law	watts	wallet	art	squall	hard
war	pa	small	mark	stall	stars

V.

watch	cart	chart	hall	arm	swamp
arm	vault	quad	was	draw	March
wash	what	wasp	calm	almost	August

Challenge Words:	ballpark	baseball	football
	[ball • park]	[base • ball]	[foot • ball]
softball	hallmark	basketball	parchment
[soft • ball]	[hall • mark]	[bas • ket • ball]	[parch • ment]

Instructions for Lesson 56

Introduce the end spelling pattern -ed which, when added to a root verb, indicates past tense and is pronounced either |ed|, |d|, or |t|, as in jolted, cleaned, and cooked, respectively.

TELL YOUR STUDENT!

This lesson introduces the three sounds for the -ed ending.
The -ed spelling is pronounced |ĕd|, |d|, or |t|, as in **added**, **zoomed**, and **jumped**.
Hint: The easiest way of saying a word is probably the correct way of saying it.

|ĕd| or |əd|

I   **NEW CONCEPT.** Today we will introduce the -**ed** ending for verbs. This ending is used to indicate that some action or behavior has already happened, often referred to as the *past tense*. This ending is pronounced |ĕd| or |əd|, as in **jolted** and **added**, and adds an additional syllable to the root word. Verbs that end in a **t** or **d** take this -**ed** ending. The -**ed** ending can be pronounced with the short-vowel **e** sound |ĕd| or more often with an unaccented schwa, |əd|. (The schwa is pronounced similarly to the shortened short-vowel **u** sound of |ŭ| in **circus**.)

|d|

II   **LEARN** the -**ed** spelling pattern pronounced |d| that is added to words ending in **n**, **m**, or any voiced letter sound. The **e** in these -**ed** ending words is silent. Examples of this pattern are **cleaned** and **zoomed**. Notice that this simple |d| sound for the -**ed** ending applies to all root words ending in a voiced letter (one causing throat vibration when the letter is pronounced). Note also that this particular tacking on of -**ed** does not add a new syllable to the root word (e.g., **roared** and **jazzed**).

|t|

III   **LEARN** the -**ed** spelling pattern applicable to root words whose last letter is voiceless (causes no throat vibration when pronounced). In these cases, -**ed** says |t|. Consider the word **cook**. The **k** is voiceless (no vibration occurs in the vocal cords when the letter is pronounced). Adding -**ed** makes it **cooked**, pronounced |kŭkt|. To illustrate this point, try this experiment: touch your Adam's apple and say the word **jump**. Notice that no vibration occurs when you pronounce the **p**. All you produce is a puff of air. Such voiceless letters to which -**ed** is added (**cooked, puffed, jumped**) are going to have -**ed** say |t|.

Review: -ed

IV & V   **REVIEW** the -**ed** ending pronounced |əd|, |d|, or |t|, as in **jolted** and **added**, **cleaned** and **zoomed**, and **cooked** and **jumped**, respectively.

Some root words end with two consonants (such as **ck**, **ff**, **ss**, **ll**, **ch**, and **sh**) or with two consonant sounds (including the |ks| sound of **x** in **fix**). Normally, we double the final consonant of a short-vowel word when adding -**ed** or –**ing** (as will be discussed more in the following lesson). This doubling is not practiced if the root word already ends in double consonants or double sounds.

116

Lesson 56

-ed

|ed| |d| |t|

───────────────────────────────────

TELL YOUR STUDENT!

This lesson introduces the three sounds for the **-ed** ending.
The **-ed** will be pronounced |ĕd|, |d|, or |t|, as in **jolted, cleaned, cooked.**

───────────────────────────────────

|ĕd| (a separate syllable)

I.

jolted	salted	lifted	greeted	charted
dusted	roasted	feasted	printed	suited
added	loaded	aided	flooded	branded

|d| (not a separate syllable)

II.

cleaned	crawled	longed	stalled	beamed
roared	jazzed	warned	buzzed	willed
zoomed	yawned	cooled	rolled	spilled

|t| (not a separate syllable)

III.

cooked	squashed	gasped	kicked	finished
puffed	helped	boxed	reached	clicked
jumped	crunched	picked	passed	blessed

Review: -ed

IV.

leaked	treated	beached	lacked	fizzed	cooled
harmed	filled	painted	gulped	courted	junked
fixed	sparked	farmed	passed	added	killed

V.

limped	gloated	pleaded	waited	poured	reached
proofed	brushed	bluffed	strayed	egged	blessed
wanted	spoofed	stretched	heaped	golfed	picked

117

Instructions for Lesson 57

> Introduce the practice of doubling a final consonant when adding the
> -ed or -ing **ending to a short-vowel word.**
>
> **The -ed ending is pronounced with one of three sounds:** |ĕd|, |d|, or |t|,
> **as in** batted, drummed, **and** snapped.
>
> **We also look at adding -s to short-vowel words, as in** bats, jogs, **and** snaps.

Adding suffixes: -ed -ing -s

When adding an **-ed** or **-ing** ending to a short-vowel word, we must double the final consonant to preserve the short vowel sound. For **hop**, we add another **p** plus the **-ed** and get **hopped**. (Otherwise, we would get **hoped** |hōpt|, which is not the word we want). Similarly, for adding **-ing**, we double the final consonant and get **hopping**.

When -ed says |əd|

I & II   NEW CONCEPT. Introduce the process of adding the **-ed** ending and doubling the final consonant for short-vowel words like **bat**. In words ending with the |d| or |t| sound, the **-ed** is pronounced as its own syllable |əd| or |ĕd|: **batted**, pronounced |bă|-|təd|. We maintain the short-vowel sound in the root word by doubling the final consonant before adding **-ed**: **kid → kidded**.

INTRODUCE the process of doubling the final consonant in short-vowel root words before adding **-ing**, as in **batting**.

INTRODUCE the practice of adding **-s** to a short-vowel word or syllable (like **bat**). When adding **-s**, there is no need to double the final consonant (**bats** not **batts**).

When -ed says |d|

III & IV   INTRODUCE adding the **-ed** ending to short-vowel words like **drum**. To preserve the short-vowel sound, we must double the final voiced consonant **m**, and then add **-ed**. **Drummed** is pronounced as a single syllable |drŭmd|.

LEARN the **-ing** and **-s** endings. Double the final consonant when adding **-ing**, as in **drumming**. We do not double the final consonant, however, when all we are doing is adding **-s** (**drums** not **drumms**).

When -ed says |t|

V & VI   LEARN the **-ed** ending that is pronounced |t|. To preserve the short-vowel sound in a word like **snap**, we must double the final consonant. The addition of **-ed** in its |t| form does not add another syllable to the word—**snapped** is pronounced |snăpt|.

LEARN the **-ing** and **-s** endings. We must double the final consonant of a short-vowel word when adding **-ing**: **snap → snapping**. This doubling will preserve the word's short-vowel sound. When adding **-s**, it is not necessary to double the final consonant—**snap** becomes **snaps**, not **snapps**.

Lesson 57
Adding Suffixes to Short-Vowel Words: -ed -ing -s

|ed|

I.	bat	batted	batting	bats
	spot	spotted	spotting	spots
	pad	padded	padding	pads
	fit	fitted	fitting	fits
II.	kid	kidded	kidding	kids
	bud	budded	budding	buds
	chat	chatted	chatting	chats
	tat	tatted	tatting	tats

|d|

III.	drum	drummed	drumming	drums
	fib	fibbed	fibbing	fibs
	scan	scanned	scanning	scans
	tan	tanned	tanning	tans
IV.	jog	jogged	jogging	jogs
	rob	robbed	robbing	robs
	dim	dimmed	dimming	dims
	slug	slugged	slugging	slugs

|t|

V.	snap	snapped	snapping	snaps
	trip	tripped	tripping	trips
	zap	zapped	zapping	zaps
	step	stepped	stepping	steps
VI.	hop	hopped	hopping	hops
	clap	clapped	clapping	claps
	slip	slipped	slipping	slips
	flap	flapped	flapping	flaps

Instructions for Lesson 58

Review the pattern of doubling the final consonant before adding the -ed or -ing suffix to a short-vowel root word.

The -ed ending is pronounced with one of three sounds—|əd|, |d|, or |t|—depending on the consonant that directly precedes it.

When adding the letter -s at the end of a word, we do not double the ending consonant.

Adding -ed -ing -s

I - V   REVIEW short-vowel words that require doubling the final consonant before -**ed** or -**ing** is added so as to preserve the word's short-vowel sound (as in **clotted** and **patting**). Knowing which pronunciation to use will start to come naturally to your student, as he will develop a sense of which sound of -**ed** is appropriate.

REVIEW the process of adding -**s** to a short-vowel word (as in **bats**). In this case (adding **s**), we never double the final consonant.

Determining the Pronunciation of Words that End in -ed

You might mention to your student that the pronunciation of the -**ed** endings is determined in most cases by which pronunciation is easiest to say. It is easier to say **sobbed** with the |d| sound for -**ed** (|sŏb-d|) than it is to say |sŏb-əd|, |sŏb-ĕd|, or |sŏb-t|. This rule of thumb is true for all three soundings of the -**ed** ending.

|ĕd| |əd|

When a root word ends with a |d| or |t| sound and we add -**ed**, the word is pronounced with the |ĕd| or |əd| forming an extra syllable (e.g., **clotted, spotted, prodded**).

|d|

When the root word ends with a voiced consonant (vibration causing) and we add -**ed** to the word, the -**ed** suffix usually is pronounced with the voiced |d| sound (**fibbed, begged, dimmed**).

|t|

Sometimes -**ed** says |t|. This is the case when the root word ends with a voiceless consonant sound, such as made by **k, ck,** or **p.** Examples of words featuring the |t| sound of -**ed** are **backed, tripped,** and **helped.**

Is your student spelling well? Is his penmanship acceptable?

Encourage him to have high standards.

Lesson 58

Short-Vowel Words
Review: Adding -ed   -ing   -s

I. clotted   nagging   kidding   zipped

     struts   crams   mapped   trapping

II. fibbed   begged   jogged   fretting

     tags   snapped   kidded   scrapped

III. tripped   dripping   bragged   tugging

     sobbed   flipped   plugs   slugged

IV. drumming   zapped   skipped   topped

     spotted   dimmed   letting   quitting

V. rotted   snapping   prodded   nodded

     patting   gutted   robbed   chipped

Instructions for Lesson 59

> **Introduce the pattern for adding the suffixes -ed, -ing, or -es
> to a long-vowel word that ends in a silent e.**
>
> **Also introduce the three possible pronunciations for the suffix -ed
> when it is added to a root word that ends in silent e.**

Adding -ed, -ing, or -es to a Long-Vowel (Silent e) Root Word

NEW CONCEPT. When we have a long-vowel silent **e** root word and want to add **-ed**, **-ing**, or **-es** to it, we drop the silent **e** and then add the suffix. See this pattern with **grade → graded, grading,** and **grades.** Depending on the root word, the **ed** ending will be pronounced |əd|, |d|, or |t|. To add **-s** to a silent **e** long-vowel word, drop the **e** and add **es.**

When -ed says |əd|

I & II   NEW PATTERN. When a root word ends with the sound of **d** or **t** and we add **-ed**, the word will be pronounced with the |əd| schwa sound as an extra syllable (**graded, voted**). Now look at the word **vote,** which ends in silent **e** preceded by a **t.** To add **-ed,** we will drop the silent **e** and add **-ed.** This creates an additional syllable, and the word is now pronounced **voted** (|vō′ • təd|). The suffix **-ed** is pronounced either |əd| or |ĕd|. The upside-down **e**, |ə|, known as a *schwa,* is pronounced like a shortened short-vowel **u** sound, |ŭ|. (See Lessons 65, 66, and 67)

When -ed says |d|

III & IV   INTRODUCE the |d| sound that comes with adding **-ed** to a long-vowel (silent **e**) word that ends with a voiced sound. Consider the word **tune.** The silent **e** in **tune** is preceded by a voiced sound, **n.** True to pattern, we drop the silent **e** and add **-ed.** The word is pronounced |tünd|. The |d| sound does not add to the syllable count.

PRACTICE dropping the silent **e** in words and adding **-ed, -ing** or **-es**, as with **tune → tuned, tuning, tunes.** When the root word ends with a voiced consonant, the **-ed** usually is pronounced with the voiced |d| sound (**tuned, shined, ruled**).

When -ed says |t|

V & VI   PRACTICE dropping the silent **e** from root words that end with a voiceless sound and add **-ed.** This suffix is pronounced with a voiceless |t| sound, as in **joked** |jōkt|.

PRACTICE the spelling pattern for an **-ed, -ing,** or **-es** suffix being added to a root word that ends in a voiceless consonant. Examples are **joke → joked, joking,** and **jokes.** In these instances, the **-ed** is pronounced with the voiceless |t| sound.

Be sure to have your student spell all of the words in this lesson. As always, discuss the meanings of the words. Mark the completion chart accordingly.

Voiced or Voiceless Sounds

A Reminder: If pronouncing a letter causes your throat to vibrate, that sound is *voiced.* If no vibration occurs, the letter is considered *voiceless.*

Lesson 59

Long-Vowel (Silent e) Words

Drop the silent **e** and add   -**ed**   -**ing**   -**es**
(-**ed** will be pronounced in one of three ways: |ĕd| |d| |t|)

|ĕd|

I. grade	graded	grading	grades
taste	tasted	tasting	tastes
code	coded	coding	codes
skate	skated	skating	skates
II. vote	voted	voting	votes
wade	waded	wading	wades
trade	traded	trading	trades
glide	glided	gliding	glides

|d|

III. tune	tuned	tuning	tunes
rule	ruled	ruling	rules
pave	paved	paving	paves
bathe	bathed	bathing	bathes
IV. shine	shined	shining	shines
score	scored	scoring	scores
prime	primed	priming	primes
weave	weaved	weaving	weaves

|t|

V. joke	joked	joking	jokes
rope	roped	roping	ropes
wipe	wiped	wiping	wipes
choke	choked	choking	chokes
VI. shape	shaped	shaping	shapes
quake	quaked	quaking	quakes
chafe	chafed	chafing	chafes
hike	hiked	hiking	hikes

Instructions for Lesson 60

> Review the procedure for adding suffixes to words.
> We revisit the practice of dropping the silent e and adding -ed, -ing, or -es.
> We also review the pronunciation patterns |əd|, |d|, and |t|.

Review: Drop the Silent e and Add -ed -ing -es

I - III   **PRACTICE** the words in rows I, II, and III. To add a suffix to each of these long-vowel words, we first have to drop the silent **e** at the end of each word before adding the intended suffix (-**ed**, -**es**, or -**ing**).

If your student struggles with the words in this lesson, ask him what the root word is. (The root of the word **naming** is **name**, for example.) Tell your student to drop the silent **e** from the root and then add -**ing**.

Sometimes -**ed** says |əd|, but other times it says |**d**| or |**t**|.

Review: -ed -ing -es

IV - VI   **REVIEW** the suffixes spelled -**ed**, -**ing**, -**es**, and -**s**. These basic patterns were introduced in Lessons 56 – 59.

The Next Lesson Introduces a New Long-Vowel Pattern

Words with a long-vowel sound are sometimes identifiable because the syllable in which the vowel appears is *open*. When a syllable ends with a vowel, it is considered an *open syllable*. In Lesson 61 we will be reading and spelling words that include open syllables. Usually the open syllable is the accented syllable, but not always. This is the third and final introduction of a pattern for words having at least one long-vowel syllable.

Let's Review
Previously Introduced Long-Vowel Patterns

As we learned in previous lessons, when two vowels are in the same syllable, the first vowel is pronounced with a long-vowel sound, and the second vowel is silent. The letters **w** and **y** sometimes act like vowels. This is a good time to review this pattern.

All of the example words below have two vowels occurring in the same syllable:

A a says |ā| as in **game** and **sail**
I i says |ī| as in **bike** and **pie**
O o says |ō| as in **froze** and **boat**
U u says |ū| as in **mule** and **cue**
E e says |ē| as in **Pete** and **meal**

One More Time . . . Short-Vowel Patterns

Short-vowel syllables contain one vowel and end with at least one consonant. The closing consonant makes the syllable *closed*. Examples of words having *closed syllables* are **pat**, **egg**, and **helpless**.

Lesson 60

Review: Long-Vowel (Silent e) Words

I.	faded	fined	stated
	heaved	planes	diving
	jokes	timed	raised

II.	ruling	caring	squared
	shined	framing	choked
	mining	bailed	quakes

III.	zoning	smiled	waved
	braked	quoted	zones
	tied	named	snoring

Review: -ed -ing -s

IV.	waved	plugged	yawned	squared
	dimmed	flagged	scooted	lumped
	naming	sized	curing	charted

V.	raided	boxed	hoped	risked
	zones	filed	parked	tapes
	junked	roasted	liked	rushing

VI.	seated	dragged	charms	blocks
	tithed	whipping	buzzing	rolled
	smiling	filled	fluffed	paved

Instructions for Lesson 61

Introduce the long-vowel pattern applicable to open syllables.
A syllable that ends with a vowel is referred to as an *open syllable.*
Words in this category are halo, open, rebate, silent, cubit, judo, **and** myself.

Open Syllables

I & II   **NEW CONCEPT.** Introduce open syllables, which produce a long-vowel sound. When a syllable ends in a vowel (**a**, **e**, **i**, **o**, or **u**), the syllable is referred to as an *open syllable.* When an open syllable is accented, the vowel in that syllable is pronounced as a long vowel. Knowing this pattern helps us pronounce words that are rich in vowels (have two or more vowels). Notice where the accent occurs in the words **ba′ • sin, o′ • pen, re′ • bate, si′ • lent, mu′ • sic,** and **ty′ • po.** In each of these words, the first syllable is open (ends with a vowel) and is accented [′]; therefore, the first syllable is pronounced with a long-vowel sound. A syllable break occurs after each long vowel in these examples.

III   **LEARN** the pattern for words whose open syllables (again, meaning a syllable ending with a vowel) are pronounced with the long-vowel sound, as in **judo**.

IV   **LEARN** words that have an open long-vowel first syllable and an accented second syllable, as in **be • gin′**.

V & VI   **REVIEW** words whose first or second syllable is accented. Each of these words has at least one open, long-vowel syllable. Some words in Lesson 61 have more than one open syllable! Prime examples of this are **violin |vī′ • ō′ • lĭn|, solo |sō′ • lō′|,** and **halo |hā′ • lō′|.** Notice that if two vowels are contiguous (side by side) in a word but they fall in different syllables, often both vowels will have a long-vowel sound. We can see this illustrated with the **eo** in **video** (|vĭd • ē′ • ō′|), the **oa** in **oasis** (|o′ • ā′ • sĭs|), the **io** in **violin** (|vī′ • ō′ • lĭn|), and the **eo** in **rodeo** (|rō′ • dē′ • ō′|). If the last syllable in a word consists of only the letter **o** (**judo, rodeo, motto**), the **o** will usually be pronounced with the long-vowel sound. The definite article **the |thē′|** follows this long-vowel pattern and is practiced in the Roman numeral V list of words. (The indefinite article **the**, pronounced |thŭ| or |thə|, will be learned in Lesson 66.)

Lesson 61
Long Vowels

The words below have at least one open, accented, long-vowel syllable.

Accent is on the first syllable, which is pronounced with a long-vowel sound.

I. halo   rayon   faking   broken   poet   robot
[ha • lo]   [ra • yon]   [fa • king]   [bro • ken]   [po • et]   [ro • bot]

open   Ozark   frozen   bonus   rotate   moment

II. rebate   female   ego   silent   diet   Friday

duplex   cubit   fluent   ruin   fluid   typo

All open syllables are pronounced using the vowel's long sound.

III. judo   motto   Plato   solo   hero   zero

veto   hippo   disco   Pluto   jumbo   Velcro™

The first syllable is pronounced with a long-vowel sound. Accent is on the second syllable.

IV. begin   react   motel   Iran   eject   describe

myself   reside   before   Noel   create   beside

Review: Long Vowels in Open Syllables

V.

unit	video	I	a	detail
the	robot	go	diet	halo
quiet	located	Oreo™	eject	monument
museum	below	even	ozone	report
direct	moment	volcano	open	we

VI.

create	Ohio	reclaim	bonus	Utah
typo	between	stamen	equator	describe
myself	remain	cameo	nitrate	being
ninth	music	profile	report	resent
equal	rodeo	prepared	zero	microwave
violin	oasis	tirade	Friday	April

Challenge Words: **United States**   **iodine**   **prognosis**
[U • ni • ted States]   [i • o • dine]   [prog • no • sis]

Instructions for Lesson 62

> Introduce the |ī| sound of *y*, as found in try and reply.
> Also introduce the sound of |ē|, as found in lady and messy.

I & II   **LEARN** the accented **y** spelling and pronunciation pattern that is pronounced |ī|. When a syllable ending in **y** is accented, the **y** is pronounced with the long-vowel **i** sound, |ī|, as in **reply** |rē • plī ′| and **myself** |mī ′ • sĕlf|. Note: English words usually do not end with a dotted letter. The dotted letter **i** at the end of a word is often changed to **y**. The reverse is true for initial (beginning) or medial (middle) positions of the **i**; in these initial and medial cases, the **y** usually is changed to an **i**. A single-syllable word can be assumed to be an accented word if the pronunciation of **y** is |ī|, as in **try**.

III & IV   **LEARN** the unaccented **y** spelling and pronunciation pattern, as in **lady**. When a syllable ending in **y** is not the accented syllable, the **y** is pronounced with a sound close to the long-vowel **e** sound |ē|, as in **lady** |lā′ • dē| and **messy** |mĕs′ • ē|.

Review: y

V & VI   **REVIEW** the spelling and pronunciation patterns for **y**, both accented and unaccented. Accented **y** is pronounced like the long-vowel **i**, |ī′|, as in **try** (|trī|) and **reply** (|rē • plī′|). Unaccented **y** is pronounced like the long-vowel **e**, |ē|, as in **penny** (|pĕn′ • ē|) and **gravy** (|grā′ • vē|).

A Better Way of Reading

Some students have spent years memorizing and guessing at words. They may at times revert to the old ingrained guess habit. Our goal is to help them acquire a new, better way of reading—one based on recognizing patterns.

Be sure your student masters each lesson. Review any lesson or pattern that has not been solidly learned.

During summer vacation, two fifth-grade students read and spelled through to Lesson 81 of 90 lessons. The following summer, these two young men were willing to start again, this time at Lesson 18, and work all the way through to the 90th lesson (including the assignment found in "Now that the Lessons Are Complete, What's Next?"). The results for these boys were nothing short of remarkable.

In another instance, an adult had successfully read and spelled through to Lesson 15. At this point, she was still struggling to accurately read and spell the words, especially the vowel sounds in the words. She was comfortable reading and spelling most of the consonants. When I suggested that we return to and begin again with Lesson 1, she was actually relieved and quite agreeable. We spent time reviewing the lessons on vowels until she read every single word with confidence. For years, she had believed that she was incapable of learning to read and spell well. Her 50-year-old ingrained habit of educated guessing was difficult to break. Her determination and her willingness to work hard ended up bringing her much joy and success. Starting over is often a very good decision for some students.

128

Lesson 62

$$y' = |\bar{\imath}|$$
$$y \text{ (unaccented)} = |\bar{e}|$$

accented **y'**: |ī|

I.	try′	by′	my	cry	fly
	sky	pry	why	spry	thy
II.	type	flying	myself	supply	defy
	reply	occupy	retry	thyself	hybrid

unaccented **y**: |ē|

III.	la′•dy	luck′•y	grimy	flashy	cheery
	penny	gravy	glossy	Emmy	crafty
IV.	messy	story	hazy	handy	nosy
	shady	baby	puffy	misty	sixty

Review: $y' = |\bar{\imath}|$ $y = |\bar{e}|$

V.	copy	sky	party	myself	army
	tiny	easy	forty	silky	body
	shy	fifty	scary	frosty	seventy
	wavy	baby	glossy	bulky	cheery
	twenty	leafy	trying	ninety	occupy
VI.	very	thy	supply	slowly	penny
	study	flaky	bumpy	hybrid	lefty
	why	salty	defy	carry	every
	happy	reply	soapy	quickly	retry
	Kentucky	Wyoming	January	February	July

Instructions for Lesson 63

> **Introduce the** i **and** y **sounds for the suffixes** -y, -iest, -iness, -ly, -liest, **and** -liness, **as in** handy, handiest, **and** handiness, **and** manly, manliest, **and** manliness.
> **Some words drop the** e (flake → flaky), **and some keep the** e (lone → lonely).

I & II   NEW CONCEPT. Introduce the pattern of adding **y** to a root word. Also introduce the pattern of changing **y** to **i** when adding a suffix. Notice that the noun **hand** can be made into the adjective **handy**, but that an **i** is used to spell **handiest** and **handiness**. In any of these cases, the sound of **y** or **i** approximates the sound of long-vowel **e** (|ē|).

III   NEW CONCEPT. Introduce dropping **e** and adding **y** or **i** to a root word. If we are adding the suffixes **est** or **ness** to a root word that used to end in **e** but now ends in **y**, we must now change the **y** to an **i**. An example of this pattern is **taste**, which can be made into **tasty**, **tastiest**, and **tastiness**. The **i** is changed to a **y** to keep the word from ending in the dotted letter **i** (not **tasti** but **tasty**).

IV   NEW PATTERN. Introduce adding **ly** to a root word and pronouncing this suffix with nearly the long-vowel |ē| sound. Adding **ly** to the noun **man** makes it into the adjective **manly**. Adding the suffixes **est** or **ness** gives us other adjectives as well. A **y** in the interior of a word must be converted to an **i** (**manliest** and **manliness**). Note: One exception to this pattern is when the meaning of the word would change if we dropped the **y**. For example, when we add **ing** to **study**, we will keep the **y** (study → **studying**).

INTRODUCE keeping the **e** and adding **ly** or **li** to a root word. We change **y** to **i** and add the suffixes **iest** and **iness**, as in **lonely**, **loneliest**, and **loneliness**. Some words drop the **e**, as is the case with **taste** → **tasty**. Some words keep the **e**, as is the case with **lone** → **lonely**. Keep a dictionary handy to confirm which pattern applies.

Review: y i

V   REVIEW the **y**, **iest**, **iness**, **ly**, **liest**, and **liness** pronunciation and spelling patterns evident in **creamy**, **creamiest**, and **creaminess**, and **manly**, **manliest**, and **manliness**.

As mentioned several times before, words in English hardly ever end with a dotted letter. Hence, English words almost never end with an **i** or **j**. Exceptions are **taxi** (from the longer word **taxicab**), and **ski** and **spaghetti** (foreign words from Norway and Italy). (**Taj Mahal** might also come to mind, but **Taj** is not really an English word.) In most cases, the end spelling will be a **y**, as in **baby**.

130

Lesson 63
y → i (pronounced |ē|)

y → i (pronounced |ē|)

I.	hand	handy	handiest	handiness
	stuff	stuffy	stuffiest	stuffiness
	mess	messy	messiest	messiness
	fuss	fussy	fussiest	fussiness

y → i (pronounced |ē|)

II.	cream	creamy	creamiest	creaminess
	trust	trusty	trustiest	trustiness
	hard	hardy	hardiest	hardiness
	show	showy	showiest	showiness

y → i (pronounced |ē|)

III.	taste	tasty	tastiest	tastiness
	bone	bony	boniest	boniness
	craze	crazy	craziest	craziness
	shine	shiny	shiniest	shininess

ly → li (pronounced |lē|)

IV.	man	manly	manliest	manliness
	kind	kindly	kindliest	kindliness
	lone	lonely	loneliest	loneliness
	love	lovely	loveliest	loveliness

Review: y → i (pronounced |ē|)

V.	itchy	aptly	fussiness	stuffiest
	showy	saltiest	looniest	bony
	lovely	messiest	kindliness	dreamiest
	shine	goofiness	craziness	manliness

Instructions for Lesson 64

Be positive and encouraging. It's worth the effort; your student is making progress!

Introduce the patterns for prefixes.

NEW CONCEPTS. Introduce spelling and pronunciation patterns for a number of prefixes in conjunction with previously introduced patterns. *Prefixes* are an extra measure of information added to a word to alter or enhance its meaning. Every dictionary has definitions of the many individual prefixes. In some cases, a prefix might have more than one connotation, so we encourage you and your student to consult your dictionary.

I - IV   **LEARN** words that have a prefix that features a short vowel, such as **upstate**, **mistake, disclose, enlist, include, admire, convert, subject,** and **undo**. Roman numeral IV introduces two long-vowel prefixes.

II   In some parts of the country, the prefixes **en-** and **in-** are pronounced nearly identically. Classic pronunciation is to be encouraged, but you may need to allow for regional differences. Understanding the differing meanings of **en-** and **in-** will help a student remember a correct spelling. Some of the **en-** and **in-** words in Roman numeral II will be pronounced with the schwa sound.

We will encounter the |ŏn| sound for the **en** spelling, as in **envoy**, in Lesson 89, Roman numeral IV.

IV & V   **LEARN** long-vowel prefixes, as found in **prevent, redo,** and **before**. Note that the initial two words (**undo, unborn**) have a short-vowel prefix.

Review: Prefixes

VI   **REVIEW** spelling and pronunciation patterns for a number of prefixes.

The Usual Reminders

Once again, remind your student to read and spell FROM LEFT TO RIGHT, blending the sounds, syllable to syllable, all the way to the end of each word. Is there a spelling or pronunciation pattern about which your student appears confused? If so, explain the concept again and provide extra practice. Always talk about the meaning of words in the lesson lists. Record your student's successful reading and spelling on his completion chart. Don't forget that a word count table for each of the lessons is included in the back of the book (page 277).

Lesson 64
Prefixes

up- mis- dis-

I.

upstate	uproot	upbeat	update	uplift	upgrade
mistake	misread	mislead	disclose	dismay	distress

en- in-

II.

enlist	encase	enclose	enfold	entire	engulf
include	inform	inquire	indoors	inspire	indent

ad- con- sub-

III.

admire	advise	advent	convert	convent	convex
subject	sublet	subtract	sublease	subscribe	subscript

un- pre- re-

IV.

undo	unborn	prevent	prepaid	preside	predate
redo	rebate	remake	react	relate	resist

be-

V.

before	begin	beware	behold	behave	beside
below	beneath	became	belittle	beyond	belong

Review: Prefixes

VI.

display	enclose	prevent	undo	upload	advise
invent	resist	engrave	berate	unleash	distaste
adhere	uplifting	beneath	indeed	invite	sublease
remake	encode	prepay	became	convex	mistake

Challenge Words:	unleashing	admiring	translated
	[un • leash • ing]	[ad • mir • ing]	[trans • la • ted]

133

Instructions for Lesson 65

Introduces the le, el, al, il, ol, **and** ul **spelling patterns for the schwa pronunciation,** |əl|, **as in** simple, travel, dental, devil, carol, **and** mogul.

Schwa Endings: |əl|

I - IV   **LEARN** the schwa spelling patterns **le, el, al, il, ol,** and **ul** pronounced |ŭl| or |əl| and used in **simple, travel, dental, devil, carol,** and **mogul,** respectively. The schwa is pronounced like a shortened short-vowel **u**, |ŭ|, as in **locust**. Surprisingly, any vowel (**a, e, i, o, u**) can produce the schwa sound. Dictionaries use the upside-down **e** (ə) to represent the schwa sound.

I   **LEARN** the **le** spelling pattern for the schwa, as in **simple** |sĭm′ • pəl|.

II   **LEARN** the **el** spelling pattern for the schwa, as in **travel** |trăv′ • əl|.

III   **LEARN** the **al** spelling pattern for the schwa, as in **dental** |děn′ • təl|.

IV   **LEARN** the **il, ol,** and **ul** spelling patterns for the schwa, as in **devil** |dě′ • vəl|, **carol** |kār′ • əl|, and **mogul** |mō′ • gəl|, respectively.

Review: |əl|

V & VI   **REVIEW** the **le, el, al, il, ol,** and **ul** spelling patterns, which have a schwa sound. Continue to pay attention to the meaning of words. We have included similar words like **capital** and **capitol** in order to prompt discussion. Keep a dictionary handy.

Every Syllable Must Have at Least One Vowel

In theory, the words in this review section could be pronounced successfully if the vowel were missing from the second syllable, e.g., **dentl** (|děn • təl|). But, since every syllable in English is supposed to have at least one vowel, these schwa endings include either an **a, e, i, o,** or **u** (**dental, simple, travel, devil, carol,** and **mogul**). The vowel may be silent, but it must appear. One exception to this vowel rule, according to some dictionaries, is the ending -**ism** (as in **capitalism**), which is usually separated into two syllables (**is • m**). The **m** is counted as a stand-alone syllable, even though it is a lone letter and not even a vowel.

Lesson 65
Schwa: |əl|

le

I.
| simple | bubble | dazzle | cattle | eagle |
| staple | giggle | uncle | tackle | pickle |

el

II.
| travel | tunnel | flannel | gospel | bushel |
| camel | nickel | level | shrivel | channel |

al

III.
| dental | rental | sandal | signal | oral |
| normal | coral | floral | metal | jackal |

il

IV.
| devil | evil | weevil | pistil | tendril |

ol   **ul**

| carol | pistol | Mongol | mogul | consul |

Review: |əl|

V.
angle	dental	mogul	camel	settle	rental
petal	table	signal	total	marble	sample
apple	oral	cruel	fumble	staple	chapel
level	little	postal	pistol	rascal	animal

VI.
middle	travel	able	Bible	dazzle	triangle
medal	battle	mammal	sandal	normal	possible
barrel	metal	dribble	novel	jewel	capital
evil	single	oval	axle	eagle	capitol

Challenge Words:	hospital	rattlesnake
	[hos • pi • tal]	[rat • tle • snake]

Instructions for Lesson 66

> **Introduce the schwa spelling and pronunciation pattern for all of the vowels. The schwa sound is found, for example, in** ago, seven, devil, lemon, **and** locust.

The Schwa

Sometimes we speak too fast to pronounce syllables accurately, or we have a lazy tongue. Whatever the reason, we fail to clearly and distinctly pronounce some vowels. The arbiters of the English language have responded to this tendency by giving us a pronunciation symbol called the *schwa*. Most dictionaries use the upside-down **e**, |ə|, to symbolize a schwa. The schwa is really quite common and follows a very predictable pattern—it usually appears in multiple-syllable words, and it is never accented.

The schwa sound can be produced by or with any vowel, including y.

I   **NEW CONCEPT.** Introduce the schwa spelling and pronunciation pattern made by the letter **a**, as in **ago**.

II   **LEARN** the schwa spelling and pronunciation pattern made by the letter **e**, as in **seven**. The indefinite article **the** is pronounced with either the short-vowel **u** or schwa sound. (The definite article **the**, |thē′|, is pronounced with the long vowel **e** sound, as we learned in Lesson 36.)

III   **LEARN** the schwa spelling and pronunciation pattern of the letter **i**, as in **devil**.

IV   **LEARN** the schwa spelling and pronunciation pattern of **o** and **ou**, as in **lemon** and **famous**.

V   **LEARN** the schwa spelling and pronunciation pattern of the letter **u**, as in **locust** and **wishful**. Notice that the word **wishful** ends with one **l**. The stand-alone word **full** is spelled with two **l**'s, but when **full** is added as a suffix to a root word, one **l** is dropped. Dictionaries might show these words with |ŭ| or |ə|.

Review: |ə|

VI   **REVIEW** the schwa spelling and pronunciation patterns for all five vowels.

There are instances where the **y** and the vowel combinations **ou** and **ai** will be pronounced with the schwa sound. In future lessons you will encounter the |ə| sound in **Maryland, Pennsylvania, famous,** and **captain**. The pattern still applies: the schwas in these words are all in the unaccented syllable of the words.

Lesson 66
Schwa: |ə|

a (pronounced |ə|)

I.   ago   alike   banana   dental   final   mental
    ado   trial   warrant   aorta   capital   woman

e (pronounced |ə|)

II.   seven   open   bagel   travel   label   problem
    camel   garden   baskets   broken   lawless   the*

i (pronounced |ə|)

III.   devil   valid   bountiful   resident   weskit   president
    rapid   family   sediment   feasible   continent   indivisible

o and **ou** (pronounced |ə|)

IV.   lemon   convene   fathom   beckon   common   reason
    nothing   compass   cotton   consult   famous   retouch

u (pronounced |ə|)

V.   locust   handful   humus   Titus   crocus   compass
    wishful   careful   gainful   difficult   monument   instrument

Review: |ə|

VI. blemish	provide	bottom	the	seventh
human	area	vibrant	poem	antenna
seventy	students	ligament	cotton	was
atlas	level	avocado	seventeen	lion
reason	moment	amazement	monument	Canada
ornament	difficult	eleven	what	reliant
president	iguana	instruments	statement	Biblical
Boston	Alabama	Wisconsin	Arizona	Alaska
Florida	Minnesota	North Dakota	Delaware	Idaho
Iowa	Montana	Washington	Nevada	America

* This is the indefinite article, pronounced |thə|. See Lesson 36 for the definite article **the**, |thē′|.
Question: Did you check your dictionary for the definition of **weskit**?

Instructions for Lesson 67

> **Introduce the** o, oe, **and** ou **spelling patterns for the** |ŭ| **or** |ə| **sound,**
> **as in** of, one, once, money, does, touch, conspire, **and** complain.

o, oe, and ou = |ŭ| or |ə| (and sometimes |wŭ|)

I - III   **NEW PATTERN.** Introduce the o, oe, and **ou** spelling patterns for words pronounced with the short vowel **u** sound, |ŭ|, or the schwa sound, |ə|, as in **of** and **front**. For **one** or **once**, pronounce the **o** as |wŭ|. Words like **does**, **one**, and **once** do follow a pattern (namely, they make use of the schwa sound). Note that the **f** in **of** is pronounced |v|. [See Lessons 86 and 89]

Review Lessons 1 – 67

IV - VI   **REVIEW** the spelling and pronunciation patterns presented in Lessons 1 – 67.

Challenge Words

The three challenge words in this lesson are technical terms for symbols used in dictionaries to tell us how to pronounce words. These symbols are pronunciation helps only and are not part of the spelling of the word.

Breve   The *breve* (pronounced |brēv|) is a curved line symbol (akin to a smile) that is placed above a vowel to indicate that the vowel says its short sound. Short-vowel sounds are indicated with the breve in dictionaries, as follows: ă, ĕ, ĭ, ŏ, and ŭ. Thus, we know the pronunciations of **săt**, **rĕd**, **bĭd**, **ŏdd**, and **sŭn**.

Macron   The *macron* is a small horizontal line that is located directly above a vowel (ā, ē, ī, ō, ū) to show a learner that the vowel is a long vowel. The word macron can be pronounced correctly either |mā′• krŏn| or |măk′• rŏn|. A long vowel is pronounced the same as the name of the vowel: **a** says |ā|; **e** says |ē|; **i** says |ī|; **o** says |ō|; and **u** says |ū|. When you look up the words **bacon**, **eagle**, **smile**, **open**, and **use** in a dictionary, you will see the macron.

Diacritical Marks   The breve (˘) and the macron (¯) are both examples of *diacritical marks*. These are purely reference marks and not part of the spelling of a word. A diacritical mark indicates how to pronounce a word, accent a syllable, or separate a word. Some common diacritical marks, in addition to the breve and macron, are the accent (′), which tells that a syllable should be stressed, and the centered dot (•), which denotes a syllable break.

When Buying a Dictionary, Opt for One with Diacritical Marks

When considering the purchase of a dictionary, buy one that features diacritical marks. Get your money's worth! A dictionary is of limited use if it does not contain these pronunciation helps. We have found to our dismay that many dictionaries do not supply diacritical marks. A good dictionary will define, spell, and show how to pronounce words.

Lesson 67
o, oe, and ou = |ŭ| or |ə| (and sometimes |wŭ|)

o (pronounced |ŭ| or |ə|)

I.
of *	some	come	from	month	son
			|wŭ| = o		
front	honey	won	one	once**	someone

o, oe, and **ou** (pronounced |ŭ| or |ə|)

II.
money	among	confess	protect	collect	lonesome
become	above	lemon	does	touch	famous

o (pronounced |ŭ| or |ə|)

III.
conspire	confine	conclude	convene
contain	confuse	contrite	compete
complain	complete	compute	compare

Review: Lessons 1 – 67

IV.
ruled	moment	does	second	careful
stoop	voted	cleaned	rodeo	chime
apply	cooked	scanned	wheel	uncle
whole	galaxy	shocking	telescope	latitude

V.
contain	happy	banana	eagle	helped
chatting	violin	zoomed	control	quiet
commute	good	dress	booth	dental
Nebraska	Oregon	Tennessee	Colorado	Kansas

VI.
zipped	mental	bulkiest	confuse	joked
horse	dozen	ornament	frozen	occupy
retouch	visited	astronomy	compute	trouble
Texas	Oklahoma	North Carolina	Monday	August

* The **f** in **of** is pronounced |v|.   ** The **ce** in **once** is pronounced |s|.

Challenge Words:	**breve**	**macron**	**diacritical marks**
	[breve]	[ma • cron]	[di • a • crit • i • cal marks]

Instructions for Lesson 68

> **Introduce the spelling and pronunciation patterns for the diphthongs**
> oi, oy, ou, **and** ow, **as in** boil, boy, out, **and** owl.

Diphthongs

NEW CONCEPT. A *diphthong* consists of two vowels that are set side-by-side, inhabiting the same syllable, and that create a unique sound. (*Di* means two.) (Diphthong may be pronounced either |dĭf′ • thông| or |dĭp′ • thông|.) The **oy** in **boy** and the **oi** in **boil** are diphthongs. The **ou** in **out** and the **ow** in **owl** are also diphthongs.

oi

I   **NEW PATTERN.** Introduce the **oi** diphthong spelling and pronunciation pattern found in **boil** and **coin**. This diphthong, pronounced |ōē| or |ōĭ|, is often encapsulated in a syllable by at least one consonant, as is the case with **boil** and **coin**. The **oi** diphthong comes to us from French. The **oi** is usually located at the beginning or in the middle of a syllable (the so-called *initial* or *medial* positions, respectively).

oy

II   **LEARN** the **oy** diphthong spelling and pronunciation pattern found in **boy** and **enjoy**. The **oy** diphthong is typically found at the end of syllables or words (final position). The **oy** letter pairing is derived from the French language.

ou

III   **LEARN** the **ou** diphthong spelling and pronunciation pattern |ow| typified in the words **out** and **proud**. Notice that the word **house** in Roman numeral III has a silent **e**.

ow

IV   **LEARN** the **ow** diphthong spelling and pronunciation pattern |ow|, as seen in the words **owl** and **down**.

Review: oi oy   ou ow

V & VI   **REVIEW** the **oi, oy, ou,** and **ow** diphthongs.

REVIEW, also, the **ou** and **ow** spelling and pronunciation patterns that make the sound of the long-vowel o, |ō|, as in **soul** and **snow**. [See Lessons 41 and 43]

The patterns for pronouncing the four points of a compass—west, east, north, south—have now been introduced (Lessons 19, 36, 43, and 68, respectively). A list of map and directional terms has been included on page 262.

Lesson 68
Diphthongs: oi oy   ou ow

oi = |ōē| or |ŏĭ|

I.
boil	join	moist	spoil	point	foil
coin	toil	oil	devoid	pointed	avoid

oy = |ōē| or |ŏĭ|

II.
boy	joy	toy	employ	soy	Troy
enjoy	coy	ploy	destroy	annoy	alloy

ou = |ow|

III.
out	count	flour	couch	pounds	cloud
proud	south	wound	ouch	loud	house

ow = |ow|

IV.
owl	brown	bow	now	town	vow
down	how	gown	crowd	drown	crown

Review: Diphthongs
oi oy   ou ow

V.
noun	shout	coin	enjoy	shown	ground
snow	house	sound	boiled	county	growth
joined	mouth	town	our	broil	alloy
soul	boiler	round	throw	found	cows

VI.
four	brown	joy	soil	mouse	pillow
south	low	vowel	around	about	outside
yellow	amount	now	without	boundary	thousand
dugout	shower	toil	cowboy	deploy	compound
South Carolina		South Dakota		Detroit	Boise

Challenge Words:	snowbound	thyroid	deployment
	[snow • bound]	[thy • roid]	[de • ploy • ment]

Instructions for Lesson 69

> Introduce eight murmur diphthongs pronounced |ər|,
> achieved with the spelling patterns er, ir, ar, or, wor, ur, yr, ear, **and** our.
> Sample words: her, first, polar, flavor, word, turn, syrup, learn, **and** journey.

Murmur Diphthongs (They Say |ər|)

NEW CONCEPT. *Murmur diphthongs* are letter pairs or trios that say |ər|. Possible spellings are **er, ir, ar, or, wor, ur, yr, ear,** and **our**. It's easy to remember how to pronounce a murmur diphthong, regardless of how it is spelled. The |ər| sound is exactly the same as the sound found in the very word itself: |mər • mər|.

I   **LEARN** the **er** and **ir** spelling patterns that say |ər|, as in **her** and **first**.

II   **LEARN** the **ar** and **or** spelling patterns pronounced |ər|, as in **polar, flavor**, and **word**. Usually, the spellings **ar** and **or** are pronounced |ər| in syllables or words that are not accented. When accented, **ar** often says |ä| or |ô| (see Lesson 55), as in **carton**. An accented **or** often says |ōr|, as in **dormant** (Lesson 43). Many **wor** words are pronounced with the murmur diphthong sound |wər|, as in **word**.

The word **record** requires us to consider context to determine its intended meaning and pronunciation. **Record** is both a noun (*"Jamaica broke the **record** at the track meet"*) and a verb (*"The head official will **record** the fastest time in the Olympic scorebook"*). The word's function (noun or verb) determines how it will be pronounced. The noun is pronounced |rĕk´ • ərd|, with a murmur diphthong in the second syllable. This second syllable is not accented. [A murmur diphthong is usually (if not always) in the unaccented syllable.] The verb, on the other hand, is pronounced |rĭ • kōrd´|, with the second syllable being accented. In context, these words seldom will be confused.

III   **LEARN** murmur diphthongs pronounced |ər| and spelled **ur, yr, ear,** and **our**, as in **turn, syrup, learn**, and **journey**.

In some regions of the country, people pronounce the words **your** or **tourist** with the |ər| murmur diphthong, but in other places, the sound used is more like a long-vowel **o**, |ōr|, or |ůr| or |ür|. Use a good dictionary and encourage your student, as much as possible, to adopt the preferred pronunciation. The contraction **you're** will be introduced in Lesson 83. How **your** is used in a sentence may also determine its correct pronunciation.

Review: |ər|

IV - VI   **REVIEW** murmur diphthongs.

Words classified as *homophones* are pronounced the same but have different meanings and spellings (e.g., **altar** and **alter**). Ensure that the word meanings are understood.

> Remember!
> Read, spell, and know the meanings of the words in this lesson.
> Mark the completion chart.

Lesson 69
Murmur Diphthongs
|ər|

er = |ər|

I.
her	clerk	terms	pepper	sermon	alter*
other	over	mother	after	number	father

ir = |ər|

first	bird	shirt	girl	third	stir

ar = |ər|

II.
polar	nectar	molar	tartar	liar	altar*

or = |ər|

flavor	record	color	doctor	motor	minor
word	work	worm	worth	worst	world

ur = |ər| **yr = |ər|**

III.
turn	purple	hurry	church	syrup	martyr

ear = |ər| **our = |ər|**

learn	search	earth	journey	nourish	journal

* The homophones **alter** and **altar** are pronounced the same but have different spellings and meanings.

Review: |ər|

IV.
actor	early	birth	lunar	perfume
surf	hinder	ester	journal	mayor
kernel	burst	flavor	thirst	murmur
water	quarter	thirteen	zipper	thirty

V.
worry	solar	mirror	dollars	yearn
quirky	earth	litter	confirm	turkey
verdict	burn	worship	serpent	myrrh
major	river	number	pattern	meters

VI.
tartar	merchant	lavender	firm	summer
verbal	disturb	further	irked	calendar
border	singer	earn	gurgle	Vermont
Thursday	October	Saturday	September	November

Challenge Words:	**grasshopper**	**interstate**	**kilometers**
	[grass • hop • per]	[in • ter • state]	[kil • o • me • ters]

Instructions for Lesson 70

> Introduce the i spelling pattern that makes the |ē| sound, as in taxi.
>
> Also introduce the o, oe, and ou spellings that are pronounced |ü|, as in do, shoe, move, and soup.
>
> Further, introduce the |ů| sound of u and ou, as in put and could.

i = |ē|

I   REVIEW the spelling and pronunciation pattern for the letter **i** where it says |ē|, as in **taxi** and **trio**. Once the **ie** and **ei** spellings have been introduced in Lessons 74 and 76, respectively, most of the spellings for the |ē| sound will have been introduced. These spellings include **-ing** (**boxing**), the silent **e** (**Pete**), **ee** (**free**), **ea** (**seat**), open syllable (**veto**), unaccented **y** (**lady**), **i** (**taxi**), **ie** (**field**), and **ei** (**ceiling**). [See Lessons 31, 33, 35, 36, 61, 62, 70, 74, and 76, respectively.]

o, oe, and ou = |ü|

II   LEARN the **o**, **oe**, and **ou** spelling patterns found in **do, shoe, move,** and **soup**. (We encountered this sound in Lesson 51 in the words **broom** and **too**.) English words are not supposed to end with the letter **v**, so words like **move** and **prove** have a silent **e** at the end. [See Lesson 89] The sound of a vowel changes slightly when the letter **r** follows it, as seen in the word **tour**.

The word **wound** with the |ü| sound is usually a noun. However, **wound** can also be a verb (**ou** = |ow|), as in *"Eva **wound** her clock."* In context, these words will not be mixed up. *"Dustin **wound** [verb] the bandage around Lance's **wound** [noun]."* [See Lesson 68]

REVIEW the |h| sound for the **wh** spelling, as in **who** and **whose**. [See Lesson 51]

u and ou = |ů|

III   LEARN the |ů| pronunciation for the spelling patterns **u** and **ou**, as in **put** and **could**. (This sound was discussed some in Lesson 51, where we talked about the **oo** in **book** and **good**.) Roman numerals II and III introduce words with an **ou** spelling, e.g., **soup** and **could**. The **ou** pattern has at least seven sounds [see Lesson 86]. The words **could, would,** and **should** have a silent **l**. [See Lesson 82]

Review: i = |ē| o and ou = |ü| o and ou = |ů|

IV - VI   REVIEW the spelling and pronunciation patterns for |ē|, |ü|, and |ů|, as in **taxi** and **trio**, **do** and **soup**, and **put** and **could**, respectively.

Vowel Sounds

Each of the five vowels has a short and long sound. We commonly refer to the sounds introduced in this lesson as the *third sounds* for **i** (|ē|), **o** (|ü|), and **u** (|ů|). Regarding the third sounds of **a** (|ä| or |ô|) and **e** (|ā|), these are covered in Lesson 55 (**ball, quad**), Lesson 76 (**veil**), and Lesson 77 (**great**), respectively. All of the vowels can make a schwa sound.

144

Lesson 70

i = |ē| o and **ou = |ü| u** and **ou = |u̇|**

i = |ē|

I.	taxi	chili	patio	audio
	trio	radio	handicap	stadium
	sodium	piano	insomnia	period

o, oe, and **ou = |ü|**

II.	do	who	loose	lose
	shoe	whose	move	prove
	soup	you	group	wound

u and **ou = |u̇|**

III.	put	push	bush	pull
	full	bull	bullet	pudding
	could	would	should	boulevard

Review: i = |ē| o and **ou = |ü| u** and **ou = |u̇|**

IV.	insomnia	full	Indian	you
	ski	butcher	period	cuisine
	tour	whose	lollipop	prove

V.	to	chili	material	radial
	question	sodium	audio	amiable
	into	movements	could	pushed

VI.	piano	stadium	patio	handicap
	Canadian	would	put	shoes
	hundred	boulevard	Monday	August
	New Mexico	Indiana	Mississippi	Louisiana

Challenge Word:	**meridian**	**millennium**
	[me • rid • i • an]	[mil • len • ni • um]

Instructions for Lesson 71

> **Introduce the** ce, ci, **and** cy **spelling patterns pronounced** |s|,
> **as seen in such words as** face, cell, city, **and** cycle.
>
> **Also introduce the** ge, gi, **and** gy **spelling patterns for words pronounced**
> |j| **and** |zh|, **as in** age, engine, gym, **and** mirage.

ce, ci, and cy = |s|

I & II   **LEARN** the **ce, ci,** and **cy** spelling patterns with the |s| pronunciation, as in **face, city,** and **cycle.** This pattern is very dependable. We are aware of only a few exceptions to this pattern, one of which is **Celtic,** can be pronounced with the |k| sound, |kĕl • tĭk|. Both |sĕl • tĭk| and |kĕl • tĭk| are correct.

ge, gi, and gy = |j| and sometimes |zh|

In the lessons to this point, words containing the letter **g** illustrate the so-called *hard sound* of **g** (|g|), as in **get, give,** and **argyle.** This lesson introduces two softer sounds for **g,** namely, |j|, as in **gem, engine,** and **gym,** and |zh|, as in **mirage.**

The **g** pattern is not as dependable as the **c** pattern (see discussion above) but is still a fairly reliable guide. Words spelled with **ga, go,** or **gu** (for example, **gap, goes, gulp**) or with **g** immediately followed by a consonant (**grade, glad**) are almost always pronounced with the hard **g** sound |g|. However, **g** will usually be pronounced with a soft **g** sound—|j|—when accompanied by **e, i,** or **y.** We see this new pattern illustrated in **germ** and **page** (ge = |j|); **engine** (gi = |j|); and **gym** (gy = |j|).

Another pronunciation of **g,** also softer than a hard **g,** is the |zh| sound found in **mirage.** The |zh| is the 47th sound of the 48 sounds covered in this book.

III & IV   **LEARN** the |j| and |zh| sounds on display in such words as **gem, age, garage, engine, gym,** and **edge.** These sounds derive from spelling patterns **ge, gi, gy,** and **dge.**

Consider discussing with your student the following particularities:

▶ The |j| sound of **g** is sometimes spelled **dge,** as in **edge** and **dodge** (see first row of words in Roman number IV); and

▶ The letter **y,** when it acts as a vowel, is often pronounced as if it were a short-vowel **i.** Such is the case in **gym.**

Review: c g

V & VI   **REVIEW** the **c** spelling patterns pronounced |k| and |s|, as in **cancel, crust, circle,** and **face.**

REVIEW the **g** spelling patterns pronounced |g|, |j|, and |zh|, as in **good, gust, grade, edge, age, gym, engine, garage,** and **mirage.**

Lesson 71
c = |s| g = |j| and sometimes |zh|

c = |s|

I.

face	twice	space	grace
cell	force	ice	percent
price	voice	juice	chance

c = |s|

II.

city	notice	fence	palace
office	practice	advice	decide
essence	recipe	cycle	lacy

ge = |j| and sometimes |zh|

III.

gem	germ	gentle	digest
age	page	stage	range
huge	urge	large	manage

dge = |j|

IV.

edge	dodge	bridge	fudge

gy, gi, and ge = |j| and sometimes |zh|

gym	clergy	energy	agile
engine	ginger	teenage	baggage
change	orange	garage	mirage

Review: c g

V.

page	cancel	ranger	force	gear	sentence
orange	grade	badge	digest	cents	ginger
brace	crust	process	product	race	teenager
gust	dance	factor	ragged	germ	exercise

VI.

calcium	circle	singing	center	since	difference
garage	strange	general	France	circus	entrance
good	face	practice	produce	surge	language
energy	baggage	decimal	distance	case	substances

Challenge Words:	**December**	**centennial**	**percentage**
	[De • cem • ber]	[cen • ten • ni • al]	[per • cent • age]
celebrated	**gyroscope**	**Genesis**	**germinate**
[cel • e • bra • ted]	[gy • ro • scope]	[Gen • e • sis]	[ger • mi • nate]
Canadian	**reconcile**	**recycle**	**cinema**
[Ca • na • di • an]	[rec • on • cile]	[re • cy • cle]	[cin • e • ma]

Instructions for Lesson 72

Introduce suffixes and end spellings.

I **NEW CONCEPT.** Introduce the suffixes and end spellings -**ful**, -**fully**, -**ac**, -**ec**, and -**ic**. When adding an **ly** ending to a word that already ends in **l** (like **joyful**), we will end up with a double **l** (**joyfully**). Adding **ly** turns a word into an *adverb*, a word that describes a verb, adjective, or another adverb.

Usually, the |**k**| sound ending of a short-vowel syllable or word is spelled **ck**. Very few syllables end with the letter **c** (**lilac**, **Aztec**, **picnic**).

II **LEARN al**, **ant**, **en**, and **ent**, as in **dental**, **vacant**, **fallen**, and **precedent**.

III **LEARN ish**, **ism**, **ance**, and **ence**, as in **finish**, **racism**, **balance**, and **absence**. The **ism** ending consists of two syllables, |**ĭz • əm**|, as in **racism**. A syllable is supposed to have at least one vowel, but the **m** in **ism** is one of the few instances in which a syllable is spelled without a vowel.

Review: Suffixes and Endings

IV & V REVIEW **ful**, **fully**, **ac**, **ec**, **ic**, **al**, **ant**, **en**, **ent**, **ish**. **ism**, **ance**, and **ence**.

Spelling

Spelling is a vital activity. Be sure that your student invests adequate time learning to spell every word in the lesson lists. Continue to discuss the meaning of words at least twice: once when your student first sees the word, and again when he spells it.

Lesson 72
Suffixes and Word Endings

-ful -fully -ac -ec -ic

I.
joyful	cupful	willful	artful	bountiful
usefully	lawfully	helpfully	skillfully	artfully
lilac	Aztec	picnic	traffic	attic

-al -ant -en -ent

II.
dental	rental	animal	bridal	carnival
vacant	distant	giant	servant	blatant
fallen	beaten	parent	precedent	accident

-ish -ism -ance -ence

III.
finish	vanish	punish	rubbish	abolish
racism	Communism	balance	entrance	finance
absence	evidence	essence	audience	commence

Review: Suffixes and Word Endings

IV.
Arctic	consent	blemish	dental
truism	normal	tropic	basic
finish	public	prism	historic

V.
economic	distance	residence	widen
Atlantic	Pacific	meridian	continental
beaten	argument	basement	fabric

VI.
hopeful	elegant	final	romance
music	influence	joyfully	electric
Hawaii	Georgia	West Virginia	Virginia

Challenge Words:	antibiotic	punishment	blemishes
	[an • ti • bi • ot • ic]	[pun • ish • ment]	[blem • ish • es]

Unit 4

Putting It All Together

Lessons 73 – 90

Sound Chart for Unit 4

|gz|

EXIT

exit sign

Instructions for Lesson 73

> **Introduce and review the various pronunciation patterns of the letter y:**
> |y|, |ē|, |ī|, |ōē| **or** |ōĭ|, silent y, |ĭ|, **and** |ər|.

If you are using the detailed completion chart, it is time for the last card. [See page 301]

All but one of the 48 sounds taught in these lessons have now been introduced. (The last sound, |gz|, will be introduced in Lesson 75.) All lists in Lesson 73 are a review of previously introduced sounds for **y**. If a student exhibits difficulty with any pattern, go back and review the lesson where the pattern was first introduced.

I   **REVIEW** the **y** sound |y|, as in **yes**. The letter **y**, when used as a consonant, is usually, if not always, the first letter in a word or syllable, as illustrated in **yes** and **beyond**. [Lessons E and 1]

II   Words in English rarely end with dotted letters like **i**. If a word would end in **i**, the **i** is usually replaced by **y**. [Lesson 63]

     REVIEW the unaccented **y** spelling pattern pronounced with the long-vowel **e** sound |ē|, as in **daily** and **funny**. [Lesson 62]

     REVIEW the accented ['] **y** spelling pattern pronounced with the long vowel **i** sound |ī|, as in **apply** and **flying**. [Lessons 45 and 62]

III   **REVIEW** the **y** spelling pattern of the **oy** diphthong pronounced |ōē| or |ōĭ|, as in **boy** and **enjoy**. (A diphthong is a pairing of two vowels that produces a unique sound within a syllable.) [See Lesson 68]

     REVIEW the silent **y** spelling pattern where **y** acts as a second vowel in a syllable, as in **day** and **play**. [Lessons 39 and 40]

IV   **REVIEW** the short-vowel **y** spelling pattern pronounced with the short-vowel **i** sound |ĭ|, as in **gym** and **myth**. This pattern was briefly introduced in Lesson 71.

     REVIEW the **yr** spelling pattern pronounced with the murmur diphthong sound |ər|, as in **syrup** and **martyr**. As always, keep a dictionary handy for looking up words. Do you know the meaning of **myrmidon**? [Lesson 69]

Review: y

V & VI   **REVIEW** seven consonant and vowel patterns for **y**. The *consonant sound* of **y** is |y|, as in **yes**. The *vowel sounds* of **y** are present in **daily**, **apply**, **boy**, **day**, **gym**, and **syrup**. When **y** acts as a vowel in a syllable or word, it often is pronounced like the letter **i**. There are very few words that use a **y** in conjunction with the schwa sound. **Maryland** and **Pennsylvania** are two of the exceptions. [Lesson 76 introduces the **ey** spelling patterns pronounced with the long-vowel **a** sound (**they**, **obey**); the long-vowel **e** sound (**key**, **money**); and the long-vowel **i** sound (**eye**, **geyser**). The |ā| and |ī| sounds for this spelling are rarely used.]

154

Lesson 73
y

y used as a consonant (pronounced |**y**|)

I.
yes	yeast	yonder	yellow
beyond	yell	yardage	yesterday

unaccented **y** used as a vowel (pronounced |ē|)

II.
daily	gravy	lefty	roomy
funny	itchy	handy	entry

accented **y** used as a vowel (pronounced |ī|)

apply	myself	reply	retype
flying	byline	hyper	cycle

diphthong **y** used as a vowel (pronounced |ōē| or |ōĭ|)

III.
boy	toy	joy	annoy
enjoy	employ	destroy	Troy

silent **y** used as a vowel

day	pray	stay	tray
play	may	clay	stray

short vowel **y** used as a vowel (pronounced |ĭ|)

IV.
gym	system	crypt	krypton
myth	cynic	bicycle	typify

yr used as a vowel (**yr** is a murmur diphthong pronounced |ər|)

syrup	myrrh	Myrtle	Smyrna
martyr	zephyr	myrmidon	martyrs

Review: y

V.
army	apply	yearly	yardage	symbol	cycle
body	crazy	daily	strays	gypsy	everyone
gym	prayed	territory	maybe	myrrh	industry
very	yeast	bicycle	shaky	retype	playground
enjoy	mystic	probably	analyst	daytime	everything

VI.
byline	tray	property	staying	itchy	hybrid
clay	myself	beyond	myth	system	employment
only	annoy	oxygen	yelling	flying	syllable
syrup	slowly	suddenly	lyric	melody	yesterday
finally	history	Milky	Way	slyly	beryllium

Instructions for Lesson 74

> Introduce the ie spelling pattern that is pronounced either |ī| or |ē|,
> as in pie and field.
>
> Also introduce homophones such as sum/some and meet/meat/mete.

ie

I   **REVIEW** the **ie** spelling pattern pronounced with the long-vowel **i** sound |ī|, as in **pie** and **fries**. [Lessons 45 and 46]

II & III   **LEARN** the **ie** spelling pattern pronounced with the long-vowel **e** sound, |ē|, as in **field** and **babies**. Note: Most words that have **ie** within the same syllable are pronounced |ē|. This is a departure from the typical long-vowel pronunciation pattern.

Review: ie

IV   **REVIEW** the **ie** spelling pattern involving either a long vowel **i**, |ī|, as in **pie**, or a long-vowel **e**, |ē|, as in **brief**. When spelling **ie** words, which comes first—the **i** or the **e**? One way to remember the proper order is to learn the phrase, *"I [comes] before e except after c, or in words that say ā, as in* **neighbor** *and* **weigh***."*

Two Additional Pronunciations for the ie Spelling Pattern

There are two very similar but unusual pronunciations for the **ie** spelling pattern that must be mentioned here. These are truly irregular and unusual, and their patterns affect very few words:

- The **ie** spelling with the long vowel **u** sound |ū|, as in **view**; and
- The **ie** spelling with the |ü| sound, as in **lieutenant** [see Lesson 89].

Listen Up! Homophones

V & VI   **REVIEW** homophones. Homophones are words that differ in spelling and meaning but sound identical. Keep a dictionary handy and discuss these words with your student. Describing, defining, or providing the word in a sentence will help your student understand homophones. Context makes homophones easy to read. From this point forward, the challenge words will sometimes be homophones. Students are usually intrigued by and enjoy learning about these words.

Lesson 74
ie = |ī| ie = |ē|

ie = |ī|

I.

pie	tried	cried	flies	vied
fries	applied	untie	relied	denies

ie = |ē|

II.

field	brief	piece	shriek	priest
yield	thief	chief	grief	siege

ie = |ē|

III.

babies	juries	shield	briefly	Julie
duties	shrieked	yielded	fielding	belief

Review: ie

IV.

pie	yield	niece	fries	chief
brief	piece	juries	pried	cries
believe	defied	grieving	shield	Julie
denied	tiers	applied	priest	fried
beliefs	fielding	yielded	prairie	relied

Homophones

V.

sum	some	meet	meat	mete	son	sun
fair	fare	for	fore	four	foul	fowl
read	reed	do	due	dew	all	awl

VI.

blue	blew	flu	flue	flew	birth	berth
sale	sail	fur	fir		here	hear
deer	dear	rays	raise	raze	tear	tier

Challenge Words:	territories	shrieking	diesel
	[ter • ri • tor • ies]	[shriek • ing]	[die • sel]

Instructions for Lesson 75

> **Introduce the letter** x, **which is pronounced** |ks|, |gz|, |z|, **or** |ksh|,
> **as in** box, exit, Xerox™, **and** complexion, **respectively.**

x

I   **REVIEW** the voiceless |ks| sound of **x**, as in **box.** Typically, this x sound appears at the end of a short-vowel syllable or word. Both the |k| and |s| sound*s* in this pronunciation of **x** are voiceless. To demonstrate to yourself that a pronunciation is voiceless, touch your throat while pronouncing the letter. Your throat will not vibrate if the letter is voiceless.

II   **NEW PATTERN.** Learn the sound of |gz| made by **x** in **exit** and **exam.** Usually, the **ex** is followed by a vowel, as in **exit.** The |g| sound and the |z| sound found in this **x** |gz| pronunciation are both voiced, meaning that the vocal cords of the speaker will vibrate. The |gz| sound is the only new sound introduced in Unit 4, and it is the last sound introduced in these lessons.

III   **NEW PATTERN.** Learn the |z| sound of **x**, as in **Xerox™.** Most words or syllables that begin with **x** are pronounced with the |z| sound. Sample words are **Xavier |Zā • vē • ər|**, **xerophytes**, and **Xerxes** (the name of the ancient king of Persia). Consult a dictionary to find out more about these words. Most students love learning about this pattern.

     NEW PATTERN. Learn the **ph** spelling pattern that says |f|. This |f| sound is found in **xylophone.**

|ksh| |gz| |ks|

IV   **NEW PATTERN.** Learn the **xion** spelling pattern that says |kshən|. Note this sound in the word **complexion.** The word **exile** can be pronounced with either |gz| or |ks|.

Review: x

V & VI   **REVIEW** the four sounds of **x:** |ks|, |gz|, |z|, and |ksh|, as in **box, exit, Xerox™**, and **complexion.**

     REVIEW the **ph** spelling that is pronounced |f|, as in **xylophone.**

Two Additional Pronunciations for X

An unusual pronunciation of **x** is |h|, as in **Xavier |Hä • vē • āir|** and **Mexico |Mĕ • hē • cō|.** The **x** in **Xaca** is pronounced with the |hw| sound, **|Hwä • hä • kə|**, and is clearly irregular. Many of the words that are unusual or irregular in English trace their origins to the languages of other countries. **Proper names** do not always follow a regular pattern. Proper nouns can be pronounced and spelled any way the originating individual, group, or nation chooses.

158

Lesson 75

x

ph = |f|

voiceless **x** = |**ks**|

I.	box	taxi	next	mixes	exclude
	Texas	index	Ajax	excuse	Mexico

voiced **x** = |**gz**|

II.	exit	exult	exist	exalt	exact
	exam	exert	example	exactly	existing

x = |**z**|

III.	Xerox™	xeric	xylem	xanthic	xebec
				|f| = ph	
	xyloid	xenon	Xanadu	xylophone	xenophobic

xi = |**ksh**|		**x** = |**gz**| or |**ks**|
IV. complexion		exile

Review: x

V.	except	exit	taxi	Texas	exile
	index	exactly	xylophone	maximum	indexed

VI.	expect	sixteenth	relax	text	extra
	suffix	explain	express	Exodus	experiment

Challenge Word:		equinox [e • qui • nox]		antioxidant [an • ti • ox • i • dant]	
Homophones:	stare	stair	team teem	steel	steal
	lone	loan	see sea	mail	male
	sore	soar	pain pane	plain	plane
	hall	haul	mall maul	pall	Paul

Instructions for Lesson 76

> **Introduce the** ei **spelling pattern found in** ceiling **and** seize;
> **and introduce the** ey **spelling pattern found in** key **and** money.
>
> **Also introduce the** ei **and** ey **spelling patterns that respectively create the sound of long-vowel** a, |ā|, **in** veil **and** they, **and the long-vowel** i, |ī|, **in** feisty **and** eye.
>
> **Review the** ei **and** ey **spellings pronounced in separate syllables,
> as in** deice (|dē • īce|) **and** beyond (|bē • yŏnd|).

ei ey

Lessons 74 and 76 focus on pronunciation and spelling patterns that follow the oft-repeated memory device: *"I [comes] before e except after c or when the letters say ā, as in **neighbor** and **weigh**."* There are only a few words that do not follow this **cei** pattern, as we will see shortly.

I   **NEW PATTERN.** Introduce the **cei** and **ei** spelling patterns. These combinations are pronounced with the long-vowel **e** sound, as seen in **ceiling** and **seize.** This faithfully follows the regular pattern for long-vowel words: the first vowel says its name while the second vowel is silent. As far as pronunciation goes, whenever **c** is followed by an **e, i,** or **y,** the **c** will be pronounced |s|—for example, **ceiling, city,** and **cycle.** [See Lesson 71] When vowels are followed by the letter **r,** there will be a slight change in their sound, as is apparent in **weird.**

II   **LEARN** the **ey** spelling with the long vowel **e** sound |ē|, as in **key** and **money.** The **y** functions as the second vowel in these words.

III   **LEARN** the **ei** and **ey** patterns that make a long-vowel **a** sound |ā|, as in **veil** and **they.** The |ā| pronunciation for **ei** and **ey** is rare. The **ei** spelling with the |ā| sound comes originally from the Greek spelling and pronunciation.

IV   **LEARN** the **ei** and **ey** spelling patterns with the long vowel **i** sound |ī|, as in **feisty** and **eye.** These are extremely rare patterns, also.

V   **REVIEW** the **ei** and **ey** spellings that involve individual syllables, as in **deice** (|dē • īs|) and **beyond** (|bē • yŏnd|).

Review: ei ey

VI   **REVIEW** the **ei** and **ey** spelling patterns found in such words as **ceiling, seize, key, money, veil, they, feisty, eye, deice,** and **beyond.**

A few words spelled with **ei** or **ey** are pronounced with the |ĕ|, |ə|, or |ĭ| sound. Among these words are **heifer, there, their, they're,** and **foreign.** A usage note regarding the homophones **there, their,** and **there** is provided in Lesson 84.

> Devote adequate time to spelling words. This is especially important
> now that the words are getting longer and more complex.

160

Lesson 76
ei   ey

ei = |ē|

I. ceiling	deceit	receive	deceiver
seize	perceives	protein	codeine
weird	conceited	*either	*neither

ey = |ē|

II. key	alley	honey	kidney
money	volley	osprey	New Jersey
hockey	keyless	donkey	valley

ei = |ā|

III. veil	reins	feint	veins

ey = |ā|

they	whey	hey	prey
obey	survey	convey	heyday

ei = |ī|

IV. feisty	seismic	stein	Geiger

ey = |ī|

eye	geysers	eyed	Popeye
walleye	Hawkeye	Buckeye	Cheyenne

ei when in separate syllables

V. deice	seeing	deist	deify
being	freeing	fleeing	atheist

ey when in separate syllables

beyond   Eeyore

Review: ei   ey

VI. veined	turkey	seizing	money	veil	Poseidon
feisty	Beirut	deceived	donkey	obey	kidney
weird	survey	receive	they	alley	Cheyenne
monkey	convey	seismic	ceiling	beige	keyboard
either	volley	whey	deceit	stein	conceited
fleeing	heist	protein	beyond	being	New Jersey

* **Either** and **neither** are words that also can be pronounced with the long **i** sound |ī|.

Challenge Words:	seismometer		honeymoon	Geiger counter
	[seis • mom • e • ter]		[hon • ey • moon]	[Gei • ger count • er]
Homophones:	pail pale	beet beat	claws clause	seller cellar
	tail tale	pray prey	shone shown	vale veil

Instructions for Lesson 77

Introduce the ea **spelling pattern that has five separate pronunciations:**
|ē|, |ĕ|, |ā|, |ər|, **and** |är|, **as in** each, ready, great, learn, **and** heart, **respectively.**

---

ea ear

I   **REVIEW** the **ea** spelling pattern with the long-vowel **e** sound |ē|, as in **each** and **clean**. [Lessons 36, 37, 38]

II   **NEW PATTERN.** Introduce the **ea** spelling pattern with the short-vowel **e** sound |ĕ|, as in **ready** and **deaf**.

Note: Roman numerals I and II introduce the word **read**. The pronunciation of **read** will have to be determined by sentence context: *"Last night I rĕad a story to Asher"* [past tense]; *"Let's rēad a story right now"* [present tense]; *"We will rēad another story tonight"* [future tense]. Noticing context and developing the habit of knowing word meanings will make your student a good reader.

III   **LEARN** the **ea** spelling pattern that has a long-vowel **a** sound |ā|, as in **great** and **steak**. Only a few words in English follow this pattern.

IV   **REVIEW** the **ear** spelling pattern with the murmur diphthong |ər|, as in **learn** and **earth**. [See Lesson 69]

V   **LEARN** the **ear** spelling pattern that says |är|, as in **heart** and **hearty**.

Review: ea ear

VI   **REVIEW** the five sounds of **ea**: |ē|, |ĕ|, |ā|, |ər|, and |är|, as in **each**, **ready**, **great**, **learn**, and **heart**.

Homonyms are words that are spelled and sound the same but have different meanings.

bat   flying mammal that lives in caves (noun); a stick used to hit the ball in the game of baseball (noun); to swat away, as in *"to bat away a wasp"* (verb).

dish   a TV satellite receiver (noun); a bowl or plate on which food is placed (noun); old-style slang used to describe an attractive woman, as in *"She's a dish!"* (noun); to give or present, as to *"dish up"* potatoes (verb).

brief   a legal document for court (noun); a short or condensed period of time, *"Please be brief in your remarks"* (adjective); a type of underpants (noun); to give information or instructions, as in *"Jimmy will brief the dog handlers"* (verb).

foul   in baseball a term referring to a ball not being hit within the baselines, as in *"Parker hit seven foul balls his last time at bat"* (adjective); an infraction of the rules in basketball, as in *"The referee called a fourth foul on the team's star player"* (noun); a bad odor, as in *"What is that foul smell?"* (adjective).

pool   swimming trough (noun); the combining of things, as in *"Let's pool our resources"* (verb); a group activity as in an *"office pool"* (noun); a game played on a special table with sticks and numbered balls, as in *"That is our pool table"* (adjective) and *"Let's play some pool"* (noun).

pat   to lightly tap on something (verb); small, flat, square piece of something, as in a *"pat of butter"* (noun); a name or nickname (as for Patricia) (proper noun); a show of approval, as in *"John received a well-deserved pat on the back"* (noun); trite, as in *"a pat answer"* (adjective).

mind   The thinking place in the head (noun); phrase referring to whether or not someone cares, as in *"Do you mind if I take the car into town?"* (verb); a verb indicating obedience, as in *"You will mind me now!"* (verb).

Lesson 77
ea   ear

ea = |ē|

I. each	lease	teach	tease
clean	beach	tear	read

ea = |ĕ|

II. ready	wear	heaven	measure
deaf	peasant	tear	read

ea = |ā|

III. great	break	steaks	greatest
steak	greatly	breaking	greatness

ear = |ər|

IV. learn	earn	pearl	heard
earth	yearn	early	search

ear = |är|

V. heart	hearth	hearken	heartier
hearty	dishearten	heartbeat	heartfelt

Review: ea ear

VI. steak	dead	hearten	really
cleaner	death	feather	head
heartache	spread	learner	heavy
searched	instead	measure	already
bread	weather	hearth	earliest
pleasant	ahead	reading	hearty

Homophones:

grate	great	bare	bear	herd	heard
hart	heart	red	read	coarse	course
brake	break	reed	read	pare	pair	pear

Homonyms are words that have identical spelling and pronunciation but have different meanings. Discuss these homonyms:

bat	bat	bat	brief	brief	brief	pat	pat	Pat
dish	dish	dish	foul	foul	foul	mind	mind	mind
			pool	pool	pool			

---

*"Beau tried to **bat** the flying black **bat** away with his baseball **bat** as he strode to home plate to **bat** at the bottom of the seventh inning."*

Instructions for Lesson 78

> **Introduce the |sh| pronunciation which has seven spelling patterns:**
> sh, ch, su, si, sc, ci, ce, **and** ti, **as in** sheep, chef, issue, Russia, crescendo, facial, ocean, **and** partial.
>
> **This lesson also introduces the sound of |shən| and |kshən|, spelled**
> sion, cean, cian, tion, **and** xion, **as in**
> session, ocean, musician, motion, **and** complexion, **respectively.**

|sh| |shŭn|

I   **REVIEW** the **sh** spelling pattern that says |sh|, as in **sheep** and **push**.

II   **LEARN** the **ch** spelling pattern that says |sh|, as in **chef**. (This variant comes to us from the French language.)

III   **LEARN** the **su, si**, and **sc** spelling patterns that say |sh|, as in **issue, Russia,** and **crescendo**. The **en** and the **in** in words like **ensure** and **insure** sound much the same, but they are indeed distinct. Check the dictionary with your student to learn the differences between these words. The word **ensure** refers to making sure something happens. The word **insure** relates to indemnification (insurance).

IV   **LEARN** the |sh| sound of **ci, ce**, and **ti**, as in **facial, ocean**, and **partial**. One word is included in this list that has the **ti** spelling pronounced |shē|, as in **negotiate**. (Syllables like **cial** or **cian** are called *final stable syllables*.)

V   **LEARN** the six ways of spelling or making the sound of |shŭn|, as in **session, ocean, musician, motion,** and **complexion**. The **tion, sion,** and **xion** spelling patterns are found at the end of a word (**motion, session,** and **complexion**). Occasionally, the **tion** and **sion** spelling patterns appear in the middle of a word (**functional, actionable, missionary**).

Review: |sh| |shŭn| |kshən|

VI   **REVIEW** the **sh, ch, su, si, sc, ci, ce,** and **ti** spelling patterns that say |sh| and |shē|.

　　REVIEW the **sion, cean, cian, tion,** and **xion** spelling patterns that say |shŭn| or sometimes |shən| or |kshən|.

Lesson 78
|sh| |shən|

sh = |sh|

I.
sheep	sharpen	dish	flashy	shuffle
push	rushed	shouted	cashew	shushed

ch = |sh|

II.
chef	chute	chagrin	charade	chiffon
schwa	brochure	machine	Michigan	Chicago

su, si, and sc = |sh|

III.
issue	sure	sugar	pressure	erasure
assure	ensure	insure	Russia	crescendo

ci, ce, and ti = |sh|

IV.
facial	musician	official	delicious	precious
special	glacier	ocean	partial	negotiate

sion, cean, cian, and tion = |shən|

V.
session	mission	tension	mansion	revulsion
admission	ocean	musician	magician	dimension
motion	direction	caption	solution	vacation
				xion = |kshən|
section	education	station	nation	complexion

Review: |sh| |shən| |kshən|

VI.
tissue	fresh	direction	nation	information
factions	mission	socially	optician	dimension
ocean	magician	crescendo	Russia	appreciate
crucial	treasure	shorten	mansion	complexion
session	aviation	eruption	caption	admission
charade	schwa	intersection	recreation	construction
special	question	elevation	sugar	population
partial	Michigan	reservation	station	education

Instructions for Lesson 79

Introduce ch, which has three different pronunciations:
|ch|, |sh|, **and** |k|, **as in** teacher, chef, **and** ache.

---

ch

I   **REVIEW** the **ch** spelling pattern with the |ch| pronunciation, as in **teacher**.

Most short-vowel words and syllables that end with the |ch| sound are spelled **tch**, but we do not include them here. Among the exceptions are **much, rich, such, touch,** and **which**.) [See Lessons 26, 27, and 67]

II   **REVIEW** the **ch** spelling pattern with the French-based |**sh**| pronunciation, as in **chef**. [See Lesson 78]

III   **LEARN** the **ch** spelling pattern with the Greek-based |**k**| pronunciation, as in **ache**.

Review: ch

IV & V   **REVIEW** the **ch** spelling with three possible pronunciations, |**ch**|, |**sh**|, and |**k**|. These constructs are found in **teacher, chef,** and **ache**.

Lesson 79

ch

ch = |ch|

I.

teacher	riches	choose	each	cheese
chapel	changing	orchard	chases	exchange

ch = |sh|

II.

chef	machine	charade	chute	Chevy
schwa	chiffon	brochure	Chicago	chagrin

ch = |k|

III.

ache	chaos	scheme	chasm	orchid
echo	mechanic	anchor	school	schedule

Review: ch

IV.

mocha	chanced	merchant	champ	chefs
Chinese	Chevy	achieving	chapter	chicken

V.

charade	technical	cheese	machine	scholarship
orchard	mechanics	chiffon	exchange	Michigan

Challenge Words:	chameleon	championship	archipelago
	[cha • me • le • on]	[cham • pi • on • ship]	[ar • chi • pel • a • go]
Homophones:	cord	chord	share	Cher

Instructions for Lesson 80

Review words that include the |k| sound spelled one of six ways—
c, k, ck(s), x, qu, **and** ch, **as in** camel, key, back(s), six, quick, **and** ache.

Six Spellings Have the |k| Sound

I   **REVIEW** the |k| sound made by **c** and **k**, as found in **camel** and **key**.
[See Lesson 13]

II   **REVIEW** the |k| sound made by **ck**, as in **back** and **jacket**.
[See Lesson 14]

   REVIEW the |ks| sound made by both **cks** and **x**, as in **locks** and **six**.
[See Lessons 1 and 14]

III   **REVIEW** the |khw| sound made by **qu**, as in **quick** and **squeak**.
[See Lessons 13, 16, and 22]

   REVIEW the |k| sound made by **ch**, as in **ache** and **mechanic**.
[See Lesson 79]

Review: |k|

IV & V   **REVIEW** words that have a **c**, **k**, **ck(s)**, **x**, **qu**, or **ch**, as in **camel**, **key**, **back**, **locks**, **six**, **quick**, and **ache**.

Challenge Words

The challenge word **mechanically** has five syllables. All of the phonemes in this word have by now been introduced as basic patterns. If your student has confidently mastered each pattern up to this point in the lessons, and if he reads properly from left to right, syllable to syllable, he will be able to read this word without assistance. Being able to read long words bolsters a student's confidence. Remember to have your student spell each and every word in the Lesson 80 list. Talk about the meaning of the words and use the dictionary when needed.

Lesson 80

|k| |ks| |khw|

I.

c = |k|

| camel | local | cloth | mascot |

c = |k|

| bacon | cactus | kind | kept |

k = |k|

| key | seek | ask | ankle |

II.

ck = |k|

| back | struck | jacket | crackers |

cks = |ks|

| locks | clocks | box | expect |

x = |ks|

| six | text | relax | complex |

III.

qu = |khw|

| quick | quiz | equal | jonquil |

| squeak | liquid | echo | anchor |

ch = |k| (above echo)

ch = |k|

| ache | mechanic | Christ | chemist |

Review: |k| |ks| |khw|

IV.

thanks	camel	index	key
quote	crackers	chaos	clocks
ticket	ache	squeak	echo

V.

cocoa	liquid	blanket	local
toxic	equal	mocha	seek
decorate	complex	blockade	crater

Challenge Words:	contraction	mechanically
	[con • trac • tion]	[me • chan • i • cal • ly]

Instructions for Lesson 81

> **Introduce silent letters. Some of the most common silent letters are**
> g, gh, b, k, h, **and** p, **as in** gnu, light, lamb, knot, hour, **and** Psalms, **respectively.**
> **(Of course, these letters are not** *universally* **silent!)**
>
> **This lesson also introduces the** eu **spelling for** |ü|, **as in** pneumonia.

Silent Letters

I   **NEW CONCEPT.** Introduce the silent letter **g**, as in **gnu** and **sign**.

II   **LEARN** the silent **gh**, as in **light** and **eight**. A sound constituted by four letters is called a *quadrigraph* or *tetragraph* and is found in such words as **eight**, **straight**, **taught**, and **though**. Examples: **eigh** says |ā| and |ī|; **aigh** says |ā|; **augh** says |ô|; and, **ough** says |ō| and |ow|, as in **eight**, **height**, **straight**, **taught**, **though**, and **bough**, respectively.

III   **LEARN** the silent **b**, as in **lamb** and **climb**.

IV   **LEARN** the silent **k**, as in **knot** and **knees**. In the word **knight**, both the **k** and **gh** are silent.

V.   **LEARN** the silent letters **h** and **p**, as in **hour**, **hemorrhage**, and **Psalms**. In the proper name **Esther**, the **h** is silent inside the **th** pattern.

       LEARN the **eu** pattern that says |ū| and |ü|, as in **Europe** and **pneumonia**.

Review: Silent Letters

VI.   **REVIEW** the (sometimes) silent letters **g, gh, b, k, h,** and **p.**

       REVIEW the **eu** spelling pronounced |ü|, as in **pneumonia**. In **feud, Europe,** and **euro,** the letters **eu** are pronounced with the long-vowel **u** sound, |ū| or |ūr|. Note that Europe is spelled with an ending silent **e**. [See Lesson 89]

Reading for Meaning and Mastering Spelling

Challenge words are provided with nearly every lesson to help your student build vocabulary. The meaning of words will usually be obvious in the context of a sentence, paragraph, page, or story.

We've said it before and we'll say it again—it is essential that your student spell words correctly! The best tool for readers is a good dictionary. Even after this course is over, your student will need to have access to a quality dictionary. Ensure that your student knows the alphabet letters in order, as this knowledge will increase his quickness and efficiency in looking up words. Knowing that letters like **h** and **k** are sometimes silent will help your student find words like **hour** and **knight**.

Lesson 81
Unpronounced (Silent) Letters

gn

I. gnu   gnash   design   gnat
    sign   gnaw   reign   gnarl

gh

II. light   taught   night   bright
    eight   straight   high   delight

b

III. lamb   thumb   comb   debt
     climb   limbs   doubt   plumber

k

IV. knot   knit   knob   knock
     knees   know   knife   knight

h and **p**

V. hour   honor   rhyme   hemorrhage
    Psalms   pterodactyl   pneumonia   psychology

Review: Silent Letters

VI. Europe	caught	aught	knew
heir	might	climbed	eighteen
pneumonia	psychology	weight	hours
doubt	eighth	Psalms	reign
right	insight	rhyming	tomb
daughter	thumbnail	gnawing	Almighty
hemorrhage	kneeling	thyme	knocked
ptomaine	Esther	sight	khaki
dishonor	knapsack	pneumatic	designed

Homophones:	mite	might	our	hour	vane	vain	vein
	wait	weight	need	knead	site	sight	cite
	way	weigh	air	heir	fain	fane	feign
	night	knight	nay	neigh	new	knew	gnu
	cot	caught	bale	bail	faint	feint	
	ate	eight	tot	taught	straight	strait	

Instructions for Lesson 82

> **Introduce more (sometimes) silent letters:** w, c, u, l, t, n, **and** s,
> **as in** write, scene, buy, half, listen, hymn, **and** isle, **respectively.**

I   **LEARN** the silent letter **w**, as in **two** and **write**.

II   **LEARN** silent letter **c**, as in **czar** and **scene**.

III   **LEARN** silent letter **u**, as in **buy** and **guest**. The silent **u** is likely included in **guest** and **guitar** to ensure that these words are pronounced with the hard **g** sound, |**g**|. [See Lesson 71]

IV   **LEARN** silent letters **l** and **t**, as in **half** and **listen**. In **walk**, the presence of the silent **l** helps achieve an |ô| sound. The **a** in **tsunami** is pronounced |ä|. [See Lesson 55]

V   **LEARN** silent letters **n** and **s**, as in **hymn** and **isle**.

Review: Silent letters

VI   **REVIEW** the sometimes silent letters **w, c, u, l, t, n**, and **s**. Students are helped by knowing that **condemn** has a silent **n** in the second syllable (|kən • děm|). However, if -**ed** is added to this word, making **condemned**, then the **n** in the second syllable is pronounced with a distinct |**n**| (|kən • děmnd|).

Homonyms

Listed below are examples of homonyms. These lists are not exhaustive.

tire	a rubber cushion encircling a wheel (noun); to exhaust or bore (verb).
bark	a noise a dog makes (noun or verb); outer covering of a tree trunk (noun).
hide	animal skin (noun); to be in a secret place, as in the game of hide-and-seek (verb).
tore	to have gone wildly fast, as in *"He tore through the room"* (verb); to have ripped something, as in *"He tore the paper in half"* (verb).
charm	a jewelry piece that dangles from a chain or bracelet (noun); the trait of grace and beauty, as in *"Lindsey could charm anyone with her personality and kindness"* (verb).
light	a lamp or other source that illuminates (noun); the opposite of darkness (noun); not heavy (adjective); God (noun).
right	direction that is opposite of left (noun); the opposite of wrong (noun); politically conservative (noun).
type	a brand or style (noun); blood type such as A positive or O negative (noun); to press letters on a keyboard (verb).
sore	a hurtful wound (noun); to be hurting or aching (adjective); a bad attitude, as in, *"We were proud that Tim was not a sore loser"* (adjective).
wear	have clothes on the body (noun or verb); to exhaust someone as, in *"Triathlons wear me out!"* (verb).
core	the center of the earth (noun); the center of an apple (noun); the main idea or the very essence of something—*"His core values were unquestionably moral"* (adjective).
harp	stringed instrument (noun); to nag or worry someone (verb).

What are some other homonyms? Consider the words **fault, plate, fan, will,** and **bug**.

Lesson 82
Unpronounced (Silent) Letters

w

I. two   wrap   wrong   wreck
    write   wrist   awry   answer

c

II. czar   scenic   ascend   scent
    scene   unscented   discern   science

u

III. buy   build   guard   guy
     guest   guitar   league   biscuit

l and **t**

IV. half   folk   walk   tsar
    listen   catch   wrestle   tsunami

n and **s**

V. hymn   column   autumn   solemn
    isle   island   Illinois   Arkansas

Review: Silent Letters

VI. wry   guarded   isle   tsunami
    could   built   rhythm   debris
    walking   vague   sword   wrinkle
    glisten   builder   scenery   unscented
    condemn   wrote   solemn   guessed
    condemned   depot   scientists   Rhode Island
    Connecticut Massachusetts Illinois   Arkansas

Homophones:	rap	wrap	him	hymn	raze	rays	raise
	gilt	guilt	aloud	allowed	wear	ware	where
	not	knot	hale	hail	sent	cent	scent
	grown	groan	rote	wrote	so	sew	sow
	sweet	suite	ring	wring	rite	right	write

Homonyms are words that are spelled and pronounced the same but have different meanings:

tire	tire	charm	charm	sore	sore
bark	bark	light	light	wear	wear
hide	hide	right	right	core	core
tore	tore	type	type	harp	harp

173

Instructions for Lesson 83

Introduce the five spellings of the |ch| sound: ch, tch, tu, te, ce, ci, **and** ti, **as in** church, kitchen, future, righteous, cello, Pacino, **and** Christian.

This lesson also introduces *contractions*, **which are words that have been combined and shortened and contain an apostrophe.**

I   REVIEW the |ch| sound made by **ch** and **tch**, as in **church** and **kitchen**. LEARN the |ch| sound made by **tu** and **te**, as in **future** and **righteous**.

II   LEARN the |ch| sound made by **ce**, **ci**, and **ti**, as in **cello**, **Pacino**, and **Christian**. The vowel sound is sometimes unaltered, as with the **e** in **cello**. In the words **Pacino** and **Christianity**, the **ci** and **ti** are separate syllables that say |chē|.

III   REVIEW the |ch| pronunciation of **ch**, **tch**, **tu**, **te**, **ce**, **ci**, and **ti**.

Contractions

IV - VI   **NEW CONCEPT.** Introduce contractions. *Contracting* is a literary technique for combining and then shortening two words, usually to make them easier to pronounce. An apostrophe (') is inserted in the word to indicate where one or more letters have been removed.

One common contraction is **isn't**. **Isn't** is the combining of the words **is + not**, followed by the removal of the letter **o** from the new word. An apostrophe is inserted to signify where the **o** was excised. When your student reads "**isn't**," have him say, *"**Isn't** means **is not**."* Continue this translation exercise through all of the words in the lists to ensure that the contraction pattern is understood.

When it is time to spell, ask your student to spell **isn't** and then recite the word. He should say, "**Isn't** means **is not**." Continue this through the lists. You might have your student use the contractions in sentences.

IV   LEARN   **n't**. It takes the place of **not**. The contraction **'ll** means **will**.

V   LEARN   **'ve** and **'d**. The contraction **'ve** stands for **have**. The contraction **'d** means **had** or **would**.

VI   LEARN   **'s** and **'re** and **'m**. The contraction **'s = is** or **has**; **'s = us**, as in **let's**; **'re = are**, as in **you're**; and **'m = am**, as in **I'm**.

Special observations about contractions:
- The word **have** ends in a silent **e**. (English words are not supposed to end in the letter **v**.)
- The first **t** in the word **mustn't** is silent.
- The contraction for **will not** is irregular. It is written **won't** and is pronounced |wōnt|.

Differentiating its, it's **and** your, you're

Please inform your student that **it's** is a contraction meaning **it is**. The presence of the apostrophe here does not indicate possession. The word **its** (no apostrophe) is a *possessive pronoun*. The sentence, *"The basketball team's mascot is a Bengal tiger"* could be expressed with the possessive pronoun equivalent, *"Its mascot is a tiger."*

The word **your** is a possessive pronoun. **You're** is a contraction meaning **you are**.

174

Lesson 83
|ch|

ch and **tch** = |ch|

I. church   orchard   chicken   impeach   cheese   cherish
teacher   chapel   spinach   chief   kitchen   catcher

tu and **te** = |ch|

future   lecture   culture   picture   capture   mature
statue   denture   stature   mutual   punctual   righteous

ce and **ci** = |ch|

II. cello   vermicelli   Pacino*   cappuccino

ti = |ch| and |chē|

Christian   Christianity* [*Chris•__ti__•an•i•ty*]

* **Ti** and **ci** are sometimes pronounced |chē| and constitute their own syllable, as in **Christianity** and **Pacino.**

III. gesture   mutual   actual   change   mixture
butcher   moisture   century   preacher   temperature
cherish   cultural   virtue   cello   intellectual
sculpture   immature   righteous   teaching   architectural

Contractions

n't = not

IV. isn't   hadn't   hasn't   haven't   didn't
don't   can't   aren't   needn't   wasn't
wouldn't   shouldn't   couldn't

'll = will

I'll   he'll   it'll   she'll   we'll
you'll   that'll   they'll

've = have

V. I've   we've   you've   they've   might've
would've   could've   should've

'd = had, would

I'd   we'd   he'd   she'd   it'd
you'd   they'd   who'd

's = is, has

VI. he's   she's   it's   there's   where's
what's   that's   who's   here's

's = us   **'re** = are   **'m** = am

let's   you're   they're   we're   I'm

Instructions for Lesson 84

> **Introduce the |zh| pronunciation for** ge, su, si, zu, **and** zi,
> **as in** garage, usual, vision, seizure, **and** glazier.

|zh|

I   REVIEW the voiced |zh| or |j| pronunciation of **ge**, as in **garage**. With your student, use a dictionary to look up all of the words on this list. The word **triage** has its syllable break between the **i** and the **a** and is pronounced |**trē • äzh′**|.

II   NEW PATTERN. Learn the voiced |zh| pronunciation of **su**, as in **usual**.

III   NEW PATTERN. Learn the voiced |zh| pronunciation of **si**, as in **vision**.

IV   NEW PATTERN. Learn the voiced |zh| pronunciation of **zu** and **zi**, as in **azure** and **glazier**, respectively.

Review: |zh| |z| |gz|

V & VI   REVIEW the voiced |zh| pronunciation of **ge, su, si, zu,** and **zi**, as in **garage, usual, vision, seizure,** and **glazier**, respectively.

        REVIEW the |z| and |gz| sounds spelled with the voiced sounds of **s, z,** and **x**, as in **his, zebra,** and **exactly**.

The word **aisle** is found in the list of homophones. This unusual word has three silent letters (**a, s,** and **e**) and is pronounced |**īl**|.

Differentiating there, their, they're **and** to, too, two

The list of challenge words for this lesson contains two extremely important sets of homophones: **there, their,** and **they're**; and **to, too,** and **two**. The members of these homophone sets are frequently mistakenly used, so we encourage you to spend time explaining their differences to your student. If he can keep clear in his mind the appropriate uses of these often misused words, he will be a star pupil!

there	=	location
their	=	possessive pronoun
they're	=	they are

to	=	location
too	=	also; more than enough; extremely
two	=	2

The differences between **its** and **it's** and **your** and **you're** were discussed in Lesson 83.

Lesson 84

|zh|

ge = |zh| and |j|

I. garage mirage triage deluge beige adage

su = |zh|

II. usual casual leisure measure pressure treasure

si = |zh|

III. vision Asia invasion decision erosion confusion

zu and **zi** = |zh|

IV. azure azures seizure seizures glazier Frazier

Review: |zh| |z| |gz|

V.			
unusual	measure	beige	pleasure
his	mirage	Xerox™	television
zebra	invasion	version	beeswax

VI.			
exactly	vision	confusion	choose
erosion	zoo	exalt	garage
casual	usually	seizures	Asia

Challenge Words: **xenophobic**
                                              [xe • no • pho • bic]

Homophones: alter   altar   there   their   they're
                    billed   build   to   too   two
                    mist   missed   isle   I'll   aisle

177

Instructions for Lesson 85

Introduce the gh spelling that is pronounced two ways:
|g| and |f|, as in ghetto and rough. Also, sometimes gh is silent, as in light.

This lesson introduces the au sound |ă|, as in laugh, and
the ou sound |ŏ|, as in ought and cough.

gh

I   NEW PATTERN. Introduce the voiced **gh** spelling pattern pronounced with a hard **g**, |g|, as in **ghetto**. Note that the word **Allegheny** in this list is a proper name, and the second **e** in **Allegheny** is pronounced |ā|.

II   REVIEW the **gh** pattern found in **light**. [Lesson 81]

         LEARN the **ou** spelling with the |ŏ| sound, as in **ought**.

III   LEARN the **gh** spelling pattern pronounced |f|, as in **rough**.

         REVIEW the **ou** spelling that makes a short-vowel **u** sound |ŭ|, as in **rough**. [Lesson 67]

         PRACTICE the **ou** spelling that makes a short-vowel **o** sound |ŏ|, as in **cough**.

         LEARN the **au** spelling that makes a short-vowel **a** sound |ă|, as in **laugh**.

Review: gh   ou   au

IV & V   REVIEW the **gh** spelling pattern pronounced |g| in **ghetto**. Also review the **gh** spelling pattern pronounced |f| in **tough**. Pay special attention to words in which the **gh** is silent (**flight** and **eighty**).

         REVIEW the **ou** spelling pronounced |ŏ|, as in **ought**.

         REVIEW the **au** spelling pronounced |ă|, as in **laugh**.

Since you are nearing the end of the program (only five lessons to go!), you should soon select a book that you and your student will read together. This is a very important part of this curriculum. You and your student will each need a copy. Select a book that is not too easy. You will take turns reading this selected book out loud after you complete the 90th lesson. [See pages 191 - 195]

Lesson 85
gh

gh = |g|

I. ghetto   gherkins   aghast   ghastly   Ghana

    afghan   spaghetti   sorghum   Allegheny   ghat

gh = silent

II. light   weight   daughter   slight   knight

    taught   highway   lightning   eight   bright

ou = |ŏ|

    ought   bought   thought   sought   wrought

gh = |f| ou = |ŭ|

III. rough   tough   enough   toughens   roughage

ou = |ŏ| **au = |ă|**

    cough   trough   laugh   laughter   laughing

Review: gh

IV. flight   highway   rougher   ghetto   knight

    eighty   tough   enough   light   caught

V. laugh   weight   daughter   afghan   bright

    eighteen   spaghetti   lightning   coughing   weigh

Challenge Words: **toughening**   **ghostwriter**   **Afghanistan**
                        [tough • en • ing]   [ghost • wri • ter]   [Af • ghan • i • stan]

Instructions for Lesson 86

> **Review the pronunciations for** ou: |ow|, |ŭ|, |ü|, |ū|, |ō|, |ōr|, |ŏ|, |u̇|, **and** |ər| **respective to** shout, rough, you, Houston, soul, four, cough, could, **and** journey.

The **ou** spelling pattern has the most pronunciations of any vowel combination. The student who correctly reads and spells all of the words in Lesson 86 will likely feel a great sense of accomplishment. All of these **ou** variants have been previously covered. To pronounce these words correctly the student will have to know the word meanings.

I   REVIEW the **ou** spelling with the diphthong pronunciation pattern |ow|, as in **shout**. [Lesson 68]

II   REVIEW the **ou** spelling with the |ŭ| or |ə| sound, as in **rough** and **famous**. [Lesson 67]

III   REVIEW the **ou** spelling with the |ü| and |ū| sound, as in **soup** and **Houston**, respectively. Words like **troupe** and **route** end with a silent **e**. [Lesson 70]

        Notice that **wound** and **route** can also be pronounced |ow|, as found above in Roman numeral I.

IV   REVIEW the **ou** spelling with the long-vowel **o** sound, |ō|, as in **soul** and **four**. [Lessons 41, 43]

        REVIEW the **ou** spelling with the short-vowel **o** sound |ŏ|, as in **cough**. The **gh** in these words makes either the |f| sound (**cough**) or is silent (**ought**). [Lessons 81 and 85]

V   REVIEW the **ou** spelling with the |u̇| sound, as in **could**. [Lesson 70]

        REVIEW the **our** spelling with the murmur diphthong sound |ər|, as in **journey**. [Lesson 69]

Review: ou

VI   REVIEW words containing **ou**.

Is **wound** being used as a noun, a verb, or an adjective? Context will determine which word is intended.

Route may be pronounced either |ü| or |ow|.

Your can be pronounced with the |ōr| or |ər| sound.

Lesson 86
ou

diphthong **ou** (pronounced |**ow**|)

I. shout	count	around	house
ground	flour	doubt	south
bout	bough	wound	route

ou (pronounced |ŭ| or |ə|)

II. rough	couple	joyous	country
famous	enough	generous	trouble
touch	precious	delicious	nervous

ou (pronounced |ü| or |ū|)

III. you	you'd	group	youth
soup	coupon	bayou	troupe
through	Houston	wound	route

ou (pronounced |ō|)   **our** (pronounced |ōr|)

IV. soul	boulder	though	source
four	mourns	bourn	gourmet

ou (pronounced |ŏ|)

cough	trough	bought	thought
ought	sought	wrought	fought

ou (pronounced |ů̇|)

V. could	would	should	boulevard

our (pronounced |ər|)

journey	nourish	courtesy	flourish
courage	tourney	journal	tournament

Review: ou

VI. numerous	court	ought	bough
wrought	fourteen	tourist	around
double	courtesy	mouth	curious
precious	outlook	shoulder	ounces
country	course	pronoun	tournament
various	although	young	southern
toughening	brought	yourself	south
Missouri	throughout	courage	though

Instructions for Lesson 87

> **Introduce** f, ff, ph, gh, **and** v, **all of which say** |f|,
> **as in** fifteen, office, phone, rough, **and** svelte.

There are several spellings for the **f** sound, **|f|**. These spellings are **f, ff, ph, gh**, and **v**. The letter **f** itself, however, has only one sound, **|f|**, with the exception of its use in the word **of**, in which case **f** makes a **|v|** sound.

|f|

I   **REVIEW** the **|f|** sound for the **f** and **ff** spelling patterns, as in **fifteen** and **office**. [Lessons C and 1]

II   **REVIEW** the **|f|** sound for the German-based **ph** spelling pattern, as in **phone** and **graph**. [Lesson 75]

III   **REVIEW** the **|f|** sound for the German-based **gh** spelling pattern, as in **rough** and **laugh**. [Lesson 85]

IV   **LEARN** the **|f|** sound for the **v** spelling pattern, as in **svelte**.

Review: |f|

V & VI   **REVIEW** the **|f|** sound made by **f, ff, ph, gh**, and **v**, as in **fifteen, office, phone, rough**, and **svelte**, respectively.

Be sure that your student understands the challenge words! Literacy is a skill that involves sound patterns (*phonics*) and spelling patterns (*orthography*). It also necessitates knowing the order of the alphabet letters (*alphabetization*) and is an occasion for developing handwriting skills (*chirography*). The correct or accepted pronunciation of words is called *orthoepy*.

All of the state names listed in this lesson have at least one slightly irregular syllable. On pages 255-265 are lists of terms and words, presented in the order in which they are introduced in these lessons. These lists include such entries as the days of the week, months of the year, number words, pronouns, map terms, states of the United States, and general science terms. These words may be useful when you devise practice and review exercises for your student.

> Three lessons from now, you will be awarding your student a certificate of completion. A master of this certificate is found on page 195. Now would be a good time to choose a nice paper on which to produce this or a certificate of your own making. Consider putting the certificate in a nice frame.

Lesson 87

|f|

f and **ff**

I.

| fifteen | alfalfa | myself | tariff | fluff |
| office | faith | belief | shelf | coffee |

ph

II.

| phone | asphalt | phonics | nephew | paragraph |
| graph | dolphins | orphan | alphabet | photograph |

gh

III.

| rough | tougher | cough | enough | troughs |
| laugh | roughly | laughing | toughest | coughing |

v

IV. svelte

Review: |f|

V.

fifteen	autograph	laughs	referee	roughrider
telephone	polygraph	coffee	laughable	alphabet
office	graphics	profit	roughage	xylophone
hemisphere	physical	coughing	geography	topographic

VI.

svelte	liftoff	elephant	phonics
orphan	phrase	enough	phone
Philadelphia	photograph	phonograph	cartography
Maryland	Pennsylvania	New Hampshire	California

Challenge Words:	**phonics**	**orthography**
	[phon • ics]	[or • thog • ra • phy]
chirography	**alphabetization**	**orthoepy**
[chi • rog • ra • phy]	[al • pha • bet • i • za • tion]	[or • tho • e • py]

Instructions for Lesson 88

Introduce words that are spelled the same but have different usages and meanings. Another name for these words is *homographs*.

If a homograph operates in a sentence as a noun, then the accent will be on the first syllable, as in con' • tract.

If a homograph functions in a sentence as a verb, then the accent will be on the second syllable, as in con • tract'.

I - V **NEW CONCEPT.** These homographs are words spelled identically but whose pronunciation depends on whether they are functioning in a sentence as a *noun* or a *verb*. A noun names a person, place, or thing. A verb indicates action or a state of being. Typically, the vowel in the unaccented syllable is pronounced |ə|.

▶ If the homograph functions as a *noun*, the accent is usually placed on the first syllable of the word.

▶ If the homograph is used as a *verb* or as part of a *prepositional phrase*, the accent is usually placed on the second syllable of the word.

Which part of speech (noun, verb, or adjective) a word functions as will dictate its pronunciation. If a student has developed the habit of comprehension, it will be easy for him to read these words in the context of a sentence.

Examples of Homographs

When your student has finished reading and spelling all of the words in this lesson, you might have him read the following sentences:

I 1. *The heat of the **desert** made us want to **desert** the caravan.*

2. *The **convert** returned home to **convert** his friends.*

II 3. *Sir Edwin feared the angry **rebel** would **rebel** against the king.*

4. *The loser of the **contest** will **contest** the outcome.*

III 5. *The difficult **subject** will **subject** the class to long hours of study.*

6. *The **produce** that we sell at the market will **produce** income for our family.*

7. *Kate's professional **conduct** enabled her to efficiently **conduct** the important meeting.*

IV 8. *The English sheep dog entered the room with the muddy **object** even though he knew that his master would **object**.*

9. *The **convict** testified to help **convict** his former co-worker in the embezzlement case.*

V 10. *The **contrast** of the bright yellow vase will **contrast** nicely with the gray walls of the room.*

11. *Drew's graduation **present** from his grandmother will be a sports car, which will **present** a dilemma for his parents.*

Lesson 88

Noun / Verb

[con´ • tract / con • tract´]

Noun Accent on the *first* syllable	**Verb** Accent on the *second* syllable (the first syllable is a schwa)	**Noun** Accent on the *first* syllable	**Verb** Accent on the *second* syllable (first syllable is a schwa or murmur diphthong)
I. des´ert	de sert´	con´ tract	con tract´
con´ vert	con vert´	per´ fume	per fume´
II. rebel	rebel	conflict	conflict
contest	contest	imprint	imprint
III. subject	subject	produce	produce
conduct	conduct	increase	increase
IV. object	object	record	record
convict	convict	insult	insult
V. contrast	contrast	converse	converse
present	present	attribute	attribute

Challenge Words: desert   desert   dessert

Instructions for Lesson 89

> **Cover irregular, unusual, and semi-phonetic spellings and pronunciations. Memorize these spellings. Use your dictionary.**

Irregular Spelling and Pronunciation Patterns

In searching for totally irregular or non-phonetic words, we have found none. This surprises some people, because they have been taught that English has lots of sight words that follow no pattern and just have to be memorized. However, every word has at least one phonetic characteristic. The task is to be on the lookout for recognizable patterns. Knowing and applying the basic patterns helps us to read and spell unusual words. Vowels seem to be the cause of most spelling and pronunciation difficulties.

In this lesson, we are going to look at several irregular but nonetheless partially phonetic words. Most contain what appears to be an unnecessary letter, such as the **u** in **fluoride** and the **e** in **give**. Each of the words in Roman numerals I, II, and III has at least one apparently unnecessary letter.

I Can you spot the seemingly extraneous vowel or vowels in these words?

II Here are 18 words that end in a silent **e** that would theoretically trigger the long-vowel sound of a preceding vowel but instead have the short-vowel or schwa sound. A silent **e** is appended to comply with the rule that English words will not end in the letter **v**.

III This list has several more words that end in **v** and silent **e**. Notice that **naïve** has two dots over the **i**. This French-based word is pronounced with two consecutive vowel sounds: |nī • ēv|. Each word has at least one silent letter or an extra consonant. For example, the **th** in **clothes** is silent; **broccoli** has an extra **c**; and the **t** in **croquet**, **bouquet**, and **sachet** is silent. The **é** in **soufflé** has a long-vowel **a** sound.

IV This list features words that have sound or spelling variations. All of these words should be part of your student's vocabulary. Pronounce the **ieu** in **milieu** either |ū| (as here in Roman numeral IV) or |ü| (as seen in Roman numeral V below).

V Even though the words **one** and **once** have already been introduced, we include them here because they are unusual. A few of the words are French-based (like **quiche**), and some are treated as exceptions because they are easier to pronounce contrary to pattern. (Try to say **pretzel** with a true **z** sound, |tz|!) A few of the words here have an **i** that is pronounced |y|. This is a role reversal, as usually a **y** mimics the **i** sound, not the other way around. Note that the **j** in **hallelujah** is pronounced |y| and that the **di** in **cordial** and **soldier** is pronounced with the |j| sound.

VI Here are just a few additional foreign-influenced or irregularly handled words to add to your student's vocabulary. Some words have previously been discussed or introduced, some have not.

Lesson 89
Unusual Spellings and Pronunciations

Extra vowel

I.

friends	Cairo	plaid	people	fluoride	are
been	were	subpoena	cayenne	gasoline	Europe

Short-vowel or schwa sound and a silent e

II.

minute	determine	opposite	doctrine	requisite	deliberate

Words that end with **v** and silent **e**

give	have	solve	active	motive	native
massive	attentive	adjective	positive	detective	submissive

More words that end with **v** and silent **e**

III.

twelve	leave	serve	observe	naïve	live

Silent or extra consonants and French influenced words

clothes	broccoli	croquet	bouquet	sachet	soufflé

A part of each of the following words has a variant vowel or consonant.

ay, ai, and **a** = |ĕ| **ee** = |ā|

IV.

says	said	again	many	matinee	fiancée

o, e, ai, and **u** = |ĭ|

women	pretty	again	busy	busied	business

ai = |ə| **en** = |ŏn|

captain	certain	mountain	encore	envoy	entourage

ew, au, and **eau** = |ō|

sew	taupe	bureau	plateau	Beau	tableau

eau, iew, and **ieu** = |ū|

beauty	beauties	beautiful	view	review	milieu

o = |wə| or |w| **ieu** = |ü|

V.

one	once	choir	memoir	lieutenant	milieu

qu = |k| **z** = |s|

mosquito	antique	quiche	pretzel	quartz	Ritz

i = |y| **j** = |y| **di** = |j|

million	onion	opinion	hallelujah	cordial	soldiers

Foreign-influenced words (irregular patterns):

VI.

j = |ē|	**ll** = |y|	**g** = *silent* **n** = |ny|	**j** = |h|	**ça** = |s|	**er** = |är| **ea** = |ə|
fjord	tortilla	vignette	jalapeño	façade	sergeant

HOMOPHONES: lock   loch   lough

187

Instructions for Lesson 90

Read and spell two-, three-, four-, five-, and six-syllable words.

This 90th lesson has 70 multiple-syllable words. The grand theme is the same: Read and spell each word FROM LEFT TO RIGHT, syllable to syllable, to the end of the word. If a spelling or pronunciation pattern causes your student to hesitate, review that particular pattern by returning to the lesson in which it was introduced. Usually, just a reminder about the pattern is enough. The schwa appears in many of these words, as it generally is found in words consisting of two or more syllables.

I	**REVIEW** words with two syllables.
II & III	**REVIEW** words with three syllables.
IV	**PRACTICE** words with four syllables.
V	**PRACTICE** words with five or six syllables.

A Word About the Challenge Words

Today's challenge words have eight and twelve syllables, respectively. The second word used to be the longest word in the dictionary. Be sure your student discovers the meaning of **sesquipedalianism**. It means "love of long words."

Congratulations!

You have just taught the last formal lesson in *Reading and Spelling Pure & Simple*! We are delighted that you and your student took this literacy journey with us. We hope you enjoyed the lessons and that your student will put to use all that he has learned. Now it's time to show your student a copy of the book you will be reading together.

Turn the page and let's begin!

Lesson 90
Multiple-Syllable Words

two-syllable words

I.

seizure	gracious	helix	oblique
excerpt	Wednesday	litmus	thorough
unctuous	wrenches	anchored	modem

three-syllable words

II.

covenant	synchronize	usury	lithograph
limerick	tectonics	division	modulate
neighborly	translucent	audience	arabesque

three-syllable words

III.

exchequer	emphasize	loneliness	tournament
dangerous	conclusion	decorum	studious
cinema	eclectic	obfuscate	epigraph

four-syllable words

IV.

orthopedics	pterodactyl	orthography	concentration
effervescent	oblivious	decrescendo	cryogenics
participle	proximity	delineate	micromanage
zoology	orthoepy	audacity	adventurous

five- or six-syllable words

V.

anticipation	skeuomorphism	occupational	inscrutability
administrator	ceremonious	creativity	deteriorate
inspirational	hematology	genetically	dialectical
psychologically	generalization	alphabetically	encyclopedia

Challenge Words: (8 syllables)	sesquipedalianism [ses • qui • pe • da • li • an • is • m]
(12 syllables)	antidisestablishmentarianism [an • ti • dis • es • tab • lish • men • tar • i • an • is • m]

Now that the Lessons Are Complete, What's Next?

Now that the Lessons Are Complete, What's Next?

First, present a certificate of completion to your student. You may use the certificate of completion found at the end of Unit 4 [page 195] or one of your own design. Make the presentation special—a big deal—because it is!

Select an inspiring, interesting, or encouraging book to read together. In making your selection, consider biographies or autobiographies about people who overcame obstacles and adversity. Exposing your student to wholesome ideas and new possibilities for his life can provide a wonderful beginning for a newly minted reader.

One of my personal favorites is a book entitled *Gifted Hands*. It is by the famous neurosurgeon, Dr. Benjamin Carson. Ben Carson grew up in a single-parent home on the edge of poverty. He faced flunking out in the fifth grade. Today, this talented black surgeon travels the world doing complex surgeries and saving lives. *Gifted Hands* is an amazing, gripping story, and my students absolutely love reading it. This book has many polysyllabic words, which students enjoy discovering they can read.

Begin reading the book out loud. You and your student may take turns reading. Read with expression! Use proper pauses and inflections. Don't read too fast; savor the material. You are providing your student with an awareness and enjoyment of his newly developed skills. During the reading, stop from time to time to ask questions and discuss the story. (For more ideas on how to assist your student in reading, see page xx.)

After just a few sessions, your student will begin to realize that he knows the meaning of a great many words (we hope all) and understands what he is reading. Prior to these lessons, his oral vocabulary was probably more extensive than his reading vocabulary. Reading a good book together allows for vocabulary building and confirms his new abilities. You don't necessarily have to finish reading the book together.

Prior to doing these lessons, your student might have been shy about answering questions in class. He still may think he can't handle questions. This is not a reading problem but a confidence problem. Before long, as he gains confidence, he will start taking the risk. He can read now, plus he knows enough about word patterns that he can take an educated guess at unfamiliar words, all the while considering the story's context. (This is the proper use of context.)

I remember one seventh-grade student who read a passage that had the words **laborious, tedious, painstaking, preparation, determination,** and **appropriate.** After discussing the paragraph, I asked him if he was aware of the big words he had just read. He looked puzzled and said no. I went back through the paragraph and showed him these words. He was genuinely surprised. Not only did he breeze through the paragraph, but he understood every word of it. All of which brings me to my point: **Real reading is effortless reading.** You will know that your student has become an accomplished reader when he reads without thinking about how to read.
[See Lesson 71]

A new math student will often begin his math work by reciting out loud (*"Two plus two is four... Four plus four is eight"*). Later, he will whisper addition facts to himself, and eventually he will handle his computations silently. The same is true for reading. Neurological research confirms that much of our learning starts externally and then trends internally. Your student will naturally progress to skilled silent reading.

Note: Just because a student has learned to read, it doesn't mean he will immediately excel in school. Keep in mind that your student probably has lots of catching up to do in school. For years, he lived in a reading fog. He might have large gaps in math, science, and other subjects because of it. Keep encouraging him to work hard and persevere. Being able to read opens up pathways of learning that were not available to him before. This student, if he continues his studies, might even end up being the best reader and speller in his class (we have seen this happen time and time again).

Poor work habits can impede progress. Some students will apply themselves only a few days out of the week. Stress the importance of being consistent and striving for excellence in all endeavors every day.

Another obstacle for some students to overcome is the idea that failure is final. They need to realize that everyone encounters difficulties and has roadblocks in life, and success comes to those who persevere. Don't quit! Never quit! *"Get up and go again!"* is the message you, as the teacher, need to emphasize. Perseverance is a strong virtue. Don't quit! The only ones who fail are those who accept failure.

The certificate of completion provided on the next page will mean a lot to your student. He has achieved something significant! Present this certificate with much fanfare.

Name of Student

Successfully Completed _____ Lessons

in

READING AND SPELLING

PURE & SIMPLE

Phonics-based Lessons for Elementary, Teen, and Adult Students

Created by Deede Hinckley Cauley

Program Director/Instructor

Completion Date

Additional Support and Information

Additional Support and Information

Ideas for the Classroom

Basic Terms

Index of Letters and Sounds

Pronunciation Guide

When Is This Word Introduced? Words Sorted According to Pattern or Category

    Common Words

    United States of America (The 50 States)

    Days of the Week

    Months of the Year

    Pronouns

    Colors

    Numbers

    Map and Direction Words

    Assorted Science Terms: Space, Trees, Plants, Fruits & Vegetables, Animals, Reptiles, Insects, Sea Creatures, Earth, and Man

Acknowledgments

Documentation

    Progress Monitoring Table (Includes Sample Table)

    Word Tabulator for Monitoring Table

    Completion Charts

        Pre-Unit Completion Chart

        Simple Completion Chart for All 90 Lessons (1 Page)

        Detailed Completion Chart (5 Pages)

Ideas for the Classroom

These lessons were developed originally for elementary-age students. The curriculum works very well for them, and it helps that they tend to be enthusiastic learners. It is important to get students reading as early as possible. Most students can and should be reading well before the end of first grade. Any reading difficulties should be resolved long before ninth grade, as this is when permanent school records start being kept. A student who is overcoming a reading deficit needs time to adjust his study habits and begin to fill in the knowledge and skill gaps that his inability to read may have caused in other disciplines (math, science, etc.). We want him to begin his high school years with everything in place for success.

Reading and Spelling Pure & Simple is equally valuable for teaching reading to teens, adults, and even ESL students. These older students usually show the most dramatic results. This curriculum is ideal for one-on-one instruction but is suitable also for small group lessons. Instructors who have used the lessons with more than one student at a time offer the following teaching tips.

The most effective use of these lessons, whether in a classroom or other setting, is when an adult works one-on-one with a student at least once a day for a minimum of twenty minutes.[1]   Naturally, a 1:1 student/teacher ratio is ideal. Group work is quite feasible, though. In one third-grade class, four students worked together through these lessons and improved their Scholastic Reading Inventory (SRI) reading scores two and three grade levels in only a few weeks. A student in Oklahoma improved from 1.6 (first grade, sixth month) to 3.2 (third grade, second month) in her SRI scores after working daily with a classroom aide for less than a month. We have seen this kind of dramatic improvement repeatedly, with consistent, daily, one-on-one or low-ratio student/adult instruction. If you do work with several students at a time, be sure that each one is getting adequate attention. Groupthink (relying on other students' answers) is not acceptable. Each pupil should be pronouncing (reading) and spelling (on paper) with immediate corrections provided.

Enlist aides and volunteers to teach the lessons.   Many concerned citizens, including the parents and grandparents of students, are willing to volunteer their time to make a difference in school classrooms and in the lives of older teens and adults. Volunteers can be found in parent/teacher organizations, churches, libraries, social clubs, community centers, and senior citizens' groups. Sometimes it is possible to get help from high school or college students who want to earn community leadership credit.

---

[1] One twelve-year-old, fifth-grade student (he had been retained once) worked on our lessons with an adult instructor for about thirty minutes a day for three weeks. Prior to using our lessons, he had scored a zero (0) on the Scholastic Reading Inventory test. After he completed Lesson 19, his SRI score jumped to a 364.5 (second grade). After completing Lesson 40, he scored 804 (sixth grade) on his next SRI test. On May 3 he scored 921 and was considered to be on grade level. When he took the Texas Assessment of Knowledge and Skills test (TAKS), he comfortably passed both math and reading (he had not been successful with either section of the TAKS before).

Our lessons can be administered daily with little prep time. Once a completion (progress) chart has been set up for the student and the person who will teach the lesson has read and understands the instructions, there is little administrative care, time, or attention needed from the lead classroom teacher. The lessons can be done in a corner of a classroom or in a school hallway, library nook, cafeteria, or wherever quiet space can be found. A quick glance at the completion chart tells the instructor which lesson is next. After that, it's just a matter of following the instructions for each lesson and marking the completion chart. Individual students can even work with different instructors from day to day and be very successful.

"Drill" for automaticity.   Begin each group session by drilling one student on the words next to a chosen Roman numeral. Rotate to the next student. If the group will be reading materials other than what is presented in these lessons, for best results, the teacher should always begin with drills. After a lesson has been read, be sure to administer the spelling test.

Assign homework.   Homework can be assigned on a schedule set by the teacher. Encourage your students to read and spell through the assigned words with their parents, grandparents, an older sibling, etc. This assignment might be sent home on Friday with a follow-up spelling test being given on Monday.

Use peer tutors in the classroom.   Class members who make a 100 on their spelling tests might serve as peer tutors. Have the peer tutor call out spelling words for other students to write on paper. Peer tutoring reinforces the tutor's own proficiency, and the struggling student gets to improve with the additional practice. One Caution: Administering the lessons solely through peer tutors, even daily, does not give the strongest results. Peer tutors younger than middle-school age often settle for less than mastery. Since each lesson builds upon the previous lessons, mastery is necessary.

Augment weekly spelling lists.   Most elementary classroom teachers give a weekly spelling test, usually featuring words from that week's reading curriculum or stories. Some spelling lists come from purchased spelling books or from lists of words determined by the school district. It is best if the words on the lists are organized along the lines of syllable patterns. A classroom teacher can use the word lists in this book to illustrate syllable and word patterns. For example, if the weekly spelling list (usually twenty words) has several words with a silent **k**, the teacher can further illustrate the silent **k** pattern by using the word list from Lesson 81, Roman numeral IV. This particular list features **knot**, **knit**, **knob**, **knock**, **knees**, **know**, **knife**, and **knight**.

Illustrate patterns with "word pictures."   There is something very powerful about seeing a list of words following the same pattern. It's like looking at a "word picture," which will often help students recognize the pattern when they see it again. Check the Index of Letters and Sounds to locate specific patterns. [See pages 215 - 223]

Start novice readers off right.   Beginning students must know the alphabet letters IN ORDER. Teaching "The Alphabet Song" is the most popular and effective way to teach the sequence of the letters (see, also, next instruction below).

It is CRITICAL, absolutely critical, that beginning students be told that we always read letters (and words) FROM LEFT TO RIGHT. Otherwise, the "soup" of letters that the students see cannot be formed into true, meaningful words. Starting on the first day of reading instruction, students must be taught that words are sounded out from left to right.

Typically, a kindergarten teacher introduces one alphabet letter a week. Creative ways are employed to teach each letter. Students practice printing the letter, use pictures to illustrate something about the letter, make collages, and so forth. A careful selecting of the order in which alphabet letters are introduced makes it possible to promote earlier-than-normal letter and sound recognition and speeds up the learning process. For example, if the first four letters that the teacher introduces are short vowel **a** and the consonants **m**, **t**, and **b**, students can immediately read **am**, **at**, **mat**, **tat**, and **bat**. If the next letters introduced are **l**, **n**, and **p**, students also can read **Al**, **an**, **lab**, **lap**, **nap**, **man**, **tan**, **pal**, **pan**, **pat**, **map**, and **tap**. As each alphabet letter is introduced, the universe of words increases greatly. Using forethought and strategy in selecting and introducing letters (as we have in our lessons) allows students' reading and spelling vocabularies to blossom quickly. Furthermore, starting new readers with a true phonics curriculum like this one also means that students will not need to spend a full week learning each alphabet letter, as they will be learning letters in meaningful, non-abstract words from Day One. By stressing the need to pay attention to every letter, in left-to-right order, we achieve continuous use and practice for each letter.

Practice out loud.   Often, I've seen a kindergarten teacher, as part of her daily routine, point to a list of words and numbers on her wall and recite these with her students. Typically, these word lists are

The days of the week:	*"Sunday, Monday, Tuesday, Wednesday ..."*
The months of the year:	*"January, February, March, April ..."*
The numbers from one to twenty:	*"One, two, three, four, five, six, seven ..."*
The numbers from 1 to 100 [by one's]:	*"1, 2, 3, 4, 5, 6, 7, 8, 9, 10, 11, 12 ..."*
The numbers from 5 to 100 [by five's]:	*"5, 10, 15, 20, 25, 30, 35, 40, 45 ..."*
The numbers from 10 to 100 [by ten's]:	*"10, 20, 30, 40, 50, 60, 70, 80 ..."*

In the same fashion, the teacher can give opportunities to learn the sounds of individual letters and to practice the words out loud. For Lesson A [featuring letters **a**, **m**, **t** and **b**], a teacher can drill with "**am**, **at**, **mat**, **tab**, **tat**, **bat** . . . ." Of course, the goal is for students to truly *read* through the lists, not just recite words from memory. The teacher can discuss or question the class about the meaning of the words being learned. She can place the words into sentences. This exercise can be used with every lesson.

Kindergarteners will be best served if their teacher introduces letters and their basic sounds exactly in the order we present them here. Only after the applicable letter sounds have been learned will the teacher present students with words that have those sounds. Start each lesson with a reminder that words are read and spelled (always!) from left to right. We require that you use a pencil to focus attention on the left side of each word. Again, we want real reading, not guesswork or word memorization.

Sentence rules and structure may be discussed at opportune times during the lessons. When students are taught, from the very beginning, to read and spell from left to right, many potential learning problems are avoided. The orderly introduction of words and patterns provides an excellent opportunity for additional instruction, such as mentioning sentence rules and structure. Early on, students will be taught the letters that comprise the name **Sam** (a proper noun) and the word **sat** (a verb, a word showing action). It is possible to make a complete sentence using these two words: *"Sam sat."* In addition to having a sentence like *"Sam sat,"* it is also possible to have the query, *"Sam sat?"* The teacher can explain to her students that every sentence must have at least one *subject*, in this case **Sam**, and at least one *verb*, in this case **sat**. A sentence must express a complete thought. Also, the teacher may want to mention that a sentence always begins with a capital letter (**S** in **Sam**) and that it ends with some kind of punctuation (a period, question mark, or other terminal punctuation mark). Essentially, the teacher can instruct her students in sentence structure along the way.

Consider using this curriculum for reading intervention. Education nomenclature changes from year to year, but the need for intervention methods and materials is constant. These 90 lessons will be helpful for Response to Intervention (RTI) instruction, tiers 1, 2, and 3.

Suggested Enrichment Activities

After your students complete a lesson, provide them with enrichment activities to reinforce the basic skills. Here are some suggestions.

1. Read aloud the definition of a word from a lesson. Ask your students to say which word it is. This game playing can also be done with incomplete sentences ("fill in the blank") or with questions. The answers can be chosen by the students, if not from the lesson list, then from selected words on an overhead, blackboard, or handout sheet or from word choices read aloud by the teacher. Have your students spell their answers on paper. The teacher might say:

> *"This is a primary color. Santa is dressed from head to ankles in this color."* (**red**)
>
> *"When tired, you might _____ on a chair to rest."* (**sit**)
>
> *"What do we call the shelf found at the bottom of a window?"* (a **sill**)

2. Provide your students with a list of nouns and a list of verbs from which to form sentences. Give points for the capitalizing of the first word in a sentence and any proper nouns. Give points for having each sentence end with an appropriate punctuation mark (a period, exclamation, or question mark). Give points for having proper sentence structure and word order (syntax). Later in this curriculum, students will have learned other parts of speech—prepositions, adjectives, conjunctions, pronouns, and adverbs—any of which they can incorporate into their sentences. Remember, these are not words to be memorized. These are words that are mastered in accordance with learned structures.

NOUNS:	VERBS:	POSSIBLE SENTENCES MADE FROM THESE WORDS:	
Sam	sat	Sam sat.	Will Bill nap?
Jim	can run	Jill can run.	Did Jim sit?
Bill	will nap	Can Jim run?	Will Jill run?
Jill	did sit	Bill will nap.	Sam will run.
	can sit	Sam can sit.	Run, Bill, run!

3. Ask students to write a poem or a few lines that rhyme, using words from the lessons.

4. Instruct students to use a dictionary to identify whether words are **nouns**, **verbs**, **pronouns**, **prepositions**, **conjunctions**, **adjectives**, or **adverbs**. Then have your student use these words to form sentences, paragraphs, or even whole stories.

5. Teach your students how to diagram a sentence. This is a phenomenal skill for them to acquire. Focus on how the parts of speech function, on the need for subject/verb agreement, and on being consistent with verb tenses.

6. Consider the orderly introduction of other disciplines when using these lessons. Consider, for example, geography and map work. One exercise might be to obtain a generic map of the United States of America with states outlined, but no state names included. After your students complete Lesson 89 (by which time they will have learned all the pronunciation patterns for the 50 states of the United States), have them label each state. Next have them insert the name of the capital city and major cities in the states. Credit would be given for proper location and correct spelling. One year, when I was teaching high school American History, I spent about ten minutes at the beginning of each class testing my students using the above activity. Those who achieved a 100 had a few minutes of free time or they could use that time to tutor students who had not yet obtained a perfect score. It took only those few minutes for a little more than a week for all the students to obtain an A. It helped us start the year with a working knowledge of the United States and provided an opportunity for students to realize the importance of studying and reviewing for success.

A listing of map and directional terms, and when in our lessons they are introduced, can be found on pages 259 and 262. For other subjects (number words or science terms), see pages 255-265.

Basic Terms

Adjective   An *adjective* is a word that changes (modifies) or describes a noun. *"A **big**, **fluffy** cat and a **small**, **friendly** dog can be fun to own."* In this sentence, **big**, **fluffy**, **small**, and **friendly** are adjectives, and **cat** and **dog** are nouns. (See also ***noun*** and ***verb***.)

Adverb   An *adverb* is a word that changes or modifies a verb, adverb, or adjective. Words that end with the suffix **ly** are usually adverbs. *"Juneau ran **quickly** and **effortlessly** to the corner."* Notice the **ly** endings in **quickly** and **effortlessly**; they provide a clue that these words are adverbs. (They are, in a manner of speaking, the vapor trail of an adverb.) The words **quickly** and **effortlessly** describe the verb **ran**. *"How did Juneau run? She ran quickly and effortlessly."*

Alphabetical   Letters that are placed in the order of the alphabet are *alphabetically* listed. The alphabet, in order, is **a b c d e f g**, **h i j k l m n o p**, **q r s**, **t u v**, **w x**, **y** and **z**. Students must learn the alphabet in order. "The Alphabet Song" is suited for this purpose. All through life, your student is going to need to look up names in a telephone book, words in a dictionary, and streets on a map index. He simply must know all 26 letters in their alphabetical order. Five of the letters in the alphabet are vowels: **a, e, i, o, u**. The rest of the letters in the alphabet function as consonants (**b, c, d, f, g, h, j, k, l, m, n, p, q, r, s, t, v, w, x, y, z**). Occasionally, the consonants **y** and **w** act as if they are vowels.

Breve   The *breve* (pronounced |**brēv**|) is a curved line symbol (looks like a smile) that is placed above a vowel to indicate that the vowel says its short sound. In dictionaries, short vowel sounds are indicated with the breve as follows: **ă, ĕ, ĭ, ŏ**, and **ŭ**. The breve instructs us how to pronounce such words as **săt, rĕd, bĭd, ŏdd**, and **sŭn**.

Chirography   *Chirography* refers to handwriting or penmanship.

Closed syllable   A *closed syllable* is one that ends with at least one consonant.

Compound word   A *compound word* consists of two or more words that could stand alone but that are combined to form a new word. Combining the two individual words **in** and **let**, for example, results in the compound word **inlet**.

Continuous   The sounds of some letters or pronunciation patterns are considered *continuous*. That means that as long as someone has breath and time, he can continue making the sound of the letter. All of the vowel sounds are continuous. Consider the vowel **a**. You can continue saying **a** in any of its variations—(|**ă**|, |**ā**|, |**ä**|)—as long as you have breath and time. A few consonants and consonant patterns are continuous, also. For example, the **sh** (|**sh**|) pattern in **push** can be expressed until one runs out of breath. These continuous letters are pronounced unbroken, without interruption. (See, also, ***noncontinuous***.)

Contractions   A *contraction* is the combination of two words subsequently shortened by the omission of one or more letters. An apostrophe is inserted where the letter or letters were omitted. Common examples are **isn't** (**is not**) and **don't** (**do not**). [There are a few irregular contractions, such as **won't** (**will not**).] Reference: Lesson 83

Diacritical marks   The breve (˘) and the macron (¯) are both examples of *diacritical marks.* Diacritical marks tell us how to pronounce a word, accent a syllable, or separate a word. Some common diacritical marks, in addition to the breve and macron, are the accent ('), which indicates that a syllable should be stressed, and the centered dot (•), which denotes a syllable break.

Digraph   A *digraph* consists of two letters, the pronunciation of which changes when they are paired. They then represent one sound. This is illustrated by **s** and **h**, which, when paired as **sh**, are pronounced |sh|, as in **ship**. The independent, individual sounds are no longer pristinely preserved by the pairing. Among the consonant digraphs are **ch**, **sh**, and **wh**. The digraph **th** in **then** is voiced (involves vibration of the speaker's vocal cords) but is not voiced in **path**. Digraphs always inhabit the same syllable (examples: **wish • ful** and **path • way**). [Do not be fooled by words like **up • hill** and **pot • hole**. These words do not have the digraphs **ph** or **th**.] There are many vowel digraphs, including, but not limited to, **oo**, **ee**, **ea**, **ai**, **ew**, **au**, **aw**, **oa**, **oe**, **ie**, and **ou**. (See, also, ***trigraph.***)

Diphthong   A *diphthong* consists of two vowels representing one sound (*di* means two). These paired vowels appear in the same syllable. Some teachers refer to these as *gliding sounds.* Examples of diphthongs are **oi**, **oy**, **ou**, and **ow**, as in **boil**, **boy**, **out**, and **cow**.

Equivalent letters   The consonants **b** and **p** are considered *equivalent letters* because the manner in which they are pronounced, considering the position of the speaker's tongue, mouth, and lips, is very similar, if not the same. However, whereas the letter **b** is voiced, the letter **p** is not. Both **b** and **p** are pronounced with the speaker's lips lightly together. The speaker releases sound when his lips open. With **b**, before the sound is released, there is a brief blockage of air as vibration builds up in the vocal cords, lips, and nose. The letter **p**, on the other hand, is expressed by the releasing of a small puff of air, and there is no vibration of the vocal cords or lips. (Again, *voiced* means that a letter is pronounced with vocal cord vibration, and *voiceless* means a letter is pronounced without vibration.) There are at least ten pairs of equivalent letters in the English language. Knowing about the equivalency of some letters may help you understand the sound confusion that some students have with certain letters.

Equivalent Letters

Voiced (with vocal cord vibration)				Voiceless (without vocal cord vibration)		
b	|b|	as in **bat**	is equivalent to	**p**	|p|	as in **pat**
d	|d|	as in **dad**	is equivalent to	**t**	|t|	as in **tat**
g	|g|	as in **gap**	is equivalent to	**k**	|k|	as in **kit**
x	|gz|	as in **exam**	is equivalent to	**x**	|ks|	as in **box**
z	|z|	as in **zip**	is equivalent to	**s**	|s|	as in **sip**
s	|z|	as in **his**	is equivalent to	**s**	|s|	as in **sis**
v	|v|	as in **vet**	is equivalent to	**f**	|f|	as in **fit**
j	|j|	as in **jam**	is equivalent to	**ch**	|ch|	as in **chum**
g	|j|	as in **gel**	is equivalent to	**ch**	|ch|	as in **chill**
th	|th|	as in **then**	is equivalent to	**th**	|th|	as in **thin**

Homographs *Homographs* are words that are spelled exactly the same but have different meanings. [Here's how to remember what a homograph is: *Homo* means *same*, and *graph* means *written*; therefore, *written the same*.] The context of a sentence or paragraph makes these words easy to read. The word **story** is a homograph. There is a **story** that is a tale to be told, for example, and there is a **story** that is a floor in a building. For more information see Lesson 88.

Homonyms *Homonyms* are words that are spelled and pronounced exactly the same but have different meanings. [Here's how to remember what a homonym is: *Homo* means *same*, and *nym* means *name*; therefore, *same name*.] The context of a sentence or paragraph makes these words easy to read. The word **bat** is a homonym. There is a **bat** that is a piece of baseball equipment, for example, and there is a **bat** that is a flying mammal. Reference: Lessons 1, 77, and 82

Homophones *Homophones* are words that sound the same but are spelled differently and mean different things. [*Homo* means *same*, and *phone* means *sound*; therefore, *same sound*.] **Road** sounds like **rode**, yet both words mean something different. *"Cody and Cory* **rode** *down the bumpy dirt* **road***."* *"The Queen of Hearts began her* **reign** *during a* **rain** *storm. The lightning strikes caused her royal guards to have to* **rein** *in their skittish horses."* Keep a dictionary handy for learning about these words. Reference: Lessons 37, 38, 42, 74, 75, 76, 77, 79, 81, 82, 84, and 89

Irregular words Even words considered to be irregular follow some recognized pattern for spelling or pronunciation for at least some part of the word. Consider the word **cousin**. The irregular part is the **ou**. In a rare departure from the usual pattern, the first vowel **o** is silent, and the second vowel, **u**, is pronounced with its short-vowel sound, |ŭ|. All of the other letters in the word **cousin** are pronounced and spelled in line with a regular pattern. Now let's look at the word **said**. The **s** and the **d** are pronounced the usual way (|s| and |d|). Only the vowels **ai** in the word **said** are irregular. In this instance they are pronounced |ĕ|. If there is an English word lacking at least a partial regular or recognized pronunciation or spelling pattern, we have not found it.

Long vowels A *long vowel* is a vowel that *says its own name.* **A** says |ā|, **e** says |ē|, **i** says |ī|; **o** says |ō|; and **u** says |ū|. For a fuller description of long vowels, see Unit 2, including the introductory pages (pages 75 – 103), and Unit 3 (specifically Lessons 60 and 61). **Aim, bacon, free, eager, bike, boat, bowl,** and **use** are all examples of long-vowel words.

Macron The *macron* is a horizontal line (‾) that is placed above a vowel to tell the reader that the vowel is a long vowel: ā, ē, ī, ō, ū. The word macron can be pronounced correctly either |mā′ • krŏn| or |măk′ • rŏn|. Reference: Lesson 67

Murmur diphthongs *Murmur diphthongs* are letter pairs or trios that say |ər|. The spellings are variant, however, and include **er, ir, ar, or, wor, ur, yr, ear,** and **our.** It's easy to remember how a murmur diphthong is pronounced. Remember this hint: The word itself—murmur—has the |ər| sound in both of its syllables |mər • mər|. Some words featuring murmur diphthongs are **her, first, polar, flavor, word, turn, syrup, learn,** and **journey.** Reference: Lesson 69

Noncontinuous   Some alphabet letters and patterns have a definite duration or stopping point. They are thus referred to as being *noncontinuous*. For example, the sound of **p** does not continue indefinitely. Notice that |p| stops the expression of **o** in the word **top**. The letter **p** is a noncontinuous sound and interrupts the flow of a preceding sound. These abrupt sounds are also referred to as quick, stop, or clipped sounds. (See ***continuous***.)

Noun   A *noun* is a person, place, or thing. Note that we capitalize proper names of people (Jenifer, President Lincoln, Mr. Magoo) and places (Eiffel Tower, Scotland, Santa Fe, Reed College, Woodland Park Zoo).

Open syllable   An *open syllable* is one that ends with a vowel.

Orthoepy   *Orthoepy* is the correct or accepted pronunciation of words. Reference: Lesson 87

Orthography   *Orthography* refers to spelling patterns. Reference: Lesson 87

Phonics   *Phonics* involves the sounds of letters. Reference: Lesson 87

Plural   If a word is *plural*, it means there is more than one of what the word represents. Most words are pluralized by adding **s**, others by adding **es**. There are only a few words in English that are pluralized by changing more than just the suffix (e.g., **mouse** → **mice**). Reference: Lessons 14, 15, 19, 20, 21, 30, 57, 59, and 60

Polysyllabic   Having more than one syllable. See ***syllable***.

Prefix   A *prefix* consists of a syllable or syllables attached to the front end of a word to qualify (further describe) its meaning. There are a great many prefixes, among them **pre**, **pro**, **ante**, **anti**, **un**, and **multi**. Reference: Lesson 64

Pronoun   A *pronoun* is a word that replaces a noun. The basic pronouns are **I**, **he**, **she**, **it**, **we**, **you** (singular or plural), and **they**.

Punctuation mark   *Punctuation marks* are like traffic signals that tell the reader what to do. A period (**.**) tells the reader to stop. A comma (**,**) tells the reader to pause. A semicolon (**;**) tells the reader to pause significantly and then finish reading the rest of the sentence. An exclamation point (**!**) tells the reader to express surprise, excitement, or emphasis. A question mark (**?**) prompts the reader to ask or inquire. A colon (**:**) signals that a list or statement meant to illustrate a point is forthcoming. Writers communicate through words *and* punctuation.

Quadrigraph   A *quadrigraph* consists of four letters pronounced as one sound; furthermore, these four letters occupy the same syllable. Some people claim that English does not have true quadrigraphs, also known as tetragraphs. However, the case for tetragraphs can be made if one counts the silent letters **gh** in **thought**, **straight**, **taught**, and **weight**. (See, also, ***digraph***, ***trigraph***.)

Schwa   The *schwa* is a sound that is pronounced with a shortened short-vowel **u** sound, |ŭ|. It is denoted in dictionaries as an upside-down **e**, |ə|. Most polysyllabic words include at least one schwa syllable. Reference: Lessons 30, 65, and 66

Why the schwa? Sometimes we speak too fast to pronounce syllables accurately, or we have a lazy tongue. Whatever the reason, we fail to clearly and distinctly pronounce some vowels. The arbiters of the English language have responded to this tendency by giving us the schwa. Most dictionaries use the upside-down e symbol |ə| to indicate a schwa. The schwa is really quite common and follows a very predictable pattern. It occurs in unaccented syllables, and most polysyllabic words include at least one schwa syllable. Reference: Lessons 65 and 66

The schwa sound can be produced by or with any vowel. It will occasionally be made with the letter **y** (as in **Maryland**) or with such combinations as **ai** or **ou** (found in **certain** and **famous**, respectively). Reference: Lessons 67 and 85

Sentence   A *sentence* is a grouping of words that expresses a complete thought. A sentence always must have at least one subject and at least one verb. The subject of a sentence is a noun (a person, place, or thing) or a pronoun (I, he, she, it, we, you, they). The subject and verb must *agree*, meaning a singular noun must have a verb that comports with its singularity (e.g., "*Hayley dances*" but "*Janie and Kyle dance*").

Short vowels   See **vowel sounds and spellings** (page 212). Reference: Unit 1 and Lessons 32 and 57

Silent letters   *Silent letters* are letters in a word that are not pronounced. In **knight**, the **k** and **gh** are silent letters. Reference: Lessons 81, 82, and page 254

Singular   In grammar, *singular* denotes one person or thing.

Stop or quick sound   Some alphabet letters and patterns have a definite stopping point. For example, the consonant **p** (|**p**|) stops rather abruptly. It is a *noncontinuous sound*. Noncontinuous sounds are also referred to as *quick*, *stop*, or *clipped* sounds. See, also, **noncontinuous sound** and **continuous sound**.

Suffix   A *suffix* is an element added to the end of a word to make another word close in meaning. In **happiness**, the **ness** is a suffix. Reference: Lessons 30, 31, 56-60, 63, and 72

Syllable   A *syllable* is a sound unit that consists of a lone letter or several letters. All English words consist of one or more syllables, and each syllable contains at least one vowel. A simple way to count syllables in a word is to count the number of times your chin drops when you pronounce the word. For example, the chin drops twice during the pronunciation of **Bat • man** and **zig • zag**. The word **encyclopedia** has six syllables. (See, also, **polysyllabic**.)

Tetragraph   A *tetragraph* consists of four letters pronounced as one sound; the four letters occur in the same syllable. Another word for tetragraph is **quadrigraph**.

Trigraph   When three letters are spelled in the same syllable and are pronounced as or represent one sound, they are referred to as a *trigraph*. One example of a trigraph is the **ing** in **sing**. Another trigraph is **eau**, as in **beauty** or **bureau**.

Verb   A *verb* is a word that indicates action or existence (a state of being). The word **am** is a state-of-being verb ("*I am a good reader*"). The word **jump** is an example of an action verb ("*Will Ross jump over the log?*").

Voiced   To determine if the sound of a letter is voiced, touch your neck over your vocal cords with your fingers, pronounce the letter, and feel if your vocal cords vibrate. If they vibrate, the letter is *voiced*. All vowel sounds are voiced. Some of the voiced consonants are **b**, **d**, **g**, **j**, **l**, **m**, **n**, **r**, **v**, **w**, **y**, and **z**, plus the so-called second sounds of the letters **s** and **x**, which are |**z**| and |**gz**|, respectively.

Some alphabet letters have more than one sound. For example, the consonant **s** has two sounds—one is voiced and the other is voiceless. The voiceless sound of **s** is found in **sat** and **boss**. The voiced (or second) sound of **s** is |**z**|, as found in **his** and **choose**. (See, also, ***voiceless***.) Reference: Lessons 27 and 59

Voiceless   If a speaker's vocal cords do not vibrate while he expresses a letter or digraph, the unit is characterized as *voiceless*. Generally, the voiceless letters are pronounced with more air than the voiced ones. Compare the voiceless **th** in **thick** and **path** with the voiced **th** in **then** and **this**. Notice that the former two produce more air and no vocal cord vibration. Among the voiceless sounds are |**f**|, |**h**|, |**k**|, |**p**|, |**t**|; the first sound of the letters **s** (|**s**|) and **x** (|**ks**|); and both sounds for the letter **c** (|**k**| and |**s**|). Notice that **ch** and **sh** are voiceless, too. (See ***voiced***.) Reference: Lessons 27 and 59

Vowel   The English alphabet has five vowels: **a**, **e**, **i**, **o**, and **u**. Every word in English contains at least one vowel. The consonants **y** and **w** sometimes function as vowels.

Vowel sounds and spellings

▶   ***Short vowels***   The short-vowel sounds are ă, ĕ, ĭ, ŏ, and ŭ, as found in **at**, **egg**, **if**, **on**, and **up**, respectively. A regularly spelled short-vowel word or syllable has one or more consonants appearing after a single vowel. When a consonant follows a vowel in a syllable, it is called a *closed syllable*. Reference: Lessons 32 and 57

▶   ***Long vowels***   The five vowels have both short and long sounds. The long sounds are ā, ē, ī, ō, and ū. Remember when encountering vowels that if two vowels are in the same syllable, the second vowel makes the first vowel say its name (its long sound), and the second vowel is silent. This pattern has few exceptions. Notice the long-vowel pattern with **bake** and **bail**. When a syllable ends with a vowel (is *open*), this syllable will often be accented and typically will be pronounced with its long sound. We see this pattern in the word **broken |brō′ • kən|**.

▶   ***Two vowels in the same syllable***   As mentioned above, when two vowels appear in the same syllable, the first vowel is usually pronounced with its long-vowel sound (the same sound as the vowel's name), and the second vowel is silent. We see this illustrated in **boat** and **meat**. The pattern (two vowels in the same syllable) holds true for **game** and **bike**, as well. It doesn't matter if the two vowels are contiguous (side by side) or separated by a consonant. If they appear in the same syllable, the first vowel will say its name, and the second vowel will be silent. Here are several more examples of two vowels appearing in one syllable:

a says |ā| as in **game** and **sail**

i says |ī| as in **bike** and **pie**

o says |ō| as in **froze** and **boat**

u says |ū| as in **mule** and **cue**

e says |ē| as in **Pete** and **meal**

212

▶ ***Open, accented syllables*** When a syllable ends with a vowel, the syllable is referred to as an *open syllable*. (Think of it this way: The syllable is not walled off by a consonant.) An accented syllable is pronounced with more emphasis than a non-accented syllable. For example, in the word **baby**, the first syllable [**ba**] is accented. The word **baby** is pronounced [**bā′ • bē**], not |bā • bē′|. When a syllable is open and accented, the vowel is usually pronounced with the long-vowel sound. An open syllable does not have to be accented to be pronounced with the long sound.

Let's look at another example of this pattern. In **bonus**, |**bō′ • nŭs**|, the first syllable [**bo**] is an open syllable since it ends with a vowel. It is also the accented syllable. The second syllable [**nŭs**] is a short-vowel syllable that ends in a consonant—i.e., it is a closed syllable—and it has no special emphasis.

If two vowels together in a word are in separate syllables, more often than not both vowels will be pronounced with their long-vowel sounds. Look at the **e** and **o** in **video**, |**vĭd • ē′ • ō′**|. Consider, also, the **o** and **a** in **oasis**, |**ō′ • ā′ • sĭs**|. Note the first **i** and the **o** in **violin**, |**vī′ • ō′ • lĭn**|. And, finally, look at the three vowels in **rodeo**, |**rō′ • dē′ • ō′**|. If the last syllable in a word ends with **o** (**judo**, **rodeo**, **motto**), the **o** will almost always be pronounced with its long-vowel sound.

Index of Letters and Sounds

Letter	Sound		Sample Words (Lessons Found in)
a	|ă|	as in	**am** (A, 1, 3, 5, 7, 9), **at** (A, 1, 3, 5, 7, 9), **bat** (A, 1), **lab** (B, 1, 3), **ban** (B, 1, 5, 7), **ram** (C, 1, 5, 9), **ax** (E, 1), **ad** (10, 11, 12), **cat** (13, 16), **back** (14, 16, 18, 34, 80), **cap** (33), **admire** (34, 64), **laugh** (85)
	|ā|	as in	**cape** (33), **game** (34), **aim** (39), **day** (39, 73), **play** (39, 40), **chain** (40), **pay** (44), **spray** (47), **quail** (47), **gray** (39, 50), **playback** (53), **maybe** (54), **graded** (59), **faded** (60), **halo** (61), **face** (71), **ache** (79), **bacon** (80)
	|ngk| and |ng|	as in	**bank** (39, 40), **sang** (39, 40)
	|âr| or |ĕr|	as in	**hair** (39, 40), **share** (39, 40)
	|ô|	as in	**ball** (55), **law** (55), **fault** (55), **quart** (55)
	|ä|	as in	**calm** (55), **watts** (55), **quad** (55), **star** (55), **heart** (77)
	|ä| or |ô|	as in	**want** (55), **quash** (55), **ma** (55)
	|ər|	as in	**polar** (69), **nectar** (69)
	|ə|	as in	**dent<u>a</u>l** (65, 66, 72), **<u>a</u>go** (66), **vac<u>a</u>nt** (72), **bal<u>a</u>nce** (72), **capt<u>ai</u>n** (89)
	silent	as in	**seat** (36), **ear** (36), **boat** (41), **Cairo** (89)
	|ō|	as in	**taupe** (89)
b	|b|	as in	**bat** (A, 1), **lab** (B, 3), **bag** (C, 1), **bit** (2, 3), **bib** (2, 3), **bob** (4, 5), **bug** (6), **buzz** (6), **bus** (6, 7, 9), **ebb** (8), **bet** (8, 9), **bell** (8), **bad** (12), **back** (14, 16), **blot** (22, 24), **brim** (22), **bless** (22, 23), **blastoff** (28)
	silent	as in	**lamb** (81), **climb** (81)
c	|k|	as in	**cat** (13, 16), **cot** (13), **cut** (13, 16), **cull** (13, 16, 18), **back** (14, 16, 80), **rocks** (14, 15), **act** (20), **class** (22), **clam** (23), **scram** (23), **cuts** (24), **scotch** (26), **cannot** (28), **cap** (33), **cost** (42), **coach** (44), **camel** (65, 66), **lilac** (72), **ache** (79, 80)

215

Letter	Sound		Sample Words (Lessons Found in)

c |ks| as in   **rocks** (14, 15, 16), **locks** (15, 21, 80)

|s| as in   **face** (71), **city** (71), **cycle** (71), **balance** (72), **absence** (72), **ceiling** (76), **façade** (89)

|ch| as in   **chop** (26), **much** (26), **inch** (26), **match** (26), **teacher** (79, 83), **church** (83), **cello** (83), **cappuccino** (83)

|sh| as in   **chef** (78, 79), **facial** (78), **ocean** (78)

|shŭn| |shən| as in   **ocean** (78), **musician** (78)

silent   as in   **czar** (82), **scene** (82)

d |d| as in   **ad** (10, 11, 12), **add** (10, 11, 12), **bad** (12), **dill**, (18), **held** (19), **land** (19), **drug** (22), **dress** (23), **address** (28), **added** (30), **dot** (33), **dream** (47), **cleaned** (56), **drummed** (57), **fibbed** (58), **tuned** (59)

|əd| as in   **added** (30, 56), **batted** (57), **kidded** (57), **faded** (60), **raided** (60)

|t| as in   **cooked** (56), **snapped** (57), **hopped** (57), **tripped** (57, 58), **joked** (59)

silent   as in   **welds** (20), **lands** (20), **mends** (20)

|j| as in   **soldier** (89)

e |ĕ| as in   **net** (8, 37), **bet** (8, 9, 18), **red** (10, 11), **led** (10, 11), **den** (10, 11), **text** (24), **met** (8, 33), **set** (8, 37), **best** (19, 37), **stretch** (26), **ready** (77), **deaf** (77)

|ĕm| |ĕn| as in   **hem** (8), **ten** (8), **den** (11), **enlist** (64)

|ē| as in   **mete** (33), **Pete** (34), **free** (35), **feet** (35), **be** (36), **we** (36), **seat** (36, 37), **meat** (37, 38), **week** (38), **weak** (38), **streamline** (53), **weekday** (54), **rebate** (61, 64), **veto** (61), **prevent** (64), **redo** (64), **before** (64), **ceiling** (76), **seize** (76), **beyond** (76), **key** (76), **money** (76), **deice** (76), **being** (76), **each** (77)

216

e |ēr| as in   here (34), deer (35), ear (36), hear (36), near (38), steer (38), seize (76), weird (76)

|ĕs| or |əs| as in   boxes (30), classes (30)

|ĕd| or |əd| as in   tested (30), added (30, 56), bunted (32), jolted (56), batted (57), kidded (57), clotted (58), graded (59), faded (60), raided (60)

|d| as in   cleaned (56), drummed (57), fibbed (57, 58), tuned (59), heaved (60)

|t| as in   cooked (56), snapped (57), tripped (57, 58), joked (59), braked (60)

silent   as in   mane (33), ride (33), bake (34), free (35), weed (37), peel (38), toe (41, 43), pie (45), bye (45), cue (48), loose (51), jolted (56), drummed (57), fibbed, (58), joked (59), shined (59), tithed (60)

|ā| as in   veil (76), they (76), great (77), eight (81)

|ī| as in   feisty (76), eye (76)

|ü| as in   new (48, 49), flew (48, 49)

|ū| and |ūr| as in   few (48), feud (48), beauty (89), Europe (89)

|ər| as in   her (69), learn (77)

|är| as in   heart (77), hearty (77), sergeant (89)

|ə| as in   simple (65), camel (65), seven (66), fallen (72), parent (72), absence (72), women (89), sergeant (89)

|ŏn| as in   envoy (89), encore (89)

|ĭ| as in   pretty (89)

|ō| as in   sew (89), bureau (89)

f |f| as in   fan (C, 1, 9), if (2), off (4, 18), gift (19), golf (21), flag (22), fled (22), fret, (23), fifteen (87), office (87)

|v| as in   of (67)

g |g| as in **gas** (C, 1, 9), **bag** (C, 1), **big** (2), **got** (4), **rug** (6), **egg** (8), **legs** (19), **glad** (22, 23), **grass** (24), **crabgrass** (28), **glint** (32), **green** (35, 47), **garage** (84), **ghetto** (85), **afghan** (85)

|ng| |ngs| as in **song** (20), **songs** (20)

|j| as in **age** (71), **engine** (71), **gym** (71), **garage** (71, 84)

|zh| as in **garage** (71, 84), **mirage** (71, 84)

|f| as in **rough** (85, 87), **cough** (85), **laugh** (85)

silent as in **gnu** (81), **sign** (81), **light** (81), **eight** (81), **taught** (81, 85), **ought** (85)

h |h| as in **hat** (D, 1, 9), **ham** (D, 3), **hip** (2, 3), **hit** (3, 5), **hog** (4), **hut** (6), **hop** (7), **hem** (8), **huff** (9)

silent as in **rhyme** (45, 81), **hour** (81), **honor** (81)

i |ĭ| as in **if** (2, 7), **it** (2, 3), **in** (2, 9), **bit** (2), **mill** (2, 3, 5), **tip** (2, 18), **sit** (3, 9), **ill** (7), **dill** (10, 11), **is** (17), **mistake** (64), **disclose** (64), **include** (64), **picnic** (72), **racism** (72)

|ī| as in **site** (33), **pile** (34), **bike** (34), **pie** (45), **kind** (45), **mild** (45), **quite** (46), **shined** (60), **silent** (61), **sign** (81), **light** (81)

|īr| as in **fire** (45), **tire** (45)

|ē| as in **boxing** (31), **batting** (57), **patting** (58), **grading** (59), **handiest** (63), **handiness** (63), **manliness** (63), **taxi** (70), **field** (74), **babies** (74)

|ə| as in **devil** (65, 66), **rapid** (66), **finish** (72)

|ər| as in **first** (69), **bird** (69)

|y| as in **million** (89), **onion** (89), **opinion** (89), **milieu** (89)

|ü| as in **milieu** (89), **lieutenant** (89)

silent as in **rain** (39), **seize** (76), **plaid** (89)

Letter	Sound		Sample Words (Lessons Found in)

j |j| as in   **jam** (D, 1, 5), **jazz** (E, 1, 3), **Jim** (2), **job** (4, 7), **jug** (6), **jet** (8), **jog** (9)

|h| as in   **jalapeño** (89)

|ē| as in   **fjord** (89)

k |k| as in   **kit** (13), **back** (14), **rocks** (14, 15, 16), **milk** (19), **ask** (19, 21), **bunk** (20), **bunks** (20, 21), **asks** (21), **skit** (22), **napkin** (29), **kind** (45, 80), **locks** (80)

silent   as in   **knot** (81), **knees** (81)

l |l| as in   **lab** (B, 1, 3), **ill** (2, 7), **lot** (4), **held** (19), **melt** (19), **milk** (19), **hulk** (19), **elm** (20), **films** (20), **helps** (20), **blot** (22), **flag** (22), **clip** (22), **black** (22), **spell** (23), **caplet** (28), **inlet** (29), **landed** (32), **quail** (47), **rule** (50), **playback** (53), **yellow** (54), **ball** (55), **joyful** (72), **usefully** (72)

|əl| as in   **simple** (65), **travel** (65), **dental** (65, 72), **devil** (65), **carol** (65), **mogul** (65)

silent   as in   **half** (82)

|y| as in   **tortilla** (89)

m |m| as in   **mat** (A, 1), **am** (A, 1, 3), **mass** (C, 1, 3, 7), **mill** (2, 3, 5), **mop** (4), **mum** (6), **met** (8), **ram** (9), **jump** (19), **films** (20), **lamps** (21), **smug** (22), **smog** (23), **drumstick** (28), **freshman** (29), **dream** (44, 47), **room** (50), **streamline** (53)

n |n| as in   **nap** (B, 1), **in** (2), **ban** (3), **not** (4, 5), **run** (6), **man** (7), **net** (8), **on** (9), **land** (19), **hints** (20), **lands** (20), **font** (21), **snap** (22), **snug** (23)

|ngk| and |ng| as in   **bunk** (20), **song** (20), **bunks** (20), **songs** (20)

silent   as in   **hymn** (82), **column** (82)

|ny| as in   **vignette** (89)

o |ä|　　　　as in　**pop** (4), **not** (4, 33)

|ô|　　　　as in　**off** (4, 18), **boss** (4)

|ŏ|　　　　as in　**pop** (4), **not** (4, 33), **off** (4, 18), **on** (4), **job** (4, 5), **top** (7, 18), **toss** (9), **hop** (33), **cost** (42), **jog** (43), **cough** (85, 86), **ought** (85, 86)

|ō|　　　　as in　**note** (33), **code** (33), **hope** (33, 41, 42), **boat** (41), **soul** (41, 86), **toe** (41), **coast** (42), **soap** (43), **quote** (43), **snow** (43), **hold** (43), **go** (43), **coach** (44), **roadside** (53), **joked** (59), **zoning** (60), **open** (61)

|ōr|　　　　as in　**score** (34), **more** (34, 41), **oar** (41), **door** (41, 42), **four** (41, 68, 86), **horse** (42, 67), **your** (43, 86), **born** (43), **offshore** (54)

|ü|　　　　as in　**moon** (48, 51), **too** (48, 51), **loose** (48, 51), **choose** (48, 51), **do** (48, 51, 70), **lose** (48, 51), **room** (48, 50, 51), **who** (51, 70), **shoe** (70), **soup** (70, 86), **you** (70, 86)

|ů|　　　　as in　**book** (51, 52), **could** (70, 86)

|ŭ| or |ə|　　as in　**blood** (51), **convert** (64), **carol** (65), **lemon** (66), **famous** (66, 67, 86), **of** (67), **front** (67), **money** (67), **does** (67), **conspire** (67), **complain** (67), **rough** (85, 86), **touch** (86)

|ər|　　　　as in　**flavor** (69), **word** (69), **journey** (69, 86), **nourish** (69, 86), **courage** (86)

|ōē| or |ōĭ|　as in　**boil** (68), **boy** (68)

|ow|　　　　as in　**out** (68), **proud** (68), **owl** (68), **down** (68), **shout** (86), **ground** (86)

|wə| or |w|　as in　**one** (67, 89), **once** (67, 89), **choir** (89), **memoir** (89)

|ĭ|　　　　as in　**women** (89)

silent　　　as in　**people** (89)

p |p|　　　　as in　**pat** (B, 1), **pass** (C, 1), **pit** (2), **top** (7), **gaps** (19), **kept** (19), **jump** (19), **helps** (20), **camps** (20), **spin** (22), **pled** (22), **sped** (23)

Letter	Sound		Sample Words (Lessons Found in)

p |f| as in   **phone** (87), **graph** (87)

    silent   as in   **Psalms** (81), **pterodactyl** (81), **pneumonia** (81), **psychology** (81)

q |khw| as in   **quiz** (13, 16), **squid** (22), **quick** (80)

    |k| as in   **mosquito** (89), **antique** (89), **quiche** (89)

r |r| as in   **ram** (C, 1), **rib** (2), **brim** (22), **trip** (22), **trust** (22), **scram** (22)

    |ər| as in   **her** (69), **first** (69), **polar** (69), **flavor** (69), **word** (69), **turn** (69), **syrup** (69), **learn** (69), **journey** (69)

s |s| as in   **Sam** (C, 1), **sat** (C, 1), **pass** (C, 1), **bus** (6), **ask** (19, 21), **gaps** (19), **pets** (19), **best** (19), **lands** (20), **bunks** (20), **songs** (20), **asks** (21), **texts** (21), **scan** (22), **skit** (22), **spin** (22), **stop** (22, 23), **scram** (22, 24), **squid** (22), **bats** (57), **struts** (58), **votes** (59)

    |z| as in   **is** (17), **tags** (58)

    |sh| as in   **dish** (25), **shop** (25), **sheep** (35, 78), **push** (70, 78), **issue** (78), **assure** (78), **Russia** (78)

    |shr| as in   **shred** (25)

    |shŭn| |shən| as in   **session** (78), **mission** (78)

    |zh| as in   **usual** (84), **vision** (84)

    silent   as in   **isle** (82), **island** (82), **Illinois** (82), **Arkansas** (82)

t |t| as in   **tat** (A, 1), **pets** (19), **kept** (19), **melt** (19), **rent** (19), **best** (19), **act** (20), **hints** (20), **text** (20), **texts** (20), **stop** (22), **strut** (22), **trip** (22), **batted** (57)

    |th| as in   **this** (27), **that** (27)

    |th| as in   **thin** (27), **path** (27)

t |sh| and |shən| as in **partial** (78), **motion** (78), **section** (78)

silent as in **match** (26), **catch** (26, 82), **listen** (82), **clothes** (89), **croquet** (89)

|ch| as in **future** (83), **statue** (83), **righteous** (83), **Christian** (83)

|chē| as in **Christianity** (83)

u |ŭ| or |ə| as in **up** (6), **hull** (6), **bus** (6, 7), **run** (6), **us** (6, 33), **cull** (13, 18), **upstate** (64), **subject** (64), **undo** (64), **mogul** (65), **locust** (66), **wishful** (66), **of** (67), **front** (67), **money** (67), **rough** (85, 86), **famous** (86)

|ūr| as in **cure** (34, 48, 49), **pure** (48)

|ū| as in **use** (33), **cute** (33, 48), **cue** (48), **cube** (48)

|ů| as in **put** (70), **full** (70), **could** (70), **joyful** (72), **usefully** (72)

|ü| as in **tube** (48), **blue** (48), **flu** (48), **truth** (48), **rule** (48), **fruit** (48, 49), **ruling** (60), **duplex** (61)

|ər| as in **turn** (69)

silent as in **buy** (82), **guest** (82), **guard** (82), **guitar** (82), **guy** (82), **league** (82), **fluoride** (89)

|ĭ| as in **busy** (89)

V |v| as in **van** (D, 1), **give** (89), **motive** (89), **leave** (89)

|f| as in **svelte** (87)

W |w| as in **wag** (D, 1), **twin** (22)

|hw̄| as in **which** (27), **why** (45)

|h| as in **who** (51), **whom** (51), **whose** (51)

|ow| as in **brown** (68)

silent as in **snow** (43), **law** (55), **two** (82), **write** (82)

X |ks| as in   **ax** (E, 1), **six** (2, 15), **box** (4, 15, 75), **text** (20), **texts** (20), **exile** (75)

|gz| as in   **exit** (75), **example** (75), **exile** (75)

|z| as in   **Xerox™** (75), **xyloid** (75)

|ksh| as in   **complexion** (75, 78)

y |y| as in   **yam** (E, 1, 7), **yes** (8, 73), **beyond** (73)

|ĭ| as in   **gym** (71, 73), **myth** (73)

silent   as in   **day** (39, 73), **play** (39, 73), **key** (76), **money** (76)

|ī| as in   **sky** (45, 62), **fly** (45), **bye** (45), **type** (45, 46), **try** (45, 46, 62), **reply** (62, 73), **myself** (62, 73), **apply** (73), **eye** (76, 89)

|īr| as in   **lyre** (45, 46)

|ē| as in   **lady** (62), **messy** (62), **handy** (63), **daily** (73), **funny** (73), **key** (76), **money** (76)

|ōē| or |ōĭ| as in   **boy** (68, 73), **enjoy** (68, 73)

|ər| as in   **syrup** (69, 73), **martyr** (69, 73)

|ə| as in   **Maryland** (87), **Pennsylvania** (87)

Z |z| as in   **zap** (E, 1, 17), **jazz** (E, 1, 17)

|zh| as in   **seizure** (84), **glazier** (84)

|s| as in   **pretzel** (89), **quartz** (89)

Pronunciation Guide

A to Z

|zh| Sound

Schwa Sound

Murmur Diphthongs

Silent Letters

This guide is strictly a support for instructors wanting more information about pronunciation and sound patterns. It is not comprehensive nor is it intended as a tool for speech therapy. Two speech therapists have reviewed this material and made corrections and suggestions, but any errors are mine. – DHC

Pronunciation Guide

A a
[Vowel]

Pronounce the **SHORT** vowel sound for the letter **a**, |ă|, by opening the mouth and tightening the corners in a tense almost smile. Lower the tongue in the mouth. The sound that issues will be like the **a** in **apple**. All vowel sounds are *continuous*, which means that as long as one has breath and time, the sound can continue uninterrupted. All vowel sounds also are *voiced*. To determine if a sound is voiced, pronounce the letter while touching the neck over the vocal cords. If the vocal cords vibrate, the letter is considered voiced. The short-vowel sound of the letter **a** is voiced.

a	|ă|	at camp lab apple
au		laugh aunt

Pronounce the **LONG** vowel sound for the letter **a**, |ā|, by holding the teeth about one-half inch apart and the facial muscles somewhat tense. The lips are not rounded but wide, and the tongue is lifted to about mid-high in the mouth. The long-vowel **a** can also be pronounced with the tongue down. As with all of the vowels, the long-vowel letter **a** is continuous and voiced. The long vowels are pronounced exactly the same as their name. Thus, **a** says |ā|, as in **ape** (|āp|).

silent e **ai**	|ā|	ape cake sail
ay a		day baby

The long-vowel **a**, when it is followed by the letters **nk** or **ng**, is pronounced with less emphasis than normal. The spelling combinations **ank**, **ang**, **are**, and **air** are pronounced a bit out of the ordinary, also. The change in sound will be stronger in words spelled with **r**, as in **stare** and **fair**. (These are called *r-controlled words*.) The modified sound is similar to the short sound of **e** (|ě|) or the slightly changed long-vowel sound of **a**. Most students will not pick up on the nuanced sound change caused by these patterns.

ank ang	|ā|	bank tank sang clang	**See: N** and **G**
are air	|ā|, |â|, or |ě|	care stare hair fair	**See: R**

Pronounce (what I often refer to as) the **THIRD** sound of **a** as |ä| or |ô|, as in **car**, **all**, **fault**, and **water**. The lips are open and rounded, the facial muscles relaxed, the tongue down, and the jaw dropped. The |ä| sound is very similar to the sound of the short-vowel **o**, |ŏ|, heard in **stop**. These additional sounds of **a** (|ä|, |ô|, and |ŏ|) are voiced.

al aw au	|ô|	all straw haul
ar a ear	|ä|	ark star ma heart
qua wa	|ä| or |ŏ|	quality water

ar	|ər|	tartar polar altar molar	**See: R**
a	|ə|	final original alone dental	**See: Schwa**
ea oa ai	*silent*	meat road boat Cairo	**See: Silent letters**

Note: The long-vowel **a** sound can also be spelled using **ei** and **ea**, as in **veil**, **eight**, and **great**.

226

B b

The letter **b** produces only one sound: $|\mathbf{b}|$. The letter **b** is silent in a few words.

To pronounce the letter **b**, $|\mathbf{b}|$, close the lips gently. Lightly build up the air pressure (including in the nasal cavity) and allow the lips, nose, and vocal cords to vibrate as pressure builds. Release the lips so that a little breath escapes along with a slight |bŭh| sound. The neck will vibrate, meaning the letter **b** is voiced. The |b| sound has a definite and fairly short lifespan; in other words, **b** is not a continuous sound.

When you pronounce **b**, it will have some |ŭh| sound, but shorten the |ŭh| sound as much as possible. In fact, coach your student to say a crisp or clipped |b|, not |bŭh|. After a word has been initially sounded out letter-by-letter, don't allow your student to continue handling the word piecemeal. For example, some students will be tempted to pronounce **bam** as |bŭh|-|ă|-|ŭmŭh| or **bat** as |bŭh|-|ă|-|tŭh|. This is a common student error that impedes understanding the meaning of words.

Encourage your student to pronounce a word (or syllable) like **bat** by blending the first two letter sounds together, |bă|, then pronouncing the third sound immediately thereafter. Thus, for **bat**, he should say, |bă| . . . |t|, and eventually |băt|. The goal is to sound the |b|, limit the |ŭh| sound as much as possible, and then quickly finish the word. Essentially, we want your student to glide through all of the letters of a syllable or word. Proper phrasing will truly aid your student's reading comprehension.

b bb	$|\mathbf{b}|$	bat ebb rabbit	
b	*silent*	debt doubt plumber thumb	**See: Silent letters**

Teaching Tip: A reading interventionist we know illustrates to her students that the sound of **b** is short and clipped by making a scissor motion with her fingers.

P and **b** are equivalent letters. This means that the configuration of the mouth and lips is the same for pronouncing both letters. Close the lips gently, and release the lips so that breath escapes to make the sound. The final result for each is different, however. With **p**, there is no vibration, no buildup of air pressure. With **b**, on the other hand, there is vibration. A partial list of equivalent letters can be found on page 208 in the Basic Terms section. Knowing about equivalent letters will often help your student pronounce words correctly.

C c

[Consonant]

The letter **c** sounds like $|k|$ when paired with the vowels **a**, **o**, or **u**. This $|k|$ sound is true also for the pairing of **c** with the consonant blends **cl** and **cr**.

c	$\|k\|$	cat cot cut clock cross	**See: K**

The **ck** spelling is common for making the $|k|$ sound at the end of short-vowel words or syllables. The letter **c** combined with the letter **k** (**ck**) is pronounced as one sound—$|k|$.

ck	$\|k\|$	back rock block	**See: K**

The **ch** digraph is pronounced $|k|$, as in **ache** and **echo**. This digraph is quite typical for words derived from Greek.

ch	$\|k\|$	ache mechanic anchor Christmas	**See: K**

There are just a few short-vowel words and syllables that end with the $|k|$ sound and are spelled with only the letter **c**.

c	$\|k\|$	picnic attic active Aztec lilac	**See: K**

The letter **c** is pronounced $|s|$ when paired with **e**, **i**, and **y**. We note this in **cell**, **city**, and **cycle**. This is a trustworthy pattern, so be on the lookout for **ce**, **ci**, and **cy**.

ce ci cy	$\|s\|$	cell city cycle	**See: S**

Pronounce the digraph **ch**, $|ch|$, with the lips rounded, open, and slightly puckered, and the teeth almost closed. Place the tip of the tongue against the roof of the mouth, just behind the upper front teeth. Block air in the nose and allow pressure to build where the tongue connects with the roof of the mouth, then drop the tongue, releasing an explosion of sound: $|ch|$.

ch	$\|ch\|$	check teacher chase church rich much such

When a short-vowel syllable or word ends in $|ch|$, the spelling usually includes a silent **t**. We see the **tch** spelling pattern in **stitch** and **patch**. (Exceptions include **rich**, **much**, **such**, **which**, and **touch**).

tch	$\|ch\|$	etch match notch stitch dispatch ratchet

The Italian word **cappuccino** is emblematic of the **ci** spelling with the $|ch|$ sound. There are a few words spelled with **ce** that make the $|ch|$ sound.

ce ci	$\|ch\|$	cello cappuccino Pacino

The **ch** spelling is pronounced $|sh|$ in words derived from French (e.g., **chef**).

ch	$\|sh\|$	chef chute schwa machine	**See: S**
ce ci		ocean special social facial	**See: S**
c	*silent*	czar scene science	**See: Silent letters**

Recap: The three sounds for the **ch** spelling pattern are $|ch|$, as in **church**; $|k|$ as in **ache**; and $|sh|$ as in **chef**.

Recap: The three sounds for the **ce** and **ci** spelling patterns are $|s|$ as in **cell** and **city**; $|ch|$ as in **cello** and **cappuccino**; and $|sh|$ as in **ocean** and **special**.

D d

Pronounce the letter **d** as |**d**|, not |**dŭh**|. To form the |**d**| sound, slightly separate the teeth while lightly pressing the tip of the tongue to the roof of the mouth, just behind the gum line of the upper front teeth. Lightly build up air pressure (including in the nasal cavity), causing the tongue, nose, and vocal cords to vibrate. Build pressure by blocking the air flow, then release the air as the tongue drops.

As mentioned above, pronounce **d** as |**d**|, not |**dŭh**|. Alone, the letter **d** will have some |**ŭh**| sound, but shorten the |**ŭh**| as much as possible. Clip the pronunciation.

The voiceless letter **t** is the equivalent letter for the voiced letter **d**.
Reference: Basic Terms, Equivalent Letters (page 208)

Encourage your student to pronounce (or phrase) a word by blending its first two letter sounds together and then sounding out the next letter in quick succession. So, for example, **dim** is read as |**dĭ**|-|**m**|, and **dad** is read as |**dă**|-|**d**|. **Dad** is not pronounced |**dŭh**|-|**ă**|-|**dŭh**|; nor is **dim** pronounced |**dŭh**|-|**ĭ**|-|**ŭmŭh**|. These two adjustments—shortening the sound of the letter **d** and instantly pronouncing the vowel that immediately follows it—will enhance student comprehension.

d dd	**|d|**	did dug daddy doll dog dell

The ending **-ed** is pronounced |**d**| when **-ed** is preceded by a voiced letter. Notice the ending sound in **cleaned**, **drummed**, and **tuned**. Note also that this particular tacking on of **-ed** does not add a new syllable to the root words.

-ed		cleaned drummed tuned

The ending **-ed** is pronounced |**t**| when **-ed** is preceded by a voiceless letter. Notice the ending sound in **pushed, hopped,** and **baked**. The root words **push** (|**sh**|), **hop** (|**p**|), and **bake** (|**k**|) end in voiceless sounds. The **-ed** ending sounds like |**t**|.

-ed	**|t|**	pushed hopped baked kicked boxed passed puffed graphed laughed punched rocked	**See: T**

The ending **-ed** is pronounced |**əd**| or |**ĕd**| when preceded by the letters **d** or **t**. This pronunciation adds an additional syllable to the root words.

ed	**|əd| or |ĕd|**	jolted dusted batted kidded graded voted

When pronouncing **land** and **end**, do say the sound of the **d**. When pronouncing the plurals of these words, however, treat the **d** as silent. The **s** sound interrupts the completion of the **d** sound, so **lands** sounds almost like |**lănz**|. Note that the **s** here is pronounced with its second sound, |**z**|.

d	*silent*	lands ends bands	**See: Silent letters**

E e
[Vowel]

To pronounce the **SHORT** sound of the letter **e**, $|\breve{e}|$, relax the muscles of the face and raise the tongue slightly to approximately mid-high in the mouth. With the lips open and the lip corners tightened, say $|\breve{e}|$. (Lips and teeth are slightly closer together than when pronouncing $|\breve{a}|$.) The sound $|\breve{e}|$ is sometimes spelled **ea**, but this is rare.

e	$|\breve{e}|$	bed egg step fell
ea		spread bread thread

When the **SHORT** vowel sound $|\breve{e}|$ is followed immediately by **m** or **n** (**em** and **en**), there will be a slight change in sound.

em en	$|\breve{e}m|$ $|\breve{e}n|$	hem ten hen spend enlist remnant

Pronounce the **LONG** vowel sound for **e**, $|\bar{e}|$, by raising and tightening the tongue against the upper side teeth. Hold the teeth close together with the facial muscles somewhat tense. The lips are less rounded and more in the shape of a widened slit, with the corner of the lips slightly tightened. The long-vowel **e** is voiced and continuous.

ee ea e	$|\bar{e}|$	week feet eat be decide
silent **e ey ei**	$|\bar{e}|$	Pete key ceiling

If the long-vowel **e** is followed by the letter **r**, a slight sound change occurs.

silent **e ear eer eir**	$|\bar{e}r|$	here hear ear steer weird

Words ending in **-ed** conclude one of three ways:

(1) An **-ed** appearing after a **d** or **t** is pronounced as a separate syllable having a short-vowel sound, $|\breve{e}|$, or schwa sound, $|\partial|$, as in **padded** and **floated**.

(2) If the root word to which **-ed** is added ends in a voiced sound, it usually is pronounced with the voiced $|d|$. Notice this pattern with the **m** in **framed** and the **b** in **stubbed**. The **e** is, therefore, treated as silent.

(3) Words that end with a voiceless sound are usually pronounced with the voiceless $|t|$ sound, as in **helped** and **boxed**. The **e** is silent in this case.

As a rule, before we add **-ed**, we double the final consonant of a root word when this root word has a short-vowel sound and ends in a single consonant. *We do this doubling in order to preserve the root word's short-vowel sound.* Examples of doubling the final consonant of the base word before adding **-ed** are **sin** → **sinned** and **trap** → **trapped**. For long-vowel (silent **e**) words, we drop the **e** and then add **-ed**, as we see with **bake** → **baked** and **style** → **styled**. Likewise, this latter pattern of spelling (dropping the **e**) keeps the long-vowel sound in the word. [See Lessons 56 – 60]

ed	$|\partial d|$ $|d|$ $|t|$	padded framed helped	**See: Schwa, D, T**
ea ey ei	$|\bar{a}|$	great steak they veil eight	**See: A**
silent e **ew eu**	$|\bar{u}|$	cute few feud	**See: U**
ew	$|\ddot{u}|$	new flew	**See: U**
er ear	$|\partial r|$	her former learn heard	**See: R**
ear	$|\ddot{a}r|$	heart hearken	**See: A**
le el e	$|\partial|$	apple nickel open	**See: Schwa**
e	*silent*	speed tie due bake rule mute	**See: Schwa**

230

F f
[Consonant]

The letter **f** produces only one sound: $|\mathbf{f}|$. (The only exception to this pattern is the word **of**. The **f** in **of** is pronounced |v|.) There are, however, five spellings that create the sound |f|: **f, ff, gh, ph,** and sometimes **v**.

To pronounce the consonant **f**, $|\mathbf{f}|$, place the top front teeth lightly on the bottom lip and blow air between the lips and teeth. The sound is voiceless. Say |f|, not |fŭh|.

The voiced letter **v** is the equivalent letter of the voiceless letter **f**.
Reference: Basic Terms

f ff |f| fan fluff office coffee

The letter **f** has one word with the |v| sound: **of**.

f |v| of   **See: V**

Note: In some words, the sound of |f| is spelled with foreign-based spellings. Examples are the **ph** found in **phonics, alphabet,** and **telephone,** and **gh** found in **rough, laugh,** and **laughter.**

Note: The |f| sound is spelled with a **v** in at least one word, **svelte.**

G g

Pronounce the letter **g**, |**g**|, by raising the middle or back of the tongue. Lightly build up air pressure, including in the nasal cavity, allowing the nose, roof of the mouth, and vocal cords to vibrate. Release air from the back of the throat and lower the tongue (now slightly hump-shaped) to emit the **g** sound, |**g**|. The sound of |**g**| is not continuous. This pronunciation is often referred to as the *hard sound* of **g**.

Pronounce **g** as |**g**|, not |**gŭh**|. Alone, the letter **g** will have some |**ŭh**| sound, but shorten the |**ŭh**| as much as possible.

Often, students will initially pronounce a word like **gap** as |**gŭh**|-|**ă**|-|**pŭh**|. Encourage your student to blend the sounds of the first two letters |**gă**|, then, as quickly as possible, pronounce the third sound: |**gă**|-|**p**|. These two adjustments—clipping the sound of the letter **g** and instantly pronouncing the vowel that follows it—will boost comprehension.

g gg	|**g**|	gate goat gum get gill argyle gagged
gh		ghetto afghan ghastly spaghetti

The **ge**, **gi**, and **gy** spelling patterns usually are pronounced |**j**|, as in **gym**, or |**zh**|, as in **mirage**. These are a softer sound than the hard **g**. Some Exceptions: **get**, **gill**, and **argyle**.

ge gi gy	|**j**|	age agile gym garage beige	**See: J**
ge	|**zh**|	garage mirage beige	**See: |zh|**

Words spelled with **ng**, |**ng**|, have a shortened hard **g** sound. The **ng** digraph is pronounced |**ng**|, which is different than the **n** and the **g** would be pronounced if appearing separately. The **n** in the **ng** spelling pattern is pronounced farther back in the mouth than is the **n** in words like **ban** and **tan**. Leave the tongue in the adjusted **n** position to complete the sound. Be sure to pronounce the **g** in the **ng** without saying |**gŭh**|. [See Lesson 20]

ng	|**ng**|	song spring gang king	**See: N and G**
gh	|**f**|	rough laugh toughen	**See: F**
gh	*silent*	sigh might lightning	**See: Silent letters**

Recap: The spelling **gh** has three sounds: |**g**|, |**f**|, and *silent*, as in **ghetto**, **rough**, and **sigh**, respectively.

H h
[Consonant]

The letter **h** produces only one sound: $|h|$. In some words, the **h** will be silent.

Pronounce **h**, $|h|$, by taking a small breath and forcing the air through the throat and out of the open mouth. This sound does not produce vibration in the vocal cords. Blend the **h** sound with the vowel that follows it (like the **a** in **hat** or **i** in **hill**). The sound of **h** is continuous. Pronounce the letter **h** with only air, |h|, not with an |ŭh| sound.

h	|h|	hat behave hill help hum hope	
h	*silent*	John oh Utah Esther	**See: Silent letters**

I i

Pronounce the **SHORT** vowel sound for the letter **i**, $|\breve{\imath}|$, by slightly opening and widening the lips while tightening the corners of the mouth almost in a smile. Raise the tongue high in the center of the mouth. (The lips and teeth will be slightly closer together and the tongue slightly pulled up from the position used when pronouncing short-vowel **e**, $|\breve{e}|$.) The letter **i** is voiced and continuous, as are all vowels.

Some students fail to differentiate between the short-vowel sounds of **i** and **e** ($|\breve{\imath}|$ vs. $|\breve{e}|$). One instructor we know uses a simple and effective technique to help students see the difference. She tells her student to stick his index finger in his mouth while he says **egg**. It is possible for him to pronounce this $|\breve{e}|$ word and get his finger past his teeth. Next, she has her student try to insert his finger past his teeth while he says a short-vowel **i** word, such as **sit**. The student will realize that his teeth are now too close together to do the maneuver. Thus, the student is able to see that these sounds are made differently.

i	$|\breve{\imath}|$	sit trim pilgrim igloo

Pronounce the **LONG** vowel sound for the letter **i**, $|\bar{\imath}|$, by opening the mouth and widening and lowering the jaw with the tongue resting in the bottom of the mouth. Close the mouth a bit while raising the back of the tongue towards the cutting edge of the back upper teeth. As the sound of **i** is projected, the vibration produced in the mouth and throat will be quite noticeable. The long-vowel **i** is actually a blend of two discrete sounds. At first the sound is a pure $|\bar{\imath}|$, but as the mouth and jaws narrow, the pronunciation concludes with the sound of long **e**, $|\bar{e}|$. The emphasis is placed on the beginning sound rather than the barely pronounced ending sound. The long-vowel **i** sound is voiced and continuous.

silent e **i**	$|\bar{\imath}|$	ride pie ice diet	
ie ild ind		tried child kind find	

i ie	$|\bar{e}|$	taxi sing police amiable kindliest field	**See: E**
ir	$|\operatorname{\mathsf{ə r}}|$	first birth third stir	**See: R**
oi	$|\bar{o}\bar{e}|$ $|\bar{o}\breve{\imath}|$	toil point join	**See: O**
i	$|y|$	onion million opinion minions	**See: Y**
i	$|\operatorname{\mathsf{ə}}|$	family bountiful sediment	**See: Schwa**
i	*silent*	sail paid weird fruit	**See: Silent letters**

J j
[Consonant]

Pronounce **j**, |**j**|, with gentle rounding of the lips, slightly separating the teeth
while placing the tongue against the roof of the mouth. (This tongue position is slightly
flatter and a little behind where the tongue is placed for the letter **d**.) Lightly build up
pressure (including in the nasal cavity) and allow the nose, roof of the mouth, and vocal
cords to vibrate as pressure builds. The release of the tongue and pressure is softer
and less crisp but similar to the release sound in |**d**|. The |**j**| release has some of the
voiced |**zh**| sound but terminates quickly; it is not a continuous sound.
The pronunciations of |**d**|, |**zh**|, and |**j**| are voiced. The voiceless |**ch**| sound
is the equivalent for the voiced |**j**| sound.

j	|j|	jet jade jump pajama	
j	|h|	Jose Javier Mojave	**See: H**
j	|hw|	Juan Joaquin	**See: W**
j	|ē|	fjord	**See: E**
j	|y|	hallelujah	**See: Y**

K k
[Consonant]

The letter **k** produces only one sound: |**k**|.

Make the sound of **k**, |**k**|, by raising and pressing the tongue towards the roof
of the mouth in front of the soft palate. Allow pressure to build, then drop and release
air over the tongue in the back of the mouth. Pronouncing this letter creates no
vibration. When appearing at the end of most short-vowel syllables or words, the |**k**|
sound is usually spelled with the **ck** spelling pattern, as in **rock** and **back**.
The voiced |**g**| sound of **g** is the equivalent sound for the voiceless |**k**| sound of **k**.

k	|**k**|	keg kid kite Kyle
ck		sick bucket

Note: The |**k**| sound has at least six spellings: **c**, **k**, **ck** (**s**), **x**, **qu**, and **ch**. Listen for the |**k**| sound
in **cat**, **kick**, **locks**, **box**, **quick**, and **ache**.

236

L l
[Consonant]

The letter **l** produces only one sound: |**l**|. In some words the letter **l** will be silent.

Pronounce the letter **l**, |**l**|, by lightly touching the tip of the tongue behind the upper front teeth while allowing air to pass around the tongue, causing a gentle vibration. When appearing at the end of a word, the **l** has a very slight |**lŭh**| sound. When pronouncing **l**, shorten the sound of |**ŭh**| so that it is barely heard.

When a word begins with **l** followed by a vowel, the tongue drops or glides into the vowel sound. **Lap** sounds like |**lă**| . . . |**p**|. Often, the letter **l** has a soft ə sound when it appears at the end of a word or syllable (e.g., **pill**, |**pĭ**|-|**lə**|). This ending **l** sound, |**lə**|, is just barely detectible.

Encourage your student to pronounce or phrase a word by blending the first two letter sounds together and then immediately adding the third sound (e.g., |**lă**|-|**b**| → **lab**).

l ll	|**l**|	lab limp pill lullaby
l le		told melt ripple
lf lk	*silent*	half calf talk walk

237

M m
[Consonant]

The letter **m** produces only one sound: $|\mathbf{m}|$.

Pronounce the letter **m**, $|\mathbf{m}|$, by lightly shutting the lips while the vocal cords, lips, and nasal passages vibrate. This is like a hum |mm| with air passing slightly through the nose. If a word or syllable ends with the letter **m**, the lips are lightly closed and will vibrate. When a word or syllable begins with **m (mat, mop)**, the lips vibrate while being lightly shut, then they open to make the sound of the vowel that follows the **m** (|mă|-|t|, |mŏ|-|p|). The letter **m** is voiced and continuous.

m mm |m| mat mop slim stamp remember drummer

238

N n
[Consonant]

Pronounce the letter **n**, $|\mathbf{n}|$, by placing the tongue just behind the upper front teeth and against the roof of the mouth. With the teeth slightly separated, allow the |n| sound to come through the nasal passages with vibration, similar to the nasal vibration and sound that occur when pronouncing the letter **m** (|m|). These two letters, **m** and **n**, both have a nasal quality. Say |n|, not |nŭh|.

When a word or syllable ends with **n**, the tongue remains lightly touching behind the teeth and on the roof of the mouth. We observe this, for example, in **pan**: |pă|-|n|. When the letter **n** begins a word or syllable, the tongue has to drop into position for the ensuing vowel sound. By way of illustration, see how this happens with the **a** in **nap**: |nă|-|p|.

n nn	|n|	nap man band numbers runner

The spelling patterns **ng**, $|\mathbf{ng}|$, and **nk**, $|\mathbf{ngk}|$, typically appear at the end of a syllable or word. Correct pronunciation requires a position change of the tongue from the normal **n** sound. To pronounce a traditional **n**, we place the front of the tongue just behind the teeth on the roof of the mouth, as when we say **pan** (|păn|). To pronounce the **ng** and the **nk** spelling patterns, however, the back of the tongue will touch the roof of the mouth farther back. The tongue touches the roof of the mouth in the same position as when the speaker pronounces the letter **g**. The patterns **n**, **ng**, and **nk** are produced somewhat nasally, with air flowing through the nose more than through the mouth.

The **ng** spelling pattern also triggers a change in how **g** is pronounced. With **ng**, instead of finishing with a small |gŭh|, leave the back of the tongue lightly touching the roof of the mouth and mute the **g** somewhat at the end. We say **sing** (|sēng|), not |sēn·gŭh|. The **nk** sound is completed by a puff of air, without vibration, showcasing the |k| sound.

ng	|ng|	song singing
nk	|ngk|	bank trunk honking

Pronounce **ñ**, $|\tilde{\mathbf{n}}|$, by holding the teeth close together and placing the tip of the tongue on the roof of the mouth for the **n** sound to begin. Then, drop the tip of the tongue into the consonant **y** pronunciation position, with the sides of the tongue pressed against the inside of the upper teeth. A hump in the middle of the tongue prevents air from easily passing over the tongue. The lips are drawn back or slightly stretched from side to side. This consonant letter is voiced (involves vibration). The **ñ** is pronounced as if it were spelled |ny|, with some shortening of the |ŭh| sound. The **n** sound in **vignette** has the same sound as the **ñ** makes. The **g** in this word is silent.

ñ gn	|ny|	piñata vignette

n	*silent*	hymn column autumn	**See: Silent letters**

O o
[Vowel]

When pronouncing the **SHORT** sound for **o**, |ŏ|, relax the facial muscles, lips, and jaw. Open and round the lips with the center of the tongue resting low in the mouth. The voiced short-vowel **o** sound comes from the throat. The posture is similar to when the doctor asks a patient to open his mouth and say *"aah"* (|ä|, |ô|, or |ŏ|). For the doctor to get a clear view of the throat, the jaw and facial and throat muscles need to be relaxed.

There are some variations in pronouncing **o**. The differences are slight, however. The sound is indicated with |ä|, |ô|, or |ŏ|. Sometimes this short-vowel **o** sound is spelled **ou**, as in **cough** and **bought**.

o	|ŏ|	hot coffee cross octopus
ou		cough sought thought

To pronounce the **LONG** sound for the vowel letter **o**, |ō|, as when saying **vote**, begin the sound with rounded, open, and slightly puckered lips (the lips, cheeks, and facial muscles will be slightly tensed). The tongue rests in the bottom of the mouth initially. Emit the |ō| sound from the throat and almost close the still-rounded mouth; pucker the lips, tightening around the dimples or the edges of the mouth; and slightly raise the back of the tongue. In fact, the long **o** is the longest expressed of all the vowels. If it were represented in musical notes, we would say that long |ō| inhabits more of a measure. The |ō| is voiced and continuous.

o *silent e*	|ō|	go broken vote
oe oa		toe road boat
ol ow		hold snow
ost oth		most both

As with all of the vowels, when followed by the letter **r**, the vowel sound will be slightly changed. These are referred to as *r-controlled* words.

or oor our	|ō|	torn door four

To pronounce the |ü| sound for the vowel letter **o**, as in **moon**, hold the muscles in the lips, cheeks, and face tight or tense with the lips rounded and more puckered than when pronouncing the long **o**. Hold the tip and back of the tongue mid-high in the mouth. In pronouncing the |ü| sound, one must not produce a |y| sound, |yū| (which would make the long-vowel sound of **u**, |ū|). The correct sound is that found in **moon**. The lips and vocal cords will lightly vibrate, making the sound voiced and continuous.

o ou	|ü|	today do soup group
oo oe		room moon balloon shoe

The letter **o** is also pronounced with the |ů| sound, as in **look**.

oo ou	|ů|	book foot could would boulevard	**See: U**

We pronounce the diphthongs **oi** and **oy** (pronounced $|\bar{o}\bar{e}|$ or $|\bar{o}\breve{i}|$) by blending their vowels. For either sound, begin with the tongue positioned low in the mouth, then raise the middle or back part of the tongue to finish the sound. With facial muscles somewhat tense, lips rounded, and tongue held in the middle of the mouth, widen the lips, raising the front of the tongue high in the mouth to almost the same position as for a long-vowel **e** or short-vowel **i**. The **oi** and **oy** spelling patterns are voiced and inhabit the same syllable.

oi	$|\bar{o}\bar{e}|$ or $|\bar{o}\breve{i}|$	toil boil coiled
oy		toy boy alloy

Pronounce the diphthong $|\mathbf{ow}|$, spelled either **ou** or **ow**, by tensing the facial muscles while opening and widening the lips. Bring the lips into a tight, almost closed, rounded position while continuing to keep the tongue down. Move the tension from the corners of the mouth and cheeks to the lips, and bring the mouth into a closed position similar to the position used when saying the $|\ddot{u}|$ in **moon**. The letters that form the **ou** and **ow** diphthongs are not split into separate syllables. They work together as a team.

ou	$|\mathbf{ow}|$	loud shout mouth cloud fountain
ow		cow down crown

The letter **o** sometimes has the murmur diphthong sound $|\partial r|$, as in **word**, **doctor**, and **journal**. (All of the vowels can function at times as a murmur diphthong.)

wor or	$|\partial r|$	word doctor record actor	**See: R**
our		journey courage tournament	

The letter **o** sometimes is pronounced with the **SHORT** sound of **u**, $|\breve{u}|$, as in **come** and **blood**, or the schwa sound $|\partial|$, as in **lemon**.

o oo	$|\breve{u}|$ or $|\partial|$	lemon nothing come money blood	**See: U or schwa**
o		compete confuse consult brother of	
ou		famous couple touch trouble	

Recap: The **oo** spelling has four sounds: $|\ddot{u}|$, $|\bar{o}|$, $|\mathring{u}|$, and $|\breve{u}|$, as in **moon**, **door**, **book**, and **flood**, respectively.

Recap: The **ow** spelling has two sounds: the diphthong $|\mathbf{ow}|$, as in **owl**, and the long-vowel **o** sound $|\bar{o}|$, as in **snow**.

Recap: The **ou** spelling has at least eight sounds: the diphthong sound $|\mathbf{ow}|$, as in **out**; the short-vowel sound of **o**, $|\breve{o}|$, as in **cough**; the long-vowel sound of **o**, $|\bar{o}|$, as in **soul**; the short-vowel sound of **u**, $|\breve{u}|$, as in **touch**; the schwa sound $|\partial|$, as in **generous**; the $|\ddot{u}|$ sound, as in **soup**; the $|\mathring{u}|$ sound, as in **could**; and the murmur diphthong sound $|\partial r|$, as in **journal**.

P p
[Consonant]

Pronounce the letter **p**, |**p**|, with the lips lightly shut, then puff out air to open
the lips. The letter **p** is voiceless, causing no vibration in the vocal cords.
The mouth is positioned the same for both the letters **b** and **p**, but there are differences
in pronunciation outcomes. The major difference is that **b** is voiced. The letter **p** is also
different from **b** because the former produces a definite puff of air. The voiced letter **b**
is the equivalent letter for the voiceless letter **p**.

p pp |**p**| pan top pull stomp mapping

ph |**ph**| phone nephew graphics   **See: F**
[Digraph]

pn ps pt   *silent*   pneumonia psychology pterodactyl   **See: Silent letters**

242

Q q
[Consonant]

The digraph **qu** expresses itself as a combination of the $|\mathbf{k}|$ and $|\mathbf{hw}|$ sounds, $|\mathbf{khw}|$, as heard in **queen** and **quilt**. Begin with the lips somewhat tense and similarly positioned as when pronouncing the voiceless sound of **wh**, |hw|. Pucker or round the lips, then gently tighten them, and blow air at the same time. The back of the tongue is touching or nearly touching the roof of the mouth in front of the soft palate at the back of the mouth. As the air starts releasing, round the lips and open the mouth and slightly drop the jaw, proceeding from the |k| sound into the |hw| sound: |k| . . . |hw|, |khw|. Both the |k| and the |wh| sounds are produced without vibration, making this letter combination voiceless.

qu |khw| quick quake queen squelch

qu |k| quiche bouquet antique mosquito   **See: K**

Only a few **q** words are spelled without the letter **u**, such as **Iraq**. A name can be spelled and pronounced however the originator wants.

q |k| Iraq   **See: K**

R r

To pronounce the letter **r**, |**r**|, have the sides of the tongue touching the insides of the top teeth and raise the back of the tongue high in the mouth. A hollow space is formed just behind the slightly raised tip of the tongue. Air passes over this hollowed space, causing the vibration (voice) required to make the |**r**|. Hold the edges of the mouth, the dimples, firmly. The letter **r** is sometimes described as a growl, like a puppy might make (|**rrr**|). The tongue is pulled slightly farther back in the mouth when pronouncing **r** than when pronouncing **w**.

When pronouncing an **r** at the beginning of a word or syllable, open the pursed lips into the vowel sound that follows, as in **ran** (|răn| . . . |n|) or **rut** (|rŭ| . . . |t|). At the end of a word or syllable, the letter **r** is pronounced |ər|.

Some students have difficulty correctly pronouncing **r**. The **r** sound is made in the middle of the mouth, making it more difficult for a teacher to help a student correct errant pronunciation. The difficulties in pronouncing are likely due to the size and shape differences of people's mouths. *Insofar as these lessons are not designed to be speech therapy of any kind, just relax and do your best to guide your student.*

r	|r|	rat run there paragraph
rr		purring stirrer

The murmur diphthong is the |**ər**| sound found in words like **molar** and **doctor**. This sound can be spelled with any of the vowels, the letter **y**, or with the **ear** or **our** spelling patterns. The murmur diphthong sound is possible when a vowel or vowel combination is followed by the letter **r**: **ar, er, ir, or, ur, yr, ear, our** or **ure**, as in **altar, term, stir, actor, murmur, syrup, learn, journal**, and **assure**, respectively.
Reference: Lesson 69

ar er ir or	|ər|	altar her first bird word
ur yr ear		turn syrup earn
ure our		assure ensure insure journal nourish

S s
[Consonant]

To make the sound of **s**, |**s**|, force breath to escape through the slightly separated upper and lower teeth and over the tongue, which is raised and almost touching the ridge on the roof of the mouth behind the teeth. The sides and tip of the tongue curl up toward the roof of the mouth, forming a groove. The escaping breath produces a hissing sound, |s|. The letter **s** is a voiceless letter (without vibration). Most words or syllables that begin with **s** are indeed pronounced with the |s| sound. The letter **s** is continuous.

Most words and syllables that end with **s** and say |s| actually have a double **s** (**hiss**, **pass**, **bass**, **mass**, and so forth). There are very few exceptions to the pattern. Among the exceptions are **Sis, gas**, and **bus** (which are actually shortened versions of **sister, gasoline**, and **omnibus**).

s ss |**s**| sat Sis gas snake stand lose mass passage missile

The second sound for the letter **s** is |**z**|. This sound is usually slightly softer than a true **z**. As a rule of thumb, whether the **s** is pronounced |s| or |z| is determined by which sound is easiest for the speaker to make. The |z| pronunciation of **s** is voiced and continuous.

s se |**z**| his choose advise   **See: Z**

To pronounce the digraph |**sh**|, pucker and slightly open the lips with the teeth together. Pull the tongue slightly back, and raise the middle groove of the tongue to mid-high in the mouth. Blow air over the tongue and between the teeth in a steady stream. The |sh| sound is pronounced nearly the same as the |s| sound, but the tongue is slightly adjusted and pulled down or back in the mouth. The |sh| sound is voiceless, without vocal cord vibration. The |zh| sound is the voiced equivalent to the voiceless |sh| sound. The **sion** and **tion** spelling patterns are pronounced |shŭn| or |shən|. The **sh** digraph is always contained within one syllable.

sh |**sh**| sheep wish cashew

si su   mission passion issue insure assure ensure

Note: The |sh| sound can be spelled **sh, si su, ch, ce, ci**, and **ti** (as in **ship, mission, tissue, chef, ocean, facial**, and **partial**, respectively).

Note: The |shən| or |kshən| sound can be spelled **sion, tion, cean**, and **xion** (as in **mission, section, ocean**, and **complexion**).

T t

[Consonant]

To pronounce the consonant **t**, |**t**|, have the tip of the tongue touch the roof of the mouth just above and behind the upper front teeth. Allow pressure to build by blocking air from passing through the nose or mouth until the tongue drops, releasing a puff or burst of air over the tip of the tongue. This letter is voiceless (without vocal cord vibration). [The voiced letter **d** is the equivalent letter for the voiceless letter **t**.] Say |**t**|, not |**tŭh**|.

t tt |**t**| tent tall tree meat listed flitted patted

VOICELESS "th"   To pronounce the voiceless **th** digraph, |**th**|, relax the facial muscles and place the front of the flattened tongue very lightly touching the cutting edge of the top front teeth. Blow air over the tongue or between the tongue and top teeth, slightly separating tongue and teeth with air. This digraph sound and spelling are found in words like **math** and **thick**. Notice how pronounced the air flow is with these words and how they do not involve the vocal cords.

th |**th**| moth pathway thumb thrift

VOICED "th"   The digraph **th**, |**th**|, can also be voiced. Relax the face and flatten the tongue and place the tongue lightly against the cutting edge of the top front teeth. To this point, the tongue is in the same position it is for the voiceless **th** digraph. Now, however, the tongue and vocal cords do not blow air between the tongue and top teeth. The voiced **th** digraph vibrates against the top teeth with very little, if any, air blowing around the tongue and teeth. The **th** spelling, pronounced |**th**|, with vibration and with little air, is found in words like **this** and **father**.

th |**th**| this that these mother father

Be aware of words that look like they contain a **th** digraph but do not. For example, **pothole** is pot · hole, with the **t** and the **h** in separate syllables. **Mother** and **path** contain true digraphs.

The **ti** spelling can be pronounced |**sh**|, as in **partial** and **motion**.

ti tion |**sh**| partial motion section vacation   **See: S**

There are a few words spelled with a **te** or **ti** that make the |**ch**| sound.

te ti |**ch**| righteous Christian   **See: C**
ti |**chē**| Christianity   **See: C**

Note: The |**t**| sound can also be spelled **-ed**, as in **helped**, **snapped**, **joked**, and **stacked**.

246

U u
[Vowel]

To pronounce the **SHORT** sound for the letter **u**, |ŭ|, relax the muscles in the face, jaw, and lower lip while lowering the tongue into the center of the mouth. The sound comes from the middle lower area of the mouth. The short-vowel **u** sound is voiced and continuous.

A few dictionaries have replaced the |ŭ| symbol with the schwa's upside-down e, |ə|, or a variation thereof.

u ou	|ŭ| or |ə|	duck upstairs rough famous

To pronounce the **LONG** sound of **u**, |ū|, hold the teeth closely together with the sides of the tongue pressed against the inside or cutting edge of the back upper teeth. A hump in the middle of the tongue prevents air from easily passing over the tongue. The lips are relaxed, with a little tension in the corners of the mouth. With the lips rounded and slightly puckered, hold the tip and back of the tongue high in the mouth. The sound of long-vowel **u** moves from the upper front area to very high in the middle or back of the mouth. The long-vowel **u** sound has a beginning sound that is similar to the consonant **y** and is pronounced much like the word **you**. Complete the pronunciation by making a sound like the **oo** in **ooze**. As with all other vowels, the long-vowel **u** sound is voiced and continuous.

u	|ū|	Utah uniform bugle cube

To pronounce the |ů| sound as heard in **book** or **put**, relax the facial muscles and round the lips almost in a pucker. Raise the tongue to mid-high in the mouth and allow air to flow over the tongue and through the almost-puckered lips. The |ů| sound of the letter **u** is similar to the short sound of the double **o** spelling **oo**, as seen in **book** and **stood**. As with all other vowel sounds, the |ů| sound is voiced and continuous.

u	|ů|	put full pulling	
ou		could would should	
ui	|ü|	fruit bruise	**See: O**
ur	|ər|	turn purple burden murmur church	**See: R**
u	|ə|	wishful focus circus locust	**See: Schwa**
bu au	*silent*	build buy haul	**See: Silent letters**
gu	*silent*	guard guess guest guy	**See: Silent letters**

Note: The **ew** and **eu** spelling patterns will sometimes make the long-vowel **u** sound, |ū|, as in **few** and **euro**.

V v

The letter **v** (except for the word **svelte**) produces only one sound: $|v|$.

To pronounce the consonant letter **v**, $|v|$, draw the lower lip inward, lightly touch
the upper front teeth to the lower lip, and allow the sound to vibrate the lips.
(The basic position is akin to that used for pronouncing **f**, $|f|$, although **f** is voiceless).
The lips and throat both vibrate when **v** is pronounced. The lip vibration is more
intense for the letter **v** than with most letters, and the vibration can cause a slight tickle
to the bottom lip. The sound of $|v|$ is continuous. The voiceless letter **f**, $|f|$,
is the equivalent letter for the voiced letter **v**, $|v|$.

One spelling pattern related to the letter **v**: A silent **e** is added to comply with the rule
that English words not end with the letter **v** (**have**, **live**, **believe**, and **leave**).

v	$\|v\|$	van valentine divide volume	
v	$\|f\|$	svelte	**See: F**

248

W w
[Consonant and Vowel]

The letter **w** is almost always a consonant, but occasionally it functions as a vowel.

To pronounce the letter **w**, |**w**|, begin by puckering or rounding the lips. From this puckered position, gently tighten and vibrate the lips, then slightly drop the jaw and open the puckered lips and position the mouth to get ready to pronounce the next letter. When pronouncing the voiced **w**, |w|, touch the neck and feel the vibration in the vocal cords. Notice that the lips and nasal cavities also will gently vibrate when the voiced |w| sound is made.

w	|**w**|	well wagon wait rewind

The **wh** spelling pattern is often pronounced with the voiceless |**hw**| sound. Purse the lips and blow air with teeth separated and the lips rounded. Move the lips into the somewhat tense and slightly puckered position. There should be no vocal cord vibration. Again, this **wh** is pronounced by combining (blending) a voiceless |h| and an air-filled and voiceless |w|.

Dictionaries indicate that both the voiced |w| and the voiceless |hw| sounds can be used to pronounce the **wh** spelling pattern. Whatever pronunciation of **wh** is used, remember that it is important to teach the **wh** spelling pattern.

wh	|**w**| or |**hw**|	which whether whistle	
wh	|**h**|	who whose whom whole	**See: H**
ow aw ew	*silent*	snow law stew	**See: Silent letters**
wr w	*silent*	write awry two	**See: Silent letters**

X x
[Consonant]

When pronouncing the voiceless sound of the letter **x**, $|ks|$, keep in mind that this letter is two sounds combined: $|k| + |s| \rightarrow |ks|$, as in **ax** and **six**. With the front of the tongue low and touching the back of the lower teeth, raise the back of the tongue to form a hump touching the roof of the mouth. Release air from the back of the throat while blocking air from escaping through the nose. When released, the air will burst over the hump-shaped tongue, producing the $|k|$ sound, followed immediately with the hissing sound of the letter **s**: $|ks|$. Both the $|k|$ and $|s|$ sounds are voiceless, making this pronunciation of **x**, $|ks|$, voiceless. The voiced second sound of **x** $|gz|$ is the equivalent for this voiceless $|ks|$ sound of **x**.

x |ks| ax six tuxedo box exile   **See: K** and **S**

To pronounce the voiced second sound for the letter **x**, $|gz|$, blend the sound equivalent of a voiced letter **g** ($|g|$) with the voiced letter **z** ($|z|$).

x |gz| example exist exit exile   **See: G** and **Z**

The letter **x** is pronounced with the **z** sound, $|z|$, only when it is used at the beginning of a syllable or word, as in **Xerox**™.

x |z| Xerox™ Xerxes xylophone   **See: Z**

The letter **x** is pronounced with a $|ksh|$ sound in at least one word, **complexion**.

x |ksh| complexion   **See: K** and **S**

Y y
[Consonant and Vowel]

The letter **y** is usually a consonant, but **y** also functions as a vowel.

The letter **y** is always in the initial position in a word or syllable when it functions as a consonant. **Y** is usually (if not always) in the medial or end position when it functions as a vowel or diphthong.

To pronounce the consonant **y**, |**y**|, hold the teeth close together with the sides of the tongue pressed against the inside of the upper teeth. A hump in the middle of the tongue prevents air from easily passing over the tongue. The lips are drawn back or slightly stretched from side to side. The sound begins with a slight or brief |ē| sound. The consonant **y** is voiced, meaning that it is pronounced with vibration. Students who have difficulty remembering how to spell words that begin with **y** (e.g., **yam**) are often helped when the instructor says, *"This letter is the same as the letter that begins the word **yes**."*

y	|y|	yes yarn yellow beyond	
y yr	|ĭ|	crypt gym system myth lyrics	**See: I**
y uy	|ī|	byline flying reply myself buy	**See: I**
y ey	|ē|	daily happy manly key money	**See: E**
oy	|ōē| or |ōĭ|	boy enjoy destroy	**See: O**
yr	|ər|	myrrh syrup martyr	**See: R**
ey	|ā|	obey they	**See: A**
ay ey	*silent*	may play daylight Saturday key	**See: Silent letters**

There are some words that are pronounced with what sounds like the consonant letter **y** but that are spelled with the letter **i** (**onion, opinion, minions, million, billion,** and **trillion**). Usually, it is the **y** that borrows the **i** pronunciation pattern, but that pattern is reversed here.

Z z

[Consonant]

The letter **z** (except in the **tz** letter combination) produces only one sound: $\big|\mathbf{z}\big|$.

To pronounce the letter **z**, $\big|\mathbf{z}\big|$, flatten and raise the front of the tongue and create a scoop or groove down the middle. Touch the sides of the upper teeth and gums with the sides of the tongue or hold the tongue just behind the teeth. Air flows over the tongue with the tongue definitely vibrating. This sound is often depicted as the |zz| sound that bees make. The consonant **z** is voiced (causes vibration) but uses less air pressure than the equivalent voiceless letter **s**. The voiceless **s** sound, |s|, is the equivalent letter for the voiced |z| sound.

When **z** is the last letter or sound in a short-vowel word, the word is often spelled with two z's (**zz**), as in **buzz** and **jazz**. There are a few short-vowel words that end with one **z** (**quiz**).

z zz |z| zap zebra quiz jazz razz

The voiceless **t** combined with the (usually voiced) letter **z** is pronounced with the voiceless equivalent sound of **z**, the |s| sound. Try to pronounce the voiced |z| sound after the voiceless |t| sound. It's just easier to pronounce both letters voicelessly.

tz |ts| pretzel Ritz quartz   **See: S**

Note: The |z| sound can also be spelled **s**, as in **his** and **choose**. This |z| sound, spelled with **s**, never appears at the beginning of a syllable or word. Often, the letter **s**, when pronounced as |z|, is followed by a silent **e**, as in **lose** and **rise**.

252

|zh| Sound

To pronounce the |**zh**| sound, slightly open the lips into a rounded, puckered shape with the teeth close together. Allow the lower lip to slightly jut forward while you relax the upper lip. Raise the middle groove of the tongue to mid-high while pressing the sides of the tongue to the cutting edges of the back top teeth. Let air flow over the tongue and between the teeth, allowing both the tongue and vocal cords to vibrate. The |**zh**| sound is voiced and continuous. The |**sh**| sound is the voiceless equivalent to the voiced |**zh**| sound.

ge su si |zh| garage mirage visual Asia

zu zi   seizure glazier

Schwa Sound

Pronounce the ***schwa sound***, symbolized in dictionaries with the upside-down **e**, |ə|, by relaxing the muscles in the face, jaw, and lower lip while lowering the tongue into the center of the mouth. The sound comes from the middle lower area of the mouth. Pronounce the schwa with a shortened short-vowel **u** sound, |ŭ|, as heard in **circus** or **locust**. When a word has two or more syllables, the schwa sound usually occurs in at least one of the syllables. The three-syllable word **banana** has two schwas—one in the first syllable and one in the last—|bə • năn • ə|. Any vowel (**a**, **e**, **i**, **o**, or **u**) can be pronounced with the schwa sound. Lesson 65 introduces the schwa spelling patterns **le**, **el**, **al**, **il**, **ol** and **ul**, as in **simple**, **channel**, **dental**, **evil**, **carol**, and **consul**. Lesson 66 introduces the schwa sound spelled with all five vowels, as in **ago**, **seven**, **devil**, **lemon**, and **locust**. The letter **y** and the **ain** spelling pattern can also be pronounced with the **schwa** sound, as in **Pennsylvania** and **certain**, respectively. The **ou** spelling can be pronounced with the schwa sound, |ə|, as in **famous**. As with all the other vowel sounds, the schwa is voiced and continuous.

a e i o u |ə| ado camel rapid nothing wishful

y ai ou   Maryland certain famous

Murmur Diphthongs

The ***murmur diphthong***, which is pronounced |ər|, can be spelled with various vowels. Notice the murmur diphthongs in **altar**, **first**, **her**, **word**, **turn**, **syrup**, **earth**, and **your** (when unstressed). Murmur diphthongs are introduced in Lesson 69.

ar er ir or wor |ər| polar her first learn flavor word   **See: R**

ur ure ear our   turn assure learn journey

Silent Letters

Silent letters sometimes serve an obvious purpose in a word, as, for example, when there is a silent **e** at the end of a short-vowel word, making it have a long-vowel sound and forming a whole new word. Examples of this function are **past** and **paste** and **hop** and **hope**. Having an ending silent **e** almost always transforms and interior short-vowel sound into a long-vowel sound.

Some words have silent letters that appear to serve no purpose. These words usually come from foreign languages, and the English language has adopted the word and kept either the spelling or the pronunciation, or both. This is true, for example with **bouquet**, a French word with a silent **t**. Some other spellings that puzzle us are **are** and **thumb**. Lessons 81 and 82 look at **thumb, sign, eight, knees, hour, Psalms, wrap, czar, buy, guest, half, listen, hymn,** and **isle**—all words having one or more silent letters.

Furthermore, there are some words in which a letter was historically pronounced but we now treat that letter as silent. Examples of this are **knee** and **knight**. These used to be pronounced |knē| and |knĭkt|, respectively.

This is not an exhaustive list of the silent letters, just a list of examples.

Silent Letter	Spelling	Sound	Sample Words
a	a	*silent*	deal dial boat ear dual Cairo
b	mb bt	"	lamb plumber doubt debt
c	ck cz sce sci c	"	back czar scene science broccoli
d	ds	"	lands melds
e	ee *silent* e ed	"	speed game drummed tuned
g	gn gh	"	gnu sign sigh eight taught straight
h	h rh	"	hour heir oh rhyme
i	ai ei eir ui	"	rain plaid seize weird fruit
k	kn	"	knot knee knave knit knuckle
l	alf alk	"	half calf talk walk
n	mn	"	hymn column
o	eo oo	"	people door
p	pn ps pt	"	pneumonia psychology pterodactyl
s	s	"	isle island Illinois Arkansas
t	st tch ts et	"	listen wrestle catch tsunami croquet
	th	"	clothes
u	bui buy au	"	build buy haul
	gua gui gue guy	"	guard guide guitar guest guy
w	w wr ow	"	two answer write awry snow
	aw ew	"	law dew

When Is This Word Introduced?
Words Sorted According to Pattern and Category

The order in which this curriculum introduces words has been carefully selected. Students will have the phonetic tools to pronounce many words by the end of each lesson. The several listings that follow are emblematic of typical phonics milestones (not all of the sample words are necessarily taught within the lessons but the sound and spelling patterns are covered).

This curriculum does not involve teaching reading through using sentences. We realize that most teachers will contemporaneously use other classroom work that does involve the reading and writing of sentences. Teachers are always free to posit sentences to test for comprehension. If your student comes across a word in his outside reading for which he has not learned one or more of the patterns and he asks you about this word, put him at ease by telling him that some patterns will be introduced later. If you want to teach the pattern early, check in the "Index of Letters and Sounds" found on pages 215 – 223 to see where the pattern is first presented. Go to the indicated lesson for an explanation of that pattern.

Some words appear simple but are actually complex. Take this sentence, which seems to consist of only easy short-vowel words: *"This math class is fun."* A student will have the phonetic tools to easily read this sentence after completing the first 27 lessons. He will have been introduced in Lessons 1, 2, and 6 to the three short-vowel sounds |ă|, |ĭ|, and |ŭ|, found in **math**, **class**, **this**, **is**, and **fun**. In Lesson 1, he will have learned **s** and **ss**, pronounced with the voiceless **s** sound, |s|, as in **this** and **class**. Lesson 17 introduced the second sound for **s**, |z|, as in **is**. Lesson 22 introduced the consonant blend **cl**, as in **class**, and Lesson 27 introduced the two sounds for the digraph **th** (voiced—**this**; and voiceless—**math**). All of the syllable patterns for this "simple" sentence are really not so simple after all. They must be intentionally and deliberately taught.

Common Words

LESSON 1	at	LESSON 13	can	LESSON 33	made
	an				use
	am	LESSON 14	back		sale
	man				
	van	LESSON 17	is	LESSON 34	came
	bag		as		time
	sat		his		like
	tax		has		name
					make
LESSON 2	in	LESSON 19	and		more
	it		left		these
	if		ask		take
	six		west		state
	big		hand		nose
	will		jump		line
	pin		just		five
	him				nine
	sit	LESSON 20	song		
			long	LESSON 35	see
LESSON 4	on				three
	off	LESSON 22	class		feet
	hot		black		
	not			LESSON 36	the
		LESSON 23	spell		be
LESSON 6	up				we
	us	LESSON 27	when		he
	but		which		she
			where		me
LESSON 8	get		that		clean
	egg		then		reach
	tell		them		east
	less		than		read
	ten		this		each
	men		there		ear
	yes		with		year
	sell		math		
	jet		sixth	LESSON 39	way
			tenth		day
LESSON 10	add				May
	dad	LESSON 30	taxes		Sunday
	had				air
	did	LESSON 31	singing		hair
		LESSON 32	address		

LESSON 43	or	LESSON 61	a	LESSON 68	boy
	for		I		toy
	old		below		out
	north		between		about
	four		April		count
	fourth		Friday		sound
	cold		ninth		south
	most				down
	toe	LESSON 62	January		now
	so		February		house
	no		July		how
	go		by		mouth
			my		thousand
LESSON 45	find		why		
	by		baby	LESSON 69	other
	my		twenty		her
	why		forty		over
			fifty		mother
LESSON 48	true		sixty		father
	truth		seventy		after
	June		ninety		number
	Tuesday				water
	to	LESSON 65	Bible		quarter
	too		rental		first
			travel		third
LESSON 51	do		channel		thirteen
	choose				thirty
	zoo	LESSON 66	the		work
	who		away		word
	room		seventh		zipper
	book		seven		September
	look		eleven		October
	door		was		November
	whole		what		Thursday
			woman		Saturday
LESSON 55	all				
	call	LESSON 67	of	LESSON 70	radio
	arm		from		shoe
	part		some		soup
	car		come		you
	start		one		could
	wash		does		would
	watch		second		put
			hundred		full
LESSON 56	reached		Monday		
	passed		August		

LESSON 71	ice	**LESSON 79**	teacher	**LESSON 84**	television
	city		school		their
	cell				they're
	age	**LESSON 81**	right		
	page		know	**LESSON 87**	phone
	large		knew		
	December		knees	**LESSON 89**	are
			hour		have
LESSON 73	yes		eight		were
	very		eighth		said
			eighty		many
LESSON 75	exit		light		any
					people
LESSON 76	money	**LESSON 82**	write		eye
	key		wrote		been
	they		answer		again
			two		busy
LESSON 77	great		buy		twelve
	bread		walk		fifth
	head		half		million
	ready		listen		billion
	earn				
	early	**LESSON 83**	don't	**LESSON 90**	Wednesday
	learn		didn't		
	heart		can't		
			I'll		
LESSON 78	question		I've		
			I'm		
			we'll		

United States of America: The 50 States

Each state is listed beside the lesson at or by which all patterns in the names have been introduced. If you want your student to read and spell by patterns, I would suggest that the names of the states not be introduced before the indicated lesson. Many state names have a schwa sound and are deceptive in their spelling or sound.

Lesson 39	Maine	**Lesson 68**	South Carolina
			South Dakota
Lesson 48	New York		
		Lesson 69	Vermont
Lesson 61	Ohio		
	Utah	**Lesson 70**	Indiana
			Louisiana
Lesson 62	Kentucky		Mississippi
	Wyoming		New Mexico
Lesson 66	Alabama	**Lesson 72**	Georgia
	Alaska		Hawaii
	Arizona		Virginia
	Delaware		West Virginia
	Florida		
	Idaho	**Lesson 76**	New Jersey
	Iowa		
	Minnesota	**Lesson 78**	Michigan
	Montana		
	Nevada	**Lesson 82**	Arkansas
	North Dakota		Connecticut
	Washington		Illinois
	Wisconsin		Massachusetts
			Rhode Island
Lesson 67	Colorado		
	Kansas	**Lesson 86**	Missouri
	Nebraska		
	North Carolina	**Lesson 87**	California
	Oklahoma		Maryland
	Oregon		New Hampshire
	Tennessee		Pennsylvania
	Texas		

When Is This Word Introduced?
Days of the Week, Months of the Year, Pronouns, and Colors

Days of the Week

Lesson 39	Sunday
Lesson 49	Tuesday
Lesson 61	Friday
Lesson 67	Monday
Lesson 69	Thursday Saturday
Lesson 90	Wednesday

Months of the Year

Lesson 39	May
Lesson 49	June
Lesson 55	March August
Lesson 61	April
Lesson 62	January February July
Lesson 69	September October November
Lesson 71	December

Pronouns

Lesson 2	it
Lesson 36	we he she me
Lesson 45	my
Lesson 61	I
Lesson 70	you
Lesson 76	they
Lesson 83	I'll I've I'm we'll

Colors

Lesson 10	red
Lesson 22	black
Lesson 34	white
Lesson 35	green
Lesson 48	blue
Lesson 54	yellow
Lesson 68	brown
Lesson 69	purple
Lesson 71	orange
Lesson 72	lilac

Numbers

Lesson 2	six	**Lesson 66**	seven
			seventeen
Lesson 8	ten		seventy
			seventh
Lesson 27	sixth		eleven
	tenth		
		Lesson 67	one
Lesson 34	five		second
	nine		
		Lesson 68	thousand
Lesson 35	three		
		Lesson 69	thirteen
Lesson 36	fifteen		first
	sixteen		third
			thirty
Lesson 39	nineteen		
		Lesson 70	hundred
Lesson 43	four		
	fourteen	**Lesson 81**	eight
	fourth		eighteen
			eighty
Lesson 61	ninth		eighth
Lesson 62	twenty	**Lesson 82**	two
	forty		
	fifty	**Lesson 89**	twelve
	sixty		million
	ninety		billion
	fifth		trillion

261

Map and Direction Words

Lesson 1	map	Lesson 45	wildlife	Lesson 70	boulevard
Lesson 10	odd	Lesson 51	loop		Canadian
					meridian
Lesson 21	west	Lesson 55	park	Lesson 71	bridge
	rest				city
		Lesson 59	paved		
Lesson 22	stop			Lesson 72	Atlantic
		Lesson 60	zones		economic
Lesson 31	camping				historic
		Lesson 61	United States		Arctic
Lesson 33	cape		even		public
	site				Pacific
		Lesson 65	between		traffic
Lesson 34	base		tunnel		tropic
	mile		hospital		
	state			Lesson 73	entry
	drive	Lesson 66	area		system
	lane		between		symbol
	lake		Canada		
	scale		America	Lesson 74	territories
	time		continental		
	campsite		capital	Lesson 75	Mexico
			hospital		
Lesson 35	street		monument	Lesson 78	construction
			atlas		elevation
Lesson 36	east		avenue		information
	sea				nation
		Lesson 68	boundary		national
Lesson 39	railway		point		international
			south		ocean
Lesson 41	coast		town		population
	road				peninsula
		Lesson 69	border		recreation
Lesson 42	railroad		interstate		reservation
	airport		kilometers		intersection
			minor		
Lesson 43	airport		major	Lesson 79	archipelago
	north		meters		
	fort		number	Lesson 81	sign
	roadside		pattern		
	coastline		river	Lesson 82	scenic
			water		island
					isle

262

Lesson 85   highway

Lesson 86   route
                    tourist
                    country

Lesson 87   cartography
                    geography
                    hemisphere
                    physical
                    topographic

Lesson 89   business
                    plateau
                    mountain

Assorted Science Terms:
Space, Trees, Plants, Fruits & Vegetables, Animals, Reptiles, Insects, Sea Creatures, Earth, and Man

Lesson 1	pass	**Lesson 36**	leaf	**Lesson 66**	avocado
					melon
Lesson 2	hill	**Lesson 37**	peach		level
	gill		peak		sediment
					stalagmite
Lesson 6	sun	**Lesson 39**	plain		lava
					forest
Lesson 19	ant	**Lesson 40**	snail		antenna
					aorta
Lesson 21	tusk	**Lesson 41**	toad		lion
					mandible
Lesson 22	twig	**Lesson 42**	horse		human
	crest				ventricles
		Lesson 43	north		pulmonary
Lesson 23	plant		pole		basin
	stem		tadpole		spinal
	stump		reptile		petal
	crab				sepal
	frog	**Lesson 45**	fly		apricot
	trunk				
		Lesson 48	moon	**Lesson 67**	galaxy
Lesson 25	shell				astronomy
	fish	**Lesson 49**	root		telescope
	shrimp				filament
		Lesson 50	shoot		stigma
Lesson 28	insect				coconut
		Lesson 55	Mars		igneous rock
Lesson 29	pumpkin		star		venomous
			fall		latitude
Lesson 30	branches		bark		
			squash	**Lesson 68**	south
Lesson 34	date		fault		magma
	cave				
	scales	**Lesson 61**	equator	**Lesson 69**	winter
			Pluto		summer
Lesson 35	tree		stamen		observatory
	seeds		volcano		Mercury
	queen				Saturn
	bee	**Lesson 65**	rattlesnake		flower

Lesson 69	conifers	**Lesson 70**	meridian	**Lesson 77**	feather
	cauliflower		radio		
	artichoke		planetarium	**Lesson 78**	crustacean
	outer core		auditorium		constellation
	inner core		bush		projection
	earthquake		scampi		partial
	magma		horseshoe		eruption
	crater				glacier
	rivers	**Lesson 71**	space		
	waterfall		longitude	**Lesson 79**	zucchini
	spider		geology		
	butterfly		epicenter	**Lesson 80**	equinox
	stinger		ridge		
	worker			**Lesson 81**	ascension
	bladder	**Lesson 72**	ecliptic		
	lobster		nectarine	**Lesson 87**	sphere
	oyster		metamorphic		hemisphere
	turtle		stalactite		amphibians
	beaver		stalagmite		morphology
	antlers				esophagus
	whiskers	**Lesson 73**	Solar		elephant
	bird		System		equinox
	tractor		chrysalis		
	rooster		Milky Way		
	pumpernickel				
	grasshopper	**Lesson 76**	seismic		
			valley		
			honey		
			kidney		
			turkey		

Acknowledgments

Since this book was years in the making, I fear that I will forget someone. God knows who you are, and I will regret not recognizing your valued contributions here.

This book really began with **Miss May**, my first grade teacher at Mayfair Heights Elementary in Oklahoma City, as she taught me to read using phonics. As an adult, I was re-introduced to the principles of phonics when I read two excellent books on the subject—**Dr. Rudolf Flesch's** *Why Johnny Can't Read* and the sequel, *Why Johnny Still Can't Read*. His work impressed upon me the importance of removing the option of guessing by teaching with lists of words instead of illustrated readers. **Millie Shropolus** of Dallas, Texas, co-founder of the Fort Worth-based Christian Educational Advancement Systems, advised me when I called her about teaching reading in September of 1983 that *"all you need is the book* Why Johnny Can't Read *by Dr. Flesch"*—and she was right. **Sister Monica Foltzer,** author of *Sound Track to Reading* and *Professor Phonics Gives Sound Advice*, graciously answered my questions after I had benefited from the insights provided in her books. **Judy** and **Neal Frey** of Educational Research Analysts, Longview, Texas, courteously answered my questions and provided research, information, and insights over a period of many years.

I owe a deep debt of gratitude to the **Federal Bureau of Investigation**, as it was at the bureau that I learned the art and importance of researching, investigating, organizing, and accurately documenting information in an easily understood format. I advanced these skills while in training at Quantico, Virginia, and later as a special agent in the Dallas Field Office. My co-workers at the F.B.I. always encouraged me to do my best and strive for excellence. Likewise, my thanks are due my many **teaching colleagues** in school districts across the states of **Texas** and **Oklahoma** who modeled not only compassion for their students but a high degree of professionalism. I especially wish to thank **Tom Henry**, a school principal, who convinced me to risk teaching reading to eighth-grade special education students in Big Spring, Texas. This was my first foray into reading instruction, without which I would not have eventually written this book.

Janet Wolfe, of Big Spring, Texas, sparked the creation of this reading program. She saw the need and obtained permission for me to teach reading as part of the Wednesday evening van ministry at **East Fourth Baptist** in Big Spring, Texas, and that became the springboard for this curriculum. Janet patiently, calmly, and effectively taught each new lesson I wrote. In addition to being a tutor, Janet prayed faithfully for the program's overall development and brought me into contact with my editor. Janet is a long-time friend and weekly prayer partner of mine (for 20 years and counting), and she has a passion for education. She served on the school board (at the time the only woman board member) in La Porte, Texas, a 5-A school district in the Houston metropolitan area. Janet believes in excellence, and her prompting, assistance, and encouragement made all the difference in this project. **Spencer Wolfe**, Janet's husband, played a role, too, opening the church for our classes, teaching lessons, and enthusiastically supporting the program. He recognizes the life change that learning to read brings to the lives of the students.

Cathrynn Novich Brown of Carlsbad, New Mexico, was my editor. She helped bring clarity to this book. Cathrynn is a lawyer and professional editor and donated her editing and legal services *pro bono publico*. We had many working sessions at her home in Carlsbad. She believes this curriculum can help improve literacy in her community and state. Cathrynn's interest in education is long-standing (she taught several of her children to read; helped start a K-12 Montessori public charter school in Carlsbad; and has taught writing and speaking workshops free of charge for home school students). While we were working on this book, Cathrynn campaigned for, was elected to, and began serving in the New Mexico House of Representatives. (Some people just have too much spare time on their hands.) I also wish to thank **Mike Brown**, Cathrynn's husband, who is a West Point alumnus and engineer. Mike helped preserve the manuscript when my computer turned uncooperative. Frequently, he graciously handled logistics for the Brown household so Cathrynn and I could concentrate on the book.

Tammy Jones gave me additional opportunities to continue writing, teaching, and refining my reading program. She is a public school teacher and was a founding administrator of the very effective after-school van ministry at **First Baptist Church** in Big Spring, Texas. The **Howard County Library** learn-to-read program, formerly known as *CAN'T READ,* allowed me to teach my first phonics workshop in the mid-1980s. **Sara Bavin, Karen Burleson, Terri Machiavello**, and **Diane Fox** variously organized, attended, and publicized these workshops. Diane helped me with the business side of producing this book, and Karen reordered some of the pages with her eye for the needs of the classroom teacher (she is also a former teacher).

Many **workshop attendees** got excited about the information presented, and I thank them for their kind words of affirmation. The **enthusiastic students** who worked hard and challenged me to stay ahead of them greatly motivated me to make improvements and refinements to each lesson. **Peggy Keane**, Las Vegas, Nevada, provided creative teaching ideas. Peggy wanted to ensure that her grandson and others learned to read and spell well. Her probing questions and drive to understand the material provided me with a vivid confirmation of the importance of teaching by patterns. I also communicated by e-mail with Peggy's thirteen-year-old granddaughter, **Elizabeth Keane**, who has a love of teaching and children that reminds me of myself when I was in the fourth grade (only she is more organized!). Elizabeth, young as she is, conducts an award winning Saturday School program.

Deehona Minton, an excellent public school teacher for nearly 30 years and former coach in Big Spring, Greenwood, and Midland, Texas, has encouraged me greatly through the years. As a secondary English teacher, she has witnessed firsthand the struggles of students who have been "socially promoted" to the junior high or high school levels without having obtained the basic reading skills needed to be successful. These students tend to struggle so much that they lose heart and soon become dropouts or are labeled as at-risk students. Since October 2010, Deehona has been tutoring using *Reading and Spelling Pure & Simple*. Her success has been phenomenal. She helped an at-risk, once-retained 5th grader to succeed in reading when nothing else was working for him. With Deehona's help, this tenacious student raised his SRI score from a zero in August to a 364 in late November, to 804 (6th grade) in early March, and then to a 921 in his May testing. He has since passed both the math and reading TAKS (Texas Assessment of Knowledge and Skills) tests for the first time, is now on grade level, and has been nationally recognized for his tremendous improvement.

Suzanne Haney, a musically talented former public high school teacher of English and Spanish, shared her excellent ear for sounds and helped me fine tune the material. My good friend **Reta Faught** understands the needs of reading instructors and greatly improved my workshops. Her eye for detail and instinctive teaching abilities improved the slides I use in the workshops and made the instructions more practical. Reta's willingness to prepare, plan, instruct, and speak in the workshops has been invaluable.

Jim Hinckley is a seasoned elementary school teacher who has contributed immensely to this reading program. Jim is one of those rare men who gives creative, caring, and talented instruction in the elementary classroom. I am grateful for his willingness to use, and improve, the lessons. **Angela Bumgarner** and **Ginger Berry**, very capable classroom aides, shared with me their delight with these lessons and became enthusiastic when students improved their SRI reading performance by two or more grade levels after only a few weeks of daily application of the lessons. We were mutually encouraged when an autistic young man responded well to Ginger's taking him through a sequence of lessons. **Tammy Stone**, the speech therapist at Tuttle Elementary in Tuttle, Oklahoma, spent her own time reading through my pronunciation instructions, making corrections and providing encouragement. **Monique Blagowsky**, a principal in Tuttle, was open to the use of the lessons in the classroom and understood the benefit of teaching reading using pattern instruction. **Susan Hinckley** made excellent observations and corrections with her logical mind and excellent ear for hearing and identifying variations in sounds.

Debbie Dillard, Murphy, Texas, willingly contributed her insights and knowledge gained from nearly a decade as an elementary teacher in public schools in Texas and Oklahoma. She listened, encouraged, shared insights, and simplified some of the material, and she reminded me to tell the instructors that one doesn't have to initially understand or know all of the patterns to be successful in teaching them. That is a good thing to know! Debbie designed the "Relax, Smile, and Keep it Simple" message that many of you will appreciate. She also helped in the design of the progress monitoring table. **Lyn Hinckley** shared her professional insights from her almost three decades as a speech pathologist at Southgate-Rippetoe Elementary School in the Moore Public School System in Oklahoma. Lyn read, corrected, provided ideas, and made the pronunciation support section of the book more accurate. **David Hinckley**, an excellent high school history teacher and talented baseball coach of 33 years who was recently inducted into the Oklahoma Baseball Hall of Fame, and **Mark Dillard**, of Murphy, Texas, a former public high school math teacher and football coach who is now serving as vice president of Public Risk Underwriters of Texas, asked good questions and were supportive.

I am thankful for **Dr. Lynn Cauley**, from Geismar, Louisiana, for coming to my aid when I had serious printer problems. (Everyone needs an IT person in the family!) **Dr. Stephanie Cauley** amazes me with her world renowned handmade dolls, *"Stephanie's Friends."* I aspire to her level of quality craftsmanship with this book. **Elizabeth Thomasson**, founder and former principal of a private school in Crockett, Texas, and now retired special education teacher from Lubbock, Texas, helped me by evaluating lessons in rough draft form and gave valuable insights regarding the instructions. **John Thomasson**, Elizabeth's husband, has encouraged me by continuing to ask when I will publish this book. (Soon, John, soon!) He is a talented, successful artist and entrepreneur and understands the creative process.

Beth Williamson, a Reading Interventionist at Liberty Hill Elementary School, Liberty Hill ISD, Texas, has worked with students with reading difficulties for the last twelve years. She served on the proofreading team, evaluated the lesson pages, and provided teacher-friendly suggestions that improved the book's usability (including the idea for the Progress Monitoring Table). **Cathy Kelton**, working on her doctorate in education, and currently employed as a teacher at Premier Academy, a Midland charter school run by the Eagle Corporation, has also encouraged me to get this book to press. **Steve Wolfe**, Houston, Texas, having previously published non-fiction books, provided a unique perspective that has improved the book's overall design. **David Wolfe**, North Carolina, contributed ideas and suggested that I reorder some of the information in Unit 4 to make the lessons more effective. I took his advice, and I'm glad I did.

Sandy Dirkes of Bakersfield, California, holds teaching credentials in the state of California and is an excellent reading instructor. She served on an early proofreading team and helped make the book better with her suggestions. Another valued member of the early proofreading team was the late **Susan Cassidy**. She was an outstanding teacher, a precious friend, and a lot of fun. She is greatly missed. I appreciate **Mike McKinley** who twice rescued my manuscript from the computer abyss into which it had fallen. **Esperanza (Hope) Porras** encouraged me, read and reread rough drafts, caught errors, and offered ideas. Hope's diligence and persistence in using the lessons with her son and another student resulted in their becoming better readers and spellers and has opened up opportunities for their futures in ways they haven't yet realized. **Hilario Ariel Ivan Porras** and **Juan Anthony Rodriquez** provided new perspectives for me as they (usually willingly) worked through the lessons. These two young men were the first students to work all the way through all 90 lessons. In addition, Hilario allowed me to demonstrate a lesson with him at one of my reading workshops. **TJ Carr**, from Midland, Texas, was one of the earliest users of the curriculum and was enthusiastic and consistent in working through the lessons with his mother during the summer and into the school year. The excitement he exhibited as he discovered the joy of reading was heartwarming.

Randy Putman, **Pete Stone** and **Stephanie Langwell** of **Action Printing** in Lubbock, Texas, were infinitely patient and helpful while my editor and I fine-tuned consecutive proofs. They gave good advice and worked extra hours to ensure that the final product would meet, and even exceed, expectations. I appreciate their efforts so much. Pete is the Director of Fun at Action Printing and Stephanie is the Associate Director of Fun.

Their titles are well-deserved. I really enjoy working with them. I wish to thank **Charlie Lewis** of the accounting firm of **Charlie Lewis and Company**, Big Spring, Texas, for enthusiastically advising me about launching The Real Reading Company. Any new business venture can be daunting, and I'm glad I had Charlie's assistance.

Many volunteers generously gave of their time to teach students to read and spell using these lessons. These people are too numerous to mention but I am no less grateful to them. A cheerleading section for the book has been my husband's office staff: **Delma Haro**, **Jackie Shelley**, **Karen Waters**, **Melinda Ruiz**, **Peggy Lee**, and **Maria Varela**. They have always asked with interest about progress on the book and, on occasion, referred me to adults and teens who needed reading help.

On a personal note, I would like to thank **Sally Stout**, Dallas, Texas, for her years of Bible Study instruction and her generous giving of time to the women she taught. She helped me realize the importance and the power of the Living Word (which I mistakenly thought that I knew already because of my parents' faith). Also, I am grateful for The Institute in Basic Life Principles, founded by **Bill Gothard**, Chicago, Illinois, for helping me understand the power of daily meditation on the Word of God, changing the direction of my life.

What can I say about a mother and father who lived their faith daily and loved me unconditionally? Their lives were spent willingly and generously giving to others with joy (and fun), and they have influenced so many lives—mine, my siblings', and the many friends and acquaintances who spent time with our family. My mother, **Dorothy Jean Hinckley** of Moore, Oklahoma, is the mother of four, grandmother of nine, and great-grandmother of six (and counting). She also was a public school teacher for many years. She has shared the *Reading and Spelling Pure & Simple* program with others, proofed the instructions, provided valuable insights, and encouraged me to get it finished and send it off. My late father, **Dr. De L. Hinckley, Jr.**, a star athlete in three sports, decorated military veteran, and brilliant and accomplished counselor and minister, loved me and let me, his "dreamer" daughter, grow and develop without crushing my free spirit. He inspired his children to always strive for excellence, be honorable, and have fun while doing it. This book is a tribute to my beloved parents.

My son, **Grayson Cauley**, tutored in the after-school program and used his God-given talent to design the book covers, the company logo, and the illustrations in the book. And, finally, this reading program would not exist without the encouragement and support of my wonderful husband, **Dr. Richard Cauley, DDS**, an excellent dentist and honorable and gifted man. Before my editor arrived on the scene, Richard spent hours reading and rereading pages, adding and deleting punctuation (mostly commas), and cleaning up "fog" in the instructions. He also sacrificially and faithfully volunteered through the years in the reading classes. Without his encouragement, this book would not exist.

Documentation

Documentation

Progress Monitoring Table

    Sample Progress Monitoring Table

    Progress Monitoring Table

    Word Tabulator

Pre-Unit Completion Chart

    Lessons A – E

Simple Completion Chart (1 Page)

    Lessons 1 – 90

Detailed Completion Chart (5 Pages)

    Lessons 1 – 18   (1 of 5)

    Lessons 19 – 36   (2 of 5)

    Lessons 37 – 54   (3 of 5)

    Lessons 55 – 72   (4 of 5)

    Lessons 73 – 90   (5 of 5)

Sample Progress Monitoring Table

Lesson Number	Roman Numeral	R or S	First Attempt	Second Attempt	Third Attempt	Fourth Attempt	Teacher Comment	Date
1	I	R	7 / 10	8 / 10	8 / 10	10 / 10	All words mastered after four times reading and spelling through the lists. Review Lesson 1, Roman Number I, next meeting.	8/12
1	I	S	6 / 10	6 / 10	8 / 10	10 / 10	All spelled correctly after 4 tries, practiced four words, bat, tat, tam, mat. Review again	8/13
1	I	R/S	10 / 10	/	/	/	No errors	8/14
1	II-VI	R/S	61 / 61	/	/	/	Excellent, No errors today	8/14
2	I-VI	R/S	57 / 58	58 / 58	/	/	Good work. Second attempt – 100 Only missed one in the first attempt (sill)	8/15
3	I-VI	R/S	80 / 85	84 / 85	85 / 85	/	Struggled with 5 words in II. Redo II next week: ban, rim, vat, fig, and gag	8/16
3	II	R/S	14 / 14	/	/	/	Reviewed II to ensure confidence. Is excited and very sure of the words.	8/19
3	I-VI	R/S	85/88	86/88	88/88	/	Student was enthusiastic about the lesson. Read all correctly. Initially misspelled 3 words: gag, gill, rig	8/20
3	I-V	R/S	/	/	/	/	Reviewed only a few words (about 10) with the letter **g**. Review until confident. Did very well with the practice.	8/21
4	All	R/S	85 / 88	86 / 88	88 / 88	/	Review: sop, lob, pox. Doing very well	8/21
			/	/	/	/		
			/	/	/	/		
			/	/	/	/		
			/	/	/	/		
			/	/	/	/		

Progress Monitoring Table

Lesson Number	Roman Numeral	R or S	First Attempt	Second Attempt	Third Attempt	Fourth Attempt	Teacher Comment	Date
			/	/	/	/		

Word Tabulator

Lesson I	II	III	IV	V	VI	Challenge	Total
PRE-UNIT							
A	2	2	2	1	4	3	-	14
B	2	5	5	5	5	5	-	27
C	4	10	6	10	10	10	-	50
D	10	7	7	7	7	7	-	45
E	10	10	10	10	10	10	-	60
UNIT 1							
1	10	10	10	10	10	8	1	59
2	10	10	10	10	10	7	1	58
3	14	14	14	14	14	14	1	85
4	10	10	10	4	6	10	1	51
5	14	14	14	14	14	16	2	88
6	10	10	10	10	5	8	1	54
7	15	15	15	15	15	21	1	97
8	7	7	7	7	7	5	2	42
9	15	15	15	15	15	32	-	107
10	10	10	10	5	10	-	-	45
11	10	10	10	10	10	-	1	51
12	14	14	14	14	14	14	1	85
13	7	14	7	24	7	-	-	59
14	6	6	6	6	6	6	3	39
15	14	14	14	14	-	-	3	59
16	6	6	12	6	6	12	-	48
17	4	12	12	12	12	-	2	54
18	15	15	15	15	15	15	2	92
19	18	18	18	18	18	18	-	108
20	10	10	12	15	12	12	-	71
21	24	12	12	12	-	-	2	62
22	12	12	12	12	12	12	3	75

Lesson I	II	III	IV	V	VI	Challenge	Total
23	12	12	12	12	12	12	2	74
24	18	18	18	18	-	-	-	72
25	10	10	10	10	10	-	3	53
26	12	3	12	12	18	18	2	77
27	13	22	12	12	12	12	2	85
28	10	10	10	10	10	-	-	50
29	10	10	10	10	10	-	-	50
30	12	12	12	12	12	12	-	72
31	10	10	10	10	-	-	-	40
32	10	10	10	10	10	-	-	50
UNIT 2							
33	32	24	16	8	16	16	2	114
34	32	24	18	18	25	25	4	146
35	10	10	10	10	10	-	-	50
36	10	10	10	5	10	7	4	56
37	16	16	16	12	28	28	-	116
38	18	10	10	10	10	10	-	68
39	10	15	15	10	10	-	7	67
40	12	12	12	12	12	12	-	72
41	12	12	12	6	12	18	-	72
42	24	15	15	15	15	-	10	94
43	20	10	10	20	28	28	7	123
44	10	10	10	10	10	10	-	60
45	14	14	14	14	7	-	4	67
46	12	12	12	12	12	-	-	60
47	10	10	10	10	10	10	4	64
48	13	13	14	4	14	-	-	58
49	6	6	6	6	6	6	4	40
50	10	10	10	10	10	10	3	63

UNIT 3

Lesson	I	II	III	IV	V	VI	Challenge	Total
51	14	14	14	14	7	-	3	66
52	12	12	12	12	-	-	3	51
53	5	10	10	10	10	-	-	45
54	15	15	15	15	-	-	-	60
55	30	25	9	18	18	-	7	107
56	15	15	15	18	18	-	-	81
57	20	20	20	20	20	20	-	120
58	8	8	8	8	8	-	-	40
59	16	16	20	20	16	16	-	104
60	9	9	9	12	12	12	-	63
61	12	12	12	12	25	30	3	106
62	10	10	10	10	25	25	-	90
63	16	16	16	16	16	-	-	80
64	12	12	12	12	12	24	3	87
65	10	10	10	10	24	24	2	90
66	12	12	12	12	12	50	-	110
67	12	12	12	20	20	20	3	99
68	12	12	12	12	24	30	3	105
69	18	18	12	20	20	20	3	111
70	12	12	12	12	12	16	2	78
71	12	12	12	16	24	24	11	111
72	15	15	15	12	12	12	3	84

UNIT 4

Lesson	I	II	III	IV	V	VI	Challenge	Total
73	8	16	16	16	30	30	-	116
74	10	10	10	25	21	20	3	99
75	10	10	10	2	10	10	26	78
76	12	12	12	12	10	36	19	113
77	8	8	8	8	8	24	40	104
78	10	10	10	10	20	40	-	100
79	10	10	10	10	10	-	7	57
80	12	12	12	12	12	-	2	62
81	8	8	8	8	8	36	40	116
82	8	8	8	8	8	28	59	127
83	24	6	25	21	16	14	-	106
84	6	6	6	6	12	12	16	64
85	10	15	10	10	10	-	3	58
86	12	12	12	16	12	32	-	96
87	10	10	10	1	20	16	5	72
88	8	8	8	8	8	-	3	43
89	12	19	10	30	18	6	3	98
90	12	12	12	16	16	-	2	70

PRE-UNIT COMPLETION CHART

A record of student achievement in Lessons A through E

INSTRUCTIONS

Use this chart to document your student's achievement if you are using the Pre-Unit (Lessons A through E). If you are not doing the Pre-Unit, disregard this chart. Adults and teens will not usually need this chart.

For each lesson, give your student a "**100**" after he correctly reads all of the words in the lesson list. Next, test him on spelling, and give him a "**100**" after he correctly spells each list. Be meticulous about keeping records!

PRE-UNIT COMPLETION CHART

Mark a "**100**" beside **R** for <u>r</u>eading
Mark a "**100**" beside **S** for <u>s</u>pelling

NAME_____   STUDENT #_____

START DATE_____   GRADE _____

LESSON	100's		STICKERS
	READING	SPELLING	

A
- I   R_____   S_____
- II   R_____   S_____
- III   R_____   S_____
- IV   R_____   S_____
- V REVIEW   R_____   S_____
- VI REVIEW   R_____   S_____   DATE_____

B
- I   R_____   S_____
- II   R_____   S_____
- III   R_____   S_____
- IV REVIEW   R_____   S_____
- V REVIEW   R_____   S_____
- VI REVIEW   R_____   S_____   DATE_____

C
- I   R_____   S_____
- II   R_____   S_____
- III   R_____   S_____
- IV REVIEW   R_____   S_____
- V REVIEW   R_____   S_____
- VI REVIEW   R_____   S_____   DATE_____

LESSON	100's		STICKERS
	READING	SPELLING	

D
- I   R_____   S_____
- II REVIEW   R_____   S_____
- III REVIEW   R_____   S_____
- IV REVIEW   R_____   S_____
- V REVIEW   R_____   S_____
- VI REVIEW   R_____   S_____   DATE_____

E
- I   R_____   S_____
- II REVIEW   R_____   S_____
- III REVIEW   R_____   S_____
- IV REVIEW   R_____   S_____
- V REVIEW   R_____   S_____
- VI REVIEW   R_____   S_____   DATE_____

COMPLETION DATE: _____

SIMPLE COMPLETION CHART

A one-page record for all 90 lessons

Note: This one-page chart is ideal for most teens and adults.

INSTRUCTIONS

Use this chart to document your student's progress through all 90 lessons. For each lesson, give your student a **"100"** after he correctly reads all of the words in the lesson list. Likewise, give him a **"100"** after he correctly spells each and every word in the lesson list.

Visual reminders like this completion chart help your student easily see, at a glance, how much he has accomplished so far. He can also see that the finish line is in sight. If you are teaching younger students, consider using the detailed color-coded completion charts instead (see next completion chart).

NAME: _____

START DATE: _____

Mark 100 beside <u>R</u> for <u>R</u>eading
Mark 100 beside <u>S</u> for <u>S</u>pelling
Mark the date beside <u>D</u>

SIMPLE
COMPLETION CHART

Unit 1

Lesson	Read	Spell	Date
1	R___	S___	D___
2	R___	S___	D___
3	R___	S___	D___
4	R___	S___	D___
5	R___	S___	D___
6	R___	S___	D___
7	R___	S___	D___
8	R___	S___	D___
9	R___	S___	D___
10	R___	S___	D___
11	R___	S___	D___
12	R___	S___	D___
13	R___	S___	D___
14	R___	S___	D___
15	R___	S___	D___
16	R___	S___	D___
17	R___	S___	D___
18	R___	S___	D___
19	R___	S___	D___
20	R___	S___	D___
21	R___	S___	D___
22	R___	S___	D___
23	R___	S___	D___
24	R___	S___	D___
25	R___	S___	D___
26	R___	S___	D___
27	R___	S___	D___
28	R___	S___	D___
29	R___	S___	D___
30	R___	S___	D___
31	R___	S___	D___
32	R___	S___	D___

Unit 2

Lesson	Read	Spell	Date
33	R___	S___	D___
34	R___	S___	D___
35	R___	S___	D___
36	R___	S___	D___
37	R___	S___	D___
38	R___	S___	D___
39	R___	S___	D___
40	R___	S___	D___
41	R___	S___	D___
42	R___	S___	D___
43	R___	S___	D___
44	R___	S___	D___
45	R___	S___	D___
46	R___	S___	D___
47	R___	S___	D___
48	R___	S___	D___
49	R___	S___	D___
50	R___	S___	D___

Unit 3

Lesson	Read	Spell	Date
51	R___	S___	D___
52	R___	S___	D___
53	R___	S___	D___
54	R___	S___	D___
55	R___	S___	D___
56	R___	S___	D___
57	R___	S___	D___
58	R___	S___	D___
59	R___	S___	D___
60	R___	S___	D___

Lesson	Read	Spell	Date
61	R___	S___	D___
62	R___	S___	D___
63	R___	S___	D___
64	R___	S___	D___
65	R___	S___	D___
66	R___	S___	D___
67	R___	S___	D___
68	R___	S___	D___
69	R___	S___	D___
70	R___	S___	D___
71	R___	S___	D___
72	R___	S___	D___

Unit 4

Lesson	Read	Spell	Date
73	R___	S___	D___
74	R___	S___	D___
75	R___	S___	D___
76	R___	S___	D___
77	R___	S___	D___
78	R___	S___	D___
79	R___	S___	D___
80	R___	S___	D___
81	R___	S___	D___
82	R___	S___	D___
83	R___	S___	D___
84	R___	S___	D___
85	R___	S___	D___
86	R___	S___	D___
87	R___	S___	D___
88	R___	S___	D___
89	R___	S___	D___
90	R___	S___	D___

DETAILED COMPLETION CHART

This longer completion chart is an alternative to the simple completion chart.

Use this particular chart for students who like bright colors and stickers and who will benefit from seeing their progress mapped out in greater detail.

LESSONS   1 – 18

LESSONS   19 – 36

LESSONS   37 – 54

LESSONS   55 – 72

LESSONS   73 – 90

INSTRUCTIONS

Use this 5-page chart to document your student's progress through all 90 lessons. For each segment of a lesson (the list marked with a Roman numeral), give your student a "100" after he has correctly read every word. Likewise, give him a "100" after he has correctly spelled every word. After he successfully completes the lists, reward your student with a sticker or stamp in the space provided. Visual reminders like this progress chart are motivating for student and teacher alike. One additional comment: At some point, usually around Lesson 40, you may also want to use the simple completion chart for your student.

Printing These Completion Charts

- We recommend that you use 65-weight card stock. It can go through most printers, including standard home printers.

- If possible, use a different color for each of these charts. We use white for Lessons A–E; yellow for Lessons 1–18; orange for Lessons 19–36; blue for Lessons 37–54; green for Lessons 55–72; and gold for Lessons 73–90. Instructors who are working with only one student might select colors that have special appeal to their student (e.g., school colors, team colors, etc.).

DETAILED COMPLETION CHART

Mark a "100" beside <u>R</u> for <u>r</u>eading
Mark a "100" beside <u>S</u> for <u>s</u>pelling

NAME_____   STUDENT #_____
START DATE_____   GRADE LEVEL_____
Review lists are shaded.

LESSON		100's					STICKERS
1	I$_R$___ II$_R$___ III$_R$___ IV$_R$___ V$_R$___ VI$_R$___						☆
	I$_S$___ II$_S$___ III$_S$___ IV$_S$___ V$_S$___ VI$_S$___						DATE___
2	I$_R$___ II$_R$___ III$_R$___ IV$_R$___ V$_R$___ VI$_R$___						☆
	I$_S$___ II$_S$___ III$_S$___ IV$_S$___ V$_S$___ VI$_S$___						DATE___
3	I$_R$___ II$_R$___ III$_R$___ IV$_R$___ V$_R$___ VI$_R$___						☆
	I$_S$___ II$_S$___ III$_S$___ IV$_S$___ V$_S$___ VI$_S$___						DATE___
4	I$_R$___ II$_R$___ III$_R$___ IV$_R$___ V$_R$___ VI$_R$___						☆
	I$_S$___ II$_S$___ III$_S$___ IV$_S$___ V$_S$___ VI$_S$___						DATE___
5	I$_R$___ II$_R$___ III$_R$___ IV$_R$___ V$_R$___ VI$_R$___						☆
	I$_S$___ II$_S$___ III$_S$___ IV$_S$___ V$_S$___ VI$_S$___						DATE___
6	I$_R$___ II$_R$___ III$_R$___ IV$_R$___ V$_R$___ VI$_R$___						☆
	I$_S$___ II$_S$___ III$_S$___ IV$_S$___ V$_S$___ VI$_S$___						DATE___
7	I$_R$___ II$_R$___ III$_R$___ IV$_R$___ V$_R$___ VI$_R$___						☆
	I$_S$___ II$_S$___ III$_S$___ IV$_S$___ V$_S$___ VI$_S$___						DATE___
8	I$_R$___ II$_R$___ III$_R$___ IV$_R$___ V$_R$___ VI$_R$___						☆
	I$_S$___ II$_S$___ III$_S$___ IV$_S$___ V$_S$___ VI$_S$___						DATE___
9	I$_R$___ II$_R$___ III$_R$___ IV$_R$___ V$_R$___ VI$_R$___						☆
	I$_S$___ II$_S$___ III$_S$___ IV$_S$___ V$_S$___ VI$_S$___						DATE___

(Page 1 of 5)

LESSON		100's					STICKERS
10	I$_R$___ II$_R$___ III$_R$___ IV$_R$___ V$_R$___						☆
	I$_S$___ II$_S$___ III$_S$___ IV$_S$___ V$_S$___						DATE___
11	I$_R$___ II$_R$___ III$_R$___ IV$_R$___ V$_R$___						☆
	I$_S$___ II$_S$___ III$_S$___ IV$_S$___ V$_S$___						DATE___
12	I$_R$___ II$_R$___ III$_R$___ IV$_R$___ V$_R$___ VI$_R$___						☆
	I$_S$___ II$_S$___ III$_S$___ IV$_S$___ V$_S$___ VI$_S$___						DATE___
13	I$_R$___ II$_R$___ III$_R$___ IV$_R$___ V$_R$___ VI$_R$___						☆
	I$_S$___ II$_S$___ III$_S$___ IV$_S$___ V$_S$___ VI$_S$___						DATE___
14	I$_R$___ II$_R$___ III$_R$___ IV$_R$___ V$_R$___ VI$_R$___						☆
	I$_S$___ II$_S$___ III$_S$___ IV$_S$___ V$_S$___ VI$_S$___						DATE___
15	I$_R$___ II$_R$___ III$_R$___ IV$_R$___ V$_R$___						☆
	I$_S$___ II$_S$___ III$_S$___ IV$_S$___ V$_S$___						DATE___
16	I$_R$___ II$_R$___ III$_R$___ IV$_R$___ V$_R$___ VI$_R$___						☆
	I$_S$___ II$_S$___ III$_S$___ IV$_S$___ V$_S$___ VI$_S$___						DATE___
17	I$_R$___ II$_R$___ III$_R$___ IV$_R$___ V$_R$___						☆
	I$_S$___ II$_S$___ III$_S$___ IV$_S$___ V$_S$___						DATE___
18	I$_R$___ II$_R$___ III$_R$___ IV$_R$___ V$_R$___ VI$_R$___						☆
	I$_S$___ II$_S$___ III$_S$___ IV$_S$___ V$_S$___ VI$_S$___						DATE___

COMPLETION DATE: _____

DETAILED COMPLETION CHART

Mark a "100" beside **R** for **r**eading
Mark a "100" beside **S** for **s**pelling

NAME_____   STUDENT #____

START DATE_____   GRADE_____

Review lists are shaded.

LESSON			100's			STICKERS
19	I R___ II R___ III R___	IV R___	V R___	VI R___	☆
	I S___ II S___ III S___	IV S___	V S___	VI S___	DATE___
20	I R___ II R___ III R___	IV R___	V R___	VI R___	☆
	I S___ II S___ III S___	IV S___	V S___	VI S___	DATE___
21	I R___ II R___ III R___	IV R___	V R___	VI R___	☆
	I S___ II S___ III S___	IV S___	V S___	VI S___	DATE___
22	I R___ II R___ III R___	IV R___	V R___	VI R___	☆
	I S___ II S___ III S___	IV S___	V S___	VI S___	DATE___
23	I R___ II R___ III R___	IV R___	V R___	VI R___	☆
	I S___ II S___ III S___	IV S___	V S___	VI S___	DATE___
24	I R___ II R___ III R___	IV R___	V R___	VI R___	☆
	I S___ II S___ III S___	IV S___	V S___	VI S___	DATE___
25	I R___ II R___ III R___	IV R___	V R___	VI R___	☆
	I S___ II S___ III S___	IV S___	V S___	VI S___	DATE___
26	I R___ II R___ III R___	IV R___	V R___	VI R___	☆
	I S___ II S___ III S___	IV S___	V S___	VI S___	DATE___
27	I R___ II R___ III R___	IV R___	V R___	VI R___	☆
	I S___ II S___ III S___	IV S___	V S___	VI S___	DATE___

LESSON			100's			STICKERS
28	I R___ II R___ III R___	IV R___	V R___	VI R___	☆
	I S___ II S___ III S___	IV S___	V S___	VI S___	DATE___
29	I R___ II R___ III R___	IV R___	V R___	VI R___	☆
	I S___ II S___ III S___	IV S___	V S___	VI S___	DATE___
30	I R___ II R___ III R___	IV R___	V R___	VI R___	☆
	I S___ II S___ III S___	IV S___	V S___	VI S___	DATE___
31	I R___ II R___ III R___	IV R___	V R___	VI R___	☆
	I S___ II S___ III S___	IV S___	V S___	VI S___	DATE___
32	I R___ II R___ III R___	IV R___	V R___	VI R___	☆
	I S___ II S___ III S___	IV S___	V S___	VI S___	DATE___
33	I R___ II R___ III R___	IV R___	V R___	VI R___	☆
	I S___ II S___ III S___	IV S___	V S___	VI S___	DATE___
34	I R___ II R___ III R___	IV R___	V R___	VI R___	☆
	I S___ II S___ III S___	IV S___	V S___	VI S___	DATE___
35	I R___ II R___ III R___	IV R___	V R___	VI R___	☆
	I S___ II S___ III S___	IV S___	V S___	VI S___	DATE___
36	I R___ II R___ III R___	IV R___	V R___	VI R___	☆
	I S___ II S___ III S___	IV S___	V S___	VI S___	DATE___

COMPLETION DATE: _____

DETAILED COMPLETION CHART

Mark a "**100**" beside <u>R</u> for <u>r</u>eading
Mark a "**100**" beside <u>S</u> for <u>s</u>pelling

NAME _____   STUDENT # _____

START DATE _____   GRADE _____

Review lists are shaded.

LESSON				100's			STICKERS
37	I R ___	II R ___	III R ___	IV R ___	V R ___	VI R ___	☆
	I S ___	II S ___	III S ___	IV S ___	V S ___	VI S ___	DATE ___
38	I R ___	II R ___	III R ___	IV R ___	V R ___	VI R ___	☆
	I S ___	II S ___	III S ___	IV S ___	V S ___	VI S ___	DATE ___
39	I R ___	II R ___	III R ___	IV R ___	V R ___		☆
	I S ___	II S ___	III S ___	IV S ___	V S ___		DATE ___
40	I R ___	II R ___	III R ___	IV R ___	V R ___	VI R ___	☆
	I S ___	II S ___	III S ___	IV S ___	V S ___	VI S ___	DATE ___
41	I R ___	II R ___	III R ___	IV R ___	V R ___	VI R ___	☆
	I S ___	II S ___	III S ___	IV S ___	V S ___	VI S ___	DATE ___
42	I R ___	II R ___	III R ___	IV R ___	V R ___		☆
	I S ___	II S ___	III S ___	IV S ___	V S ___		DATE ___
43	I R ___	II R ___	III R ___	IV R ___	V R ___	VI R ___	☆
	I S ___	II S ___	III S ___	IV S ___	V S ___	VI S ___	DATE ___
44	I R ___	II R ___	III R ___	IV R ___	V R ___	VI R ___	☆
	I S ___	II S ___	III S ___	IV S ___	V S ___	VI S ___	DATE ___
45	I R ___	II R ___	III R ___	IV R ___	V R ___		☆
	I S ___	II S ___	III S ___	IV S ___	V S ___		DATE ___

LESSON				100's			STICKERS
46	I R ___	II R ___	III R ___	IV R ___	V R ___		☆
	I S ___	II S ___	III S ___	IV S ___	V S ___		DATE ___
47	I R ___	II R ___	III R ___	IV R ___	V R ___	VI R ___	☆
	I S ___	II S ___	III S ___	IV S ___	V S ___	VI S ___	DATE ___
48	I R ___	II R ___	III R ___	IV R ___	V R ___		☆
	I S ___	II S ___	III S ___	IV S ___	V S ___		DATE ___
49	I R ___	II R ___	III R ___	IV R ___	V R ___	VI R ___	☆
	I S ___	II S ___	III S ___	IV S ___	V S ___	VI S ___	DATE ___
50	I R ___	II R ___	III R ___	IV R ___	V R ___	VI R ___	☆
	I S ___	II S ___	III S ___	IV S ___	V S ___	VI S ___	DATE ___
51	I R ___	II R ___	III R ___	IV R ___	V R ___		☆
	I S ___	II S ___	III S ___	IV S ___	V S ___		DATE ___
52	I R ___	II R ___	III R ___	IV R ___	V R ___		☆
	I S ___	II S ___	III S ___	IV S ___	V S ___		DATE ___
53	I R ___	II R ___	III R ___	IV R ___	V R ___		☆
	I S ___	II S ___	III S ___	IV S ___	V S ___		DATE ___
54	I R ___	II R ___	III R ___	IV R ___	V R ___		☆
	I S ___	II S ___	III S ___	IV S ___	V S ___		DATE ___

COMPLETION DATE: ___

DETAILED COMPLETION CHART

Mark a "**100**" beside <u>R</u> for <u>r</u>eading
Mark a "**100**" beside <u>S</u> for <u>s</u>pelling

NAME _____   STUDENT # _____

START DATE _____   GRADE _____

Review lists are shaded.

LESSON				100's			STICKERS
55	I_R ___ II_R ___	III_R ___	IV_R ___	V_R ___			☆
	I_S ___ II_S ___	III_S ___	IV_S ___	V_S ___			DATE ___
56	I_R ___ II_R ___	III_R ___	IV_R ___	V_R ___			☆
	I_S ___ II_S ___	III_S ___	IV_S ___	V_S ___			DATE ___
57	I_R ___ II_R ___	III_R ___	IV_R ___	V_R ___	VI_R ___		☆
	I_S ___ II_S ___	III_S ___	IV_S ___	V_S ___	VI_S ___		DATE ___
58	I_R ___ II_R ___	III_R ___	IV_R ___	V_R ___			☆
	I_S ___ II_S ___	III_S ___	IV_S ___	V_S ___			DATE ___
59	I_R ___ II_R ___	III_R ___	IV_R ___	V_R ___	VI_R ___		☆
	I_S ___ II_S ___	III_S ___	IV_S ___	V_S ___	VI_S ___		DATE ___
60	I_R ___ II_R ___	III_R ___	IV_R ___	V_R ___	VI_R ___		☆
	I_S ___ II_S ___	III_S ___	IV_S ___	V_S ___	VI_S ___		DATE ___
61	I_R ___ II_R ___	III_R ___	IV_R ___	V_R ___	VI_R ___		☆
	I_S ___ II_S ___	III_S ___	IV_S ___	V_S ___	VI_S ___		DATE ___
62	I_R ___ II_R ___	III_R ___	IV_R ___	V_R ___	VI_R ___		☆
	I_S ___ II_S ___	III_S ___	IV_S ___	V_S ___	VI_S ___		DATE ___
63	I_R ___ II_R ___	III_R ___	IV_R ___	V_R ___			☆
	I_S ___ II_S ___	III_S ___	IV_S ___	V_S ___			DATE ___

(Page 4 of 5)

LESSON				100's			STICKERS
64	I_R ___ II_R ___	III_R ___	IV_R ___	V_R ___	VI_R ___		☆
	I_S ___ II_S ___	III_S ___	IV_S ___	V_S ___	VI_S ___		DATE ___
65	I_R ___ II_R ___	III_R ___	IV_R ___	V_R ___	VI_R ___		☆
	I_S ___ II_S ___	III_S ___	IV_S ___	V_S ___	VI_S ___		DATE ___
66	I_R ___ II_R ___	III_R ___	IV_R ___	V_R ___	VI_R ___		☆
	I_S ___ II_S ___	III_S ___	IV_S ___	V_S ___	VI_S ___		DATE ___
67	I_R ___ II_R ___	III_R ___	IV_R ___	V_R ___	VI_R ___		☆
	I_S ___ II_S ___	III_S ___	IV_S ___	V_S ___	VI_S ___		DATE ___
68	I_R ___ II_R ___	III_R ___	IV_R ___	V_R ___	VI_R ___		☆
	I_S ___ II_S ___	III_S ___	IV_S ___	V_S ___	VI_S ___		DATE ___
69	I_R ___ II_R ___	III_R ___	IV_R ___	V_R ___	VI_R ___		☆
	I_S ___ II_S ___	III_S ___	IV_S ___	V_S ___	VI_S ___		DATE ___
70	I_R ___ II_R ___	III_R ___	IV_R ___	V_R ___	VI_R ___		☆
	I_S ___ II_S ___	III_S ___	IV_S ___	V_S ___	VI_S ___		DATE ___
71	I_R ___ II_R ___	III_R ___	IV_R ___	V_R ___	VI_R ___		☆
	I_S ___ II_S ___	III_S ___	IV_S ___	V_S ___	VI_S ___		DATE ___
72	I_R ___ II_R ___	III_R ___	IV_R ___	V_R ___	VI_R ___		☆
	I_S ___ II_S ___	III_S ___	IV_S ___	V_S ___	VI_S ___		DATE ___

COMPLETION DATE: _____

DETAILED COMPLETION CHART

Mark a "**100**" beside <u>R</u> for <u>reading</u>
Mark a "**100**" beside <u>S</u> for <u>spelling</u>

NAME _____

START DATE _____

STUDENT # _____

GRADE _____

Review lists are shaded.

LESSON			100's			STICKERS
73	I R ___ II R ___ III R ___	IV R ___	V R ___	VI R ___	★
	I S ___ II S ___ III S ___	IV S ___	V S ___	VI S ___	DATE ___
74	I R ___ II R ___ III R ___	IV R ___	V R ___	VI R ___	★
	I S ___ II S ___ III S ___	IV S ___	V S ___	VI S ___	DATE ___
75	I R ___ II R ___ III R ___	IV R ___	V R ___	VI R ___	★
	I S ___ II S ___ III S ___	IV S ___	V S ___	VI S ___	DATE ___
76	I R ___ II R ___ III R ___	IV R ___	V R ___	VI R ___	★
	I S ___ II S ___ III S ___	IV S ___	V S ___	VI S ___	DATE ___
77	I R ___ II R ___ III R ___	IV R ___	V R ___	VI R ___	★
	I S ___ II S ___ III S ___	IV S ___	V S ___	VI S ___	DATE ___
78	I R ___ II R ___ III R ___	IV R ___	V R ___	VI R ___	★
	I S ___ II S ___ III S ___	IV S ___	V S ___	VI S ___	DATE ___
79	I R ___ II R ___ III R ___	IV R ___	V R ___	VI R ___	★
	I S ___ II S ___ III S ___	IV S ___	V S ___	VI S ___	DATE ___
80	I R ___ II R ___ III R ___	IV R ___	V R ___	VI R ___	★
	I S ___ II S ___ III S ___	IV S ___	V S ___	VI S ___	DATE ___
81	I R ___ II R ___ III R ___	IV R ___	V R ___	VI R ___	★
	I S ___ II S ___ III S ___	IV S ___	V S ___	VI S ___	DATE ___

LESSON			100's			STICKERS
82	I R ___ II R ___ III R ___	IV R ___	V R ___	VI R ___	★
	I S ___ II S ___ III S ___	IV S ___	V S ___	VI S ___	DATE ___
83	I R ___ II R ___ III R ___	IV R ___	V R ___	VI R ___	★
	I S ___ II S ___ III S ___	IV S ___	V S ___	VI S ___	DATE ___
84	I R ___ II R ___ III R ___	IV R ___	V R ___	VI R ___	★
	I S ___ II S ___ III S ___	IV S ___	V S ___	VI S ___	DATE ___
85	I R ___ II R ___ III R ___	IV R ___	V R ___	VI R ___	★
	I S ___ II S ___ III S ___	IV S ___	V S ___	VI S ___	DATE ___
86	I R ___ II R ___ III R ___	IV R ___	V R ___	VI R ___	★
	I S ___ II S ___ III S ___	IV S ___	V S ___	VI S ___	DATE ___
87	I R ___ II R ___ III R ___	IV R ___	V R ___	VI R ___	★
	I S ___ II S ___ III S ___	IV S ___	V S ___	VI S ___	DATE ___
88	I R ___ II R ___ III R ___	IV R ___	V R ___	VI R ___	★
	I S ___ II S ___ III S ___	IV S ___	V S ___	VI S ___	DATE ___
89	I R ___ II R ___ III R ___	IV R ___	V R ___	VI R ___	★
	I S ___ II S ___ III S ___	IV S ___	V S ___	VI S ___	DATE ___
90	I R ___ II R ___ III R ___	IV R ___	V R ___	VI R ___	★
	I S ___ II S ___ III S ___	IV S ___	V S ___	VI S ___	DATE ___

COMPLETION DATE: _____